LANDSCAPES
AND SEASONS
OF THE
MEDIEVAL
WORLD

LANDSCAPES AND SEASONS OF THE MEDIEVAL WORLD

Derek Pearsall and Elizabeth Salter

University of Toronto Press

Published in Great Britain by
Elek Books Ltd
London

First published in Canada and the United States
by University of Toronto Press
Toronto and Buffalo

ISBN 0–8020–2110–7
LC 73–85089

Printed in Great Britain

CONTENTS

LIST OF PLATES

The illustration on the jacket is *The Virgin and Unicorn in an Enclosed Garden*. Fitzwilliam Museum, Cambridge, MS 99, f. 11v.

ACKNOWLEDGEMENTS

We are indebted to the following Museums, Galleries, Libraries, and other institutions, for the supply of photographs, and for permission to reproduce in this volume illustrations from works in their possession:

Aachen, the Central Treasury (Photo: Ann Münchow)	I
Amsterdam, Rijksmuseum	22
Berlin, Staatliche Museen	5, VII
Brussels, Bibliothèque Royale Albert Ier	47a,b
Cambridge, the Fitzwilliam Museum	34b, II, III, IV
Cambridge, the Master and Fellows of Corpus Christi College	41a–e
Cambridge, the Master and Fellows of Trinity College (Photo: University Library, Cambridge)	19
Châteauroux, Bibliothèque Municipale	49
Cologne, Wallraf-Richartz-Museum (Photo: Rheinisches Bildarchiv, Kölnisches Stadtsmuseum)	32b
Epernay, Bibliothèque Municipale (Photo: Bibl. Nat., Paris)	16
Ferrara, Musei Civici d'Arte Antica	38a,b
Frankfurt/M., Städelsches Kunstinstitut	21
Istanbul, Topkapu Saray Library	15a,b
Lisbon, Museu Calouste Gulbenkian	34a
London, the Trustees of the British Museum	18, 23b, 24b, 25a, 29, 30a,b, 31, 40a,b, 42a–f, 43a,b, V, VI
London, the National Gallery	58, 62, VIII
Madrid, Museo del Prado	58
New York, the Frick Collection	64
New York, the Metropolitan Museum of Art	26, 44c, 46b, 52a
Oxford, the Ashmolean Museum, University of Oxford, Department of Western Art	63
Oxford, Bodleian Library, University of Oxford	24a, 25b
Palestrina, Museo Nazionale	7

Paris, Bibliothèque Nationale	11, 12, 20, 35a, 44a,b, 45a–d, 46a, 52b, 61
Paris, Musée Condé, Chantilly (Photo: Bibl. Nat., Paris)	23a, 50a, 51a
Paris, Musée Jacquemart-André (Photo: Bulloz)	48a,b
Paris, Musée du Louvre (Cliché des Musées Nationaux)	56
Piazza Armerina, Sicily	6
Trento, Torre dell'Aquila, Castello Buonconsiglio	39, 50b
Utrecht, Bibliotheek der Rijksuniversiteit	17
Vatican City, Biblioteca Apostolica Vaticana	4, 10, 13, 14
Venice, Biblioteca Nazionale Marciana	35b, 51b, 52c
Venice, Museo Civico Correr (Photo: Toso Venezia)	66
Verona, Museo di Castelvecchio: Comune di Verona, Musei e Gallerie d'Arte	32a
Vienna, Kunsthistorisches Museum	36, 37
York, the University of York (Photo: David Whiteley)	33

We are similarly indebted to the following art-photographic agencies:

Fratelli Alinari, S. A. Istituto di Edizioni Artistiche, Florence	28
André Held, Documentation Photographique, Ecublens VD	1, 2, 3, 8, 9, 53, 55, 60
Scala Istituto Fotografico Editoriale, Florence	27, 54, 59, 65

We are also grateful to the following publishers, authors and copyright holders for permission to quote from their publications: Edward Arnold (Publishers) Ltd for R. A. Waldron's edition of *Sir Gawain and the Green Knight*; the Cambridge University Press for *Studies in Early Celtic Nature Poetry* by K. Jackson; the Clarendon Press, Oxford, for J. Norton-Smith's edition of Lydgate *Poems*, J. Kinsley's edition of Dunbar *Poems*, C. Elliott's edition of Henryson *Poems*, E. V. Gordon's edition of *Pearl*, and for *Tradition and Originality in Roman Poetry* by G. Williams, *A History of Secular Latin Poetry in the Middle Ages* by F. J. E. Raby, and C. R. Dodwell's translation of Theophilus *De Diversis Artibus*; Constable Publishers and Harper and Row, Publishers, Inc. for *Medieval Latin Lyrics* by Helen Waddell; J. M. Dent and Sons Ltd (Publishers) and E. P. Dutton and Co., Inc. for translations by R. K. Gordon of *Anglo-Saxon Poetry*, by J. M. Rigg of Boccaccio's *Decameron*, and by G. A. Hight of *The Saga of Grettir the Strong*; Harvard University Press for *Early Netherlandish Painting* by E. Panofsky; David Higham Associates Ltd and A. Watkins, Inc. for translations by Dorothy Sayers of *The Song of Roland* and *The Divine Comedy*; Indiana University Press for the translation by M. Bishop of *Petrarch's Letters*; The Loeb Classical Library (Harvard University Press: William Heinemann) for editions and translations of Virgil's *Aeneid*, *Georgics* and *Eclogues*, Ovid's *Metamorphoses*, *Tristia* and *Fasti*, Pliny's *Natural History*, Vitruvius *On Architecture*, the poems of Claudian and Ausonius, the *Pervigilium Veneris*, Cicero *De Inventione*, Statius' *Thebaid* and *Silvae*; John Murray (Publishers) Ltd and Charles Scribner's Sons for *From Glory to Glory: texts from Gregory of Nyssa's Mystical Writings*, selected by J. Daniélou and translated by H. Musurillo; Penguin Books Ltd for translations by E. V. Rieu of Homer's *Iliad* and *Odyssey*, by A. T. Hatto of Gottfried von Strassburg's *Tristan*, by R. E. Latham of Lucretius *De Rerum Natura*, by M. Magnusson and H. Pálsson of *Njal's Saga*, and *Painting in Britain: the Middle Ages* by M. Rickert, and *The Leaves of Southwell* by N. Pevsner; the Phaidon Press Ltd for *French Painting in the time of Jean de Berry* by M. Meiss; Princeton University Press for *Early Christian Art* by C. R. Morey, and *The Vision of Landscape in Renaissance Italy* by A. R. Turner; the Scottish Text Society for Gavin Douglas's translation of Virgil's *Aeneid*, edited by D. F. C. Coldwell; Thames and Hudson and Harry N. Abrams, Inc. for *Italian Gardens* by Georgina Masson; and Wayne State University Press for *Vagabond Verse* by E. H. Zeydel. The translations in R. Aldington, *A Wreath for San Gemignano*, are copyright Madame Catherine Guillaume 1946.

This book is dedicated to Kenneth Clark, whose *Landscape into Art* provided us with both model and inspiration

INTRODUCTION

The natural world presented to medieval man aspects of paradise, and of
perdition: it was simultaneously the garden of God, and the 'terra Babylonis',
the land of confusion and sterility into which he had been sent after the Fall.
His attitudes to it were various, and, at times, ambiguous: his desire was to
enjoy it, to delight in it as a stimulus to the senses, but he was equally anxious
to control and limit it, as a means of exercising the faculties of reason.
Consequently, in life as in art, we see him moving always from the 'real' to
the ideal, in an effort to preserve and conceptualize what was, by definition,
transient and sensuous. Creating a garden out of the wilderness reassured
him of his god-given power over the mindless luxuriance of nature. Tilling
and reaping, in the steady cycle of the year's weather, reassured him of a
divine order, a rhythmic and meaningful pattern of planets, and seasons, to
be interpreted and utilized by man.

Medieval 'nature poetry' has, therefore, a power that is easier to recognize
than to define clearly. Our models are the wrong models, and comparison
with the verse of later centuries can be misleading. 'Realism' is no criterion,
nor, in many cases, is 'originality': wealth of reference and source material
can legitimately outweigh freshness of observation. There is a close relationship between such medieval poetry and the visual arts: to describe a landscape, either overtly, or by implication, in terms of paint, or stone, or
precious metal, is to go one stage further in the creation of an enduring
image out of the fading materials of leaf and flower. The artefact is an
approximation to the eternal.

Within the period, there is change and counterchange: the landscape of
the mind begins to attract poets and painters less than the landscape of the
eye. The ideal seems to recede before the real. But realism quickly establishes
its own conventional syntax, and the vision of the natural world in the later
Middle Ages draws upon a highly complex set of assumptions about 'inner
and outer weather'.

With such a subject, it would be foolhardy for the authors to claim that
this study of medieval poems and paintings which deal with the natural
world should be considered a definitive treatment. Rather, it offers a series of
approaches to the subject of medieval landscape, and some tentative notions
about the interrelationships of art, literature, life, and the life of the intellect.
Its scope is necessarily wide, for the medieval centuries had no cloistered view
of history and were receptive, though not uncritical, of a long-established
classical heritage. We begin with Homer, and end with poets and artists who

I

lived on the very boundaries of the modern world. Yet total comprehensiveness is not our aim, nor, it must be said, is total consistency of method and opinion. For such is the richness of the theme, that variations must be free and subtle. The general survey must be both confirmed and questioned by the more searching particular enquiry; the truth of individual discoveries must be tested in larger cultural settings.

We have not, therefore, sought a superficial unanimity, content instead with a deeper agreement about the power and beauty of the materials, and the need to communicate something of those qualities, however imperfectly, to the reader.

Chapter One

CLASSICAL TRADITIONS

Landscape backgrounds play a minor but significant part in classical art and literature, and attain a high degree of representational realism, though they are never truly more than backgrounds. The themes of landscape description that were developed, in poetry, wall decoration and manuscript illumination, provided the fundamental sources of medieval treatment of landscape until the fourteenth century, even though in eroded and stylized forms, and the emergence of landscape painting as an independent art form in the fifteenth and sixteenth centuries was inspired, in Italy at least, partly by a return to classical models.

The origins of landscape portrayal are in Hellenistic and Roman art, rather than Greek. The figure art of classical Greece, with its anthropocentric belief in man as the measure of all things, disdained the trivial particularity of landscape, as did Michelangelo later. Greek paintings and friezes approximate always to the free-standing sculpted figure, intensely real yet universal, circumscribed neither in space nor time. Pliny has many anecdotes concerning the illusionistic effect of Greek painting—Parrhasius paints a runner so lifelike that he seems to be panting for breath; Protogenes paints portraits so accurate that they can be used for physiognomical prognostication; and in the picture by Apelles of Alexander holding the thunderbolt, his fingers appear to project from the surface[1]—but they nearly all have to do with figure modelling.

In the same way the *Iliad* concentrates on human action and the human event. There is no landscape here, only land—the bloody littoral of Troy, where Nestor has task enough to find an open place amid the unburied dead for his night parley.[2] Yet the landscape of reality finds its place in the *Iliad*, like most other kinds of reality: not in the actual narrative, but in similes such as those of the cranes in the water meadows, or the long waves breaking on the shore, or the sea in a dark swell before a storm.[3] There is a keenly observant eye here, but it is as if natural description were an inferior art, which had to be enclosed within the literary formula of the simile. The marvellous night scene at the end of book VIII is framed as a simile, even though reality and similitude are the same:

'There are nights when the upper air is windless and the stars in heaven stand

3

out in their full splendour round the bright moon; when every mountain-top and headland and ravine starts into sight, as the infinite depths of the sky are torn open to the very firmament; when every star is seen, and the shepherd rejoices. Such and so many were the Trojans' fires.'[4]

A similar allusiveness is seen in the description of the shield of Hephaestus, made for Achilles when he returns to battle, and decorated with its images of the world: of the field being ploughed, depicted so that the gold fallowland grows black behind the plough—'The artist here achieved a miracle'; of the field being reaped; of the vineyard, done in gold and silver, with a ditch of blue enamel and a fence of tin; a grazing ground for cattle, of gold and tin; and a sheep pasture.[5] It is the world of good order and rural government, such as we shall see again in the frescoes of Ambrogio Lorenzetti in Siena, but described indirectly in terms of what an artist in another medium was trying to portray, with constant reminders of the limitations of that portrayal. It is a humane pastoral landscape, but still half-playfully encapsulated and distanced, so as to preserve the epic foreground. Later, descriptions of pictures were to be used more frankly in narrative as opportunities to introduce landscape motifs for their own sake: the Thracian wilderness around the temple of Mars in Chaucer's *Knight's Tale*, where consciousness of 'picture' soon recedes, is at the end of a line of development running through Virgil, Statius and Boccaccio.

The *Odyssey*, in a less elevated genre, as much romance as epic, is different. Here landscape description functions as part of the narrative, and the long-leaved olive tree at the head of the cove where Odysseus lands on the island of Ithaca, and the thicket of alder where he meets the rancorous Melantheus on the way to his house, have as particular and necessary an identity as 'the dense undergrowth of marshland reeds' where Odysseus describes himself crouching one frosty night at Troy.[6] Typically, we have to look in the *Odyssey* for the scenery of the *Iliad*. More extended descriptions, such as that of the uninhabited goat island near the land of the Cyclopes, with its rich soil and safe anchorage, or that of Odysseus' struggle with Poseidon's raging seas,[7] unfold into narrative what the *Iliad* enclosed in simile and picture. More significantly, the *Odyssey* introduces into Western literature the idealized landscape: in the garden of Alcinous, with its orchard, vineyard, kitchen garden and irrigation ditches, where the trees bear fruit all the year and the west wind always blows,[8] it is still fairly closely tied to the realities of everyday life. But it is openly romantic in the grotto of Calypso on the island of Ogygia, shaded by alders, aspens and cypresses, haunted by birds, with a rich grape vine trailing luxuriantly around the mouth of the cave, four crystal rivulets elegantly conduited, and soft meadows around of iris and parsley. 'It was indeed a spot where even an immortal visitor must pause to gaze in wonder and delight.'[9] This self-conscious flourish, and the pause which Hermes makes to 'view the scene', are events of some moment, marking as they do the emergence of the *locus amoenus* as one of the delights of poetry.

Virgil develops in a consciously 'poetic' manner all the themes of landscape description present in Homer. His similes are more contrived and decorous, without the Greek poet's touch of homeliness. The soldiers of Achaea swarm in the *Iliad* 'as many and as restless as the unnumbered flies that swarm round the cowsheds in the spring'.[10] But the throngs on the banks of Acheron are 'thick as the leaves of the forest that at autumn's first frost dropping fall',

'quam multa in silvis autumni frigore primo
lapsa cadunt folia'[11]

thick as migrating birds. Virgil's image of Turnus rushing headlong into battle as the loosened boulder hurtling downhill is directly imitated from Homer, but it has again this self-consciously epic quality. Homer's boulder, 'misbegotten thing', rolls down and 'runs on unchecked till it reaches level ground, where it stops rolling, much against its will'.[12] But Virgil's rock is aware of its epic rôle 'and bounds over the earth, rolling with it trees, herds and men':

'exsultatque solo, silvas, armenta virosque
involvens secum.'[13]

Virgil's storm at sea is similarly more elaborate than the corresponding description in Homer,[14] more of a set-piece, depicted on a larger canvas with more detail. It is also more careful. Homer has Poseidon hurl all four winds together at Odysseus, his interest being in the god's rage and the man's suffering rather than meteorological likelihood, but Virgil speaks more precisely of the wind shifting suddenly from south-east to south-west, as is said to be characteristic of Mediterranean cyclonic storms.[15]

Homer also provides the hints for Virgil's harbour scene, where Aeneas and his followers first set foot on the Libyan shore. Virgil borrows details not only from the goat island of the Cyclopes and the harbour of the Laestrygonians, but also from the cove in Ithaca where the Phaeacians put Odysseus ashore.[16] Gordon Williams points out that the last passage is part of the poet's narrative, whereas the other two are dramatic narration within the narrative, and is marked by a deliberately digressive quality and by its present tense—*there is*.

'The literary point of this device is to enable the poet to turn the reader's or listener's attention deliberately for a short time, away from the narrative to enjoy a type of digression that invites poetic treatment on its own account.'[17]

Virgil uses this device in a more elaborately self-conscious way to create the fully-developed epic *topographia*:

> 'est in secessu longo locus: insula portum
> efficit obiectu laterum, quibus omnis ab alto
> frangitur inque sinus scindit sese unda reductos.
> hinc atque hinc vastae rupes geminique minantur
> in caelum scopuli, quorum sub vertice late
> aequora tuta silent; tum silvis scaena coruscis
> desuper, horrentique atrum nemus imminet umbra;
> fronte sub adversa scopulis pendentibus antrum,
> intus aquae dulces vivoque sedilia saxo,
> Nympharum domus. hic fessas non vincula navis
> ulla tenent, unco non alligat ancora morsu.'[18]

('There in a deep inlet lies a spot, where an island forms a harbour with the barrier of its sides, on which every wave from the main is broken, then parts into receding ripples. On either side loom heavenward huge cliffs and twin peaks, beneath whose crest far and wide is the stillness of sheltered water; above, too, is a background of shimmering woods with an overhanging grove, black with gloomy shade. Under the brow of the fronting cliff is a cave of hanging rocks; within are fresh waters and seats in the living stone, a haunt of Nymphs. Here no fetters imprison weary ships, no anchor holds them fast with hooked bite.')

The difference between Homer's brief sketch and Virgil's richly landscaped cove with its overhanging cliffs is like the difference between an artist's sketch and the amplitude of the finished painting, with the same loss of immediacy, the same subordination of graphic fact to scenic harmony. Virgil's eye lingers on the scene, composing it into a picturesque whole, just as it lingers on the reflection of the leaves in the water as Aeneas and his men row upstream to Latium.[19] Virgil returns again and again to this particular scenic landscape, the cove or vale amid high wooded hills. There is the enclosed valley where Turnus plans to lay ambush for Aeneas, or the sacred grove of Silvanus, girdled with dark fir trees,[20] and above all the vale of Ampsanctus, introduced with a hush of awe,

> 'est locus Italiae medio sub montibus altis . . .'[21]

('There is a place in the heart of Italy beneath high hills . . .')

and described in terms that suggest some vestigial symbolic value for the sacred landscape which might modify one's view of the essential unimportance of landscape to the Romans.

There is the strong possibility that landscapes such as these may have been inspired by pictures. Mackail points out that the word *scaena*, used in the Libyan harbour scene, is generally applied to the back wall or backcloth of a stage,[22] and landscapes certainly played some part in scene painting. Vitruvius tells us that perspective was introduced into the dramatic *scaena* as early as 456 BC by Agatharcus, in connection with a performance of the *Oresteia* of Aeschylus, and that this caused a revolution in Greek painting,[23] though he adds elsewhere that landscape backgrounds are associated with the satyric genre,[24] another indication of their inferior status. Scene painting no doubt had an influence on Hellenistic landscape painting, stage settings and backgrounds for the actors giving an impetus to scenes in perspective in the Pompeiian 'Second style'.[25] There is a temptation to see close connections between Virgil's epic landscapes and the epic narrative painting fashionable in his day, such as the Odyssey Landscapes,[26] four of which portray the arrival of Odysseus in the land of the Laestrygonians (Plate 4). However, a general current of taste, in both poetry and painting, for the picturesque landscape is what one would wish to identify.

Virgil has an eye as keen as any painter's for the natural world, for effects of light and shade, the shimmer of moonlight on water,[27] or of flickering light reflected from water, in a simile for Aeneas' confused thoughts:

> 'sicut aquae tremulum labris ubi lumen aënis
> sole repercussum aut radiantis imagine lunae
> omnia pervolitat late loca iamque sub auras
> erigitur summique ferit laquearia tecti.'[28]

('As a flickering light from water, flung back by the sun or the moon's glittering form, flits far and wide o'er all things, and now mounts high and smites the fretted ceiling of the roof aloft.')

Pliny records similar experiments with chiaroscuro in Greek painting, as in the picture of a boy blowing a fire, by Antiphilus, where the room is lit by the reflection of the fire and the light on the boy's face.[29] This interest in light effects had long ago been echoed by Hellenistic poets such as Apollonius of Rhodes.[30]

But it is worth noting that Virgil's rendering of observed nature is most exact when under the precise formal control of simile. Virgil's realism is always rigorously objective, is always subdued to the larger concerns of his story, has always the epic universality. The Tunisian coast has been scoured for Aeneas' harbour, fruitlessly, one would think, and desperate attempts have likewise been made to challenge the artifice of the *Eclogues* by moving

Virgil to a place where such scenery as he describes can be found, to Naples, for instance, rather than Mantua, or the site of his farm from Pietole to Calvisano.[31] Virgil's larger concerns in the *Aeneid* are well seen in the contrast between the shield of Vulcan and that of Hephaestus in the *Iliad*. The decoration of the shield in Homer embraces vignettes of town and country life; Aeneas' shield, on the other hand, is painted with the whole history and triumph of Rome down to the battle of Actium.[32] The *land* has become the *state*, and the passage, like the poem, celebrates the victory and peace of Augustan Rome. Its truest analogue in art is the *Ara Pacis Augustae*, or Altar of Peace, dedicated by Augustus in 9 BC.[33] The walled precinct of this open-air altar is decorated with friezes of Roman society in procession, highest and lowest, oldest and youngest, real and allegorical figures, and the carving is done with a strong sense of perspective, the figures at the front in high relief casting shadows on those at the back in low relief, so as to give an impression of distance. There is naturalistic carving of fruits and leaves, hints of background, even of landscape, but the realism of the parts is subdued to the measured political and religious statement of the monumental whole.

The *Georgics* have a similar view of the fulfilment of Roman destiny, and of the importance of the well-ordered land to the well-governed state, and it is no surprise therefore to find that the nearest they approach to landscape description is the long eulogy of Italy in book II, which praises its soil, its climate, its cities, its mineral wealth, and when it speaks of eternal spring, speaks with Roman practicality of two fruit crops a year.[34] Eduard Fraenkel, in his book on Horace, has a passage in which he speaks of Horace's description of Anxur, 'perched up on rocks that can be seen shining for miles around' ('impositum saxis late candentibus'), as 'perhaps the first time in the history of European poetry that so faithful and so suggestive a picture of a definite piece of landscape was given in a few words'.[35] This may be true, and, if so, apt to the genre of satire, but it would be a mistake to associate Horace's particularity here with Virgil's description of towns piled high on steep crags, with streams gliding beneath their ancient walls,[36] lines which, as Fraenkel says, 'irresistibly conjure up the vision of countless Italian townlets'.[37] It is precisely this generalized objectivity which characterizes Virgil.

Other Roman poets, except for Lucretius, lack Virgil's steady eye. Statius imitates Virgil's favourite *scaena*, the vale set around with wooded hills, as a natural amphitheatre for the funeral games of Opheltes. He can describe the landscape carefully when need be, as in the setting for the ambush of Tydeus, or the drought-parched land through which the Argives pass to Thebes.[38] But elsewhere description provides the opportunity for rhetorical extravaganzas, all hectic colour and violence. The unbridgeable

8

gap between *poesis* and *pictura*, subtly hinted at in Homer and Virgil, is crossed and recrossed, and many of Statius' prize passages of description hover fantastically between the two: in the temple of Mars, he appears now to describe carvings, now real things, and in the domain of Sleep a thousand likenesses of the god precede the real one—*Hae species*.[39] His extravagance and fantasy made a direct appeal to the Middle Ages, and vestigial versions of both these passages are to be found in Chaucer, in the *Knight's Tale* and the *Book of the Duchess*.

Propertius is even further from Virgil, and nearer to the Middle Ages, in the way he accumulates detail to give a rich ornamental effect rather than to stimulate the visual imagination with accuracy of perception. The effect can be seen in his description of the sanctuary of Bona Dea,[40] where Housman's much-admired conjecture *glaucis* (grey-green) for *longis*, of poplar leaves, is quite opposed to the non-visual bias of the description.[41] At the other extreme, the poetry of Lucretius embodies visual perception of extraordinary accuracy, as in his description of the play of motes in a sunbeam, or of a flock of sheep moving over a hillside but seen as still from a distance[42] (here there is perspective in poetry long before McLuhan's cliff at Dover), but both passages are enclosed as similitudes for atomic theory. The blending of landscape reality into a comprehensive poetic vision seems therefore to be Virgil's peculiar achievement; for other poets landscape provides a series of motifs for poetic ornamentation and elaboration. One would be wary of attributing to them any desire for particularity or for accuracy for its own sake, and more than wary of Fraenkel's romantic interpretation of Horace's ode *O fons Bandusiae* in terms of 'the poetic directness that comes from the close contact with tree and fountain, rocks and hilly woodlands'.[43] One would think, rather, in this poem, of poetic effects poetically achieved, and, fondly, of the ubiquity of nature feeling since Wordsworth.

In one kind of poetry, however, the cultivation of a feeling for nature is generic to the type, that is, in pastoral. The image of a landscape offered by nature as a refuge from reality is present already in Homer's island of Ogygia, but the features of the pastoral landscape—flowers, birds, breezes, above all the dominant motif of the tree-shaded waters—are first systematically developed in the *Idylls* of the poet Theocritus (*c.* 280 BC). Here, in the work of a man who knew only the parched lands of Sicily and Egypt, we find the origins of a vision of landscape which was to dominate the next two thousand years, to dominate poets writing even in far Northern lands where shade and water are by no means difficult to come by. So it is to the sacred stream beside the altar in the grove sacred to Demeter that Simichidas and his friends come, after competing in praise of their boy loves, to celebrate the festival

9

(Idyll 7). The waters are shaded by poplars and elms; pears and apples lie strewn on the ground, and the air is full of the chatter of cicadas, the hum of bees and the song of the lark, goldfinch and turtledove. In Idyll 22, Castor and Pollux, like Hylas in Idyll 13, go in search of water, and find under a smooth cliff an ever-flowing spring, shaded by pine, poplar, plane and cypress, and filled with pure water, so that the pebbles gleam like crystal or silver from the depths. Such descriptions, which may derive something of their self-consciously 'composed' air from imitation of the bowers and grottoes of contemporary Alexandrian country art,[44] are already developing the richness of ornament which, systematized, is the basis of the medieval convention of the *locus amoenus*.

It is, however, Virgil's *Eclogues*, deeply influenced by Theocritus, which fixed for ever in the European mind the idyllic landscape of pastoral tradition. All study of ancient Latin poetry in the Middle Ages began with Tityrus under the beech tree's shade, and continued with the cooling streams, the murmur of the breeze through the hedgerows, the moaning of doves in the elms, of the first Eclogue:

'hic inter flumina nota
et fontis sacros frigus captabis opacum.'[45]

('Here, amid familiar streams and sacred springs, you shall court the cooling shade.')

Pastoral landscape in Virgil is strictly confined to the pastoral genre, the business, for all its literary affiliations, of shepherds. The medieval division of the three styles, high, middle and low, according to the reflection of society in Virgil's three poems, the *Aeneid*, the *Georgics* and the *Eclogues*,[46] enforces this association of pastoral landscape with homely life. Such landscape, as we have seen already, and shall see again in painting and accounts of painting, is essentially trivial, a minor and digressive ornament in the serious business of life. The scenery of the *Aeneid* is by contrast grand in the epic manner, and in the *Georgics* Virgil rejects an opportunity to describe garden cultivation as irrelevant to his matter, saying that if he did he would describe the delights of having flowers and fruits in season, the first roses in spring, apples in autumn, loading the board with unbought dainties.[47] In other words he concentrates on the garden not as an opportunity to re-create the idyllic scenery of pastoral, but in terms of purposeful good husbandry.

It is therefore to Ovid, with his essentially unserious view of life, that one would turn for the fully-developed models of the *locus amoenus*. Ovid has a sense of the natural world as sharp as Virgil's, in the way he directs attention in this night scene, for instance, to sensory detail:

'inmotaeque silent frondes, silet umidus aer,
sidera sola micant.'[48]
('The leaves were mute and motionless, the dewy air was still, only the stars
twinkled.')

Or in his description of the sickle-shaped bay of shallow water, with firm
sand, free from seaweed, where the sand retains no footprints, yet does not
clog one's steps.[49] But in contrast to Virgil's steadiness of gaze, it is a free
and wanton eye that Ovid has, delighting itself in the embroidery of fantastic
possibilities in the account of the Flood, where a man takes fish caught in the
elm's upper branches, the keels brush the vineyard's top, and the dolphins
swim between the high branches of the oak trees.[50] This is 'imagination' of a
high order, in its way, but purely decorative, meaningless in the sense in
which Virgil has meaning, or in comparison with the Christian interpretation
of the biblical Flood, which never distracted itself with such detail. It was the
innate triviality of content in Ovid which made him such a hunting ground
for medieval readers, a wealth of matter crying out for sense. (We may think
it a symbolic accident that the Middle Ages did not know Lucretius.) The
irresponsibility of the professional rhetorician can be seen too in the way
Ovid will abandon reality for extravagance of effect. Virgil has some justi-
fication, as we have seen, for his contrary winds, and Homer too, but in
Ovid's sea storm[51] not only do the winds blow from all four quarters, but
mountainous seas seem to reach the stars, and yawn to reveal black Tartarus.

Ovid, partly for these reasons, develops the idyllic landscape of the *locus
amoenus* with a tender and elaborate detail which makes him a major source
for all subsequent landscape description. It is again the seductive image of
tree-shaded waters that dominates: the cool grove with gentle stream where
Diana comes; the pool of Narcissus, with grass to the edge, fed by the water,
and surrounding coppice; the pool of Pergus, where Proserpine is seized,
and where trees crown the heights around to keep the sun off like an awning;
the grotto of Diana in the vale of Gargaphie; or Arethusa's description of the
river Alpheus, flowing without eddy, crystalline so that the very pebbles in
its bed can be counted, and shaded by poplars and silvery willows.[52] Above
all, there is Ovid's decorative version of the Virgilian enclosed vale, the
valley through which thunders the river Peneus, clouding the air with spray,
the most famous of all classical landscapes:

'Est nemus Haemoniae, praerupta quod undique claudit
silva: vocant Tempe . . .'[53]
('There is a vale in Thessaly which steep-wooded slopes surround on every side,
Men call it Tempe . . .')

Even Pliny, amidst his lists of place names and distances, allows himself to be touched by the traditional poetry of the scene:

'Part of the course of the Peneus is called the Vale of Tempe, five miles long and nearly an acre and a half in breadth, with gently sloping hills rising beyond human sight on either hand, while the valley between is verdant with a grove of trees. Along it glides the Peneus, glittering with pebbles and adorned with grassy banks, melodious with the choral song of birds.'[54]

Pliny subdues the grandeur of Ovid's 'praerupta silva', in which the influence, again, of picturesque landscape paintings, such as those of the Vatican Odyssey, has been seen.[55]

The ubiquity of the pastoral landscape, which we shall see systematized in late Roman and medieval poetry, is illustrated in Horace's warning against allowing bravura descriptions of this kind to usurp the proper function of poetry in non-pastoral genres.[56] His own Roman contempt for such romantic idylls we can see in the second Epode, where a brilliant pastiche of pastoral motifs is sharply turned back on the reader at the end, with the unexpected attribution of the poem's sentiments to the usurer Alfius, who talks like this every time business is bad.[57] We shall find a similar condescension in the response of some writers to the current vogue for landscape painting.

Alexandria was the source of this Hellenistic tradition of landscape painting, though almost all the surviving examples, apart from the mosaics in Syrian Antioch, are Italian, principally from Pompeii, Herculaneum and Rome. It was, in its origins, a pastoral tradition, the product of an urban culture, with some influence from the parks and gardens of the orient. There is a characteristic range of features—rocky hills in the background, trees, bits of monumental architecture, such as an arch or colonnade, above all the *stele*, or column, with its associated tree, which together are almost a 'signature' of Hellenistic landscape. Perspective is often elaborately developed, though not systematic in the strictest Brunelleschian sense.[58] Such painting was popular in Rome from the second century BC onwards, and was introduced into Pompeii towards the middle of the first century BC (Plates 1, 2) where it swiftly superseded the first Pompeiian or 'Incrustation' style, the imitation in paint of marble revetting and veneers. It was a genre on its own, probably executed by professional landscape painters, such as the Demetrius Topographos of an earlier period mentioned by Valerius Maximus,[59] and often added, as in fifteenth-century Italy, to copies of famous classical figure pictures or mythological scenes, which the rich of Pompeii would have in

their villas like Old Masters.[60] The illusion of depth, perhaps fortified by
scene painting in drama, is allied to an impressionistic rendering of tree
foliage and a strong sense of light and shade, later developed in the portrayal
of rocky landscape to produce the characteristically dramatic 'broken
terrace' structure[61] which is the most distinctive single legacy of Hellenistic
landscape painting to the Middle Ages. A favourite fashion was to paint the
walls of the villa with pilasters or columns, with landscape vistas between, as
if to reveal the open country beyond the wall. Pliny speaks of this fashion
being introduced into Rome by one Spurius Tadius (or Ludius) in the reign
of Augustus:

'painting walls with pictures of country houses and porticoes and landscape
gardens, groves, woods, hills, fish-ponds, canals, rivers, coasts, and whatever
anybody could desire, together with various sketches of people going for a stroll or
sailing in a boat or on land going to country houses riding on asses or in carriages,
and also people fishing or fowling or hunting or even gathering the vintage.'[62]

Vitruvius speaks in very similar terms of how painters solved the problem
of wall decoration in large villas by using

'the varieties of landscape gardening, finding subjects in the characteristics of
particular places; for they paint harbours, headlands, shores, rivers, springs, straits,
temples, groves, hills, cattle, shepherds.'[63]

There are many survivals of these continuous prospect pictures (Plate 3),
opening out walls into romantic countrysides adorned with interesting villas,
shrines, streams and seacoasts—the villa of Boscoreale and the house of
M. Lucretius Fronto in Pompeii, the villa of Quintili on the Appian Way
and the house of Augustus which was known as Livia's after he died.[64]
    Pliny, however, is very conscious of landscape painting as a minor and
inferior art, elegant and pleasing ('qualia quis optaret'), but not of great
significance. He expresses regret that wall painting has become so popular,
since it is neither public not portable, and seems on the whole to regard it as
a harmless fad of the rich middle classes. There is a strong echo here of the
low-style status of literary pastoral, and we should remember that imperial
Rome had a high-style monumental art to set against the trivial prettiness of
painted pastoral. The reliefs of the Arch of Titus, the Arch of Trajan at
Beneventum, and many other monuments, but above all of Trajan's Column,
with their strong sense of perspective and complete illusionism, are the
characteristic Roman response to the Alexandrian manner, the 'adaptation
of Hellenistic style to the rendering of historical events'.[65] The illusionism of

Trajan's Column is part of a stable 'Virgilian' realism, a steadiness of vision which can record the Emperor's Dacian campaigns in their horrors (the surgeons attending to the wounded, the Dacian women torturing Roman prisoners), as well as their glories and triumphs. The crowding of figure and action is all politically meaningful, since the ultimate dedication is not to truth of appearance but to fact.

At the same time one should not dismiss Roman landscape painting as altogether unrepresentative of this larger realism. The continuous sense of villa and garden, of garden and landscape, the harmony of man's world and the world of nature, is an important expression of classical realism, as against the medieval tendency to close off the garden against the wilderness. The medieval view of landscape is of a series of pockets of civilization in an alien or indifferent surround, the walled garden in the midst of the wild wood, the castle complex rather than the country villa. Landscape outside the enclosure can have only a symbolic identity. Classical painting and garden art, however, sees no barrier between inner and outer. The house opens out into the garden, partly through Persian influence, where the city of Cyzicus gave its name to a kind of room with folding windows opening on to gardens.[66] Where this is not possible, rooms are painted with illusionistic gardens, as in the villa of Livia at Prima Porta near Rome, where, in an underground room with garden frescoes, the walls have disappeared completely: the garden retreats from the base of the painted wall into a tangle of flower beds, drawn with minute accuracy. The garden in its turn was a vestibule to the surrounding landscape, as in Pliny's garden at his Tuscan villa:

'Box cut in the form of steps conceals the outside walls, so as to obliterate the appearance of a separation of garden and open country. For it is always an object of desire that the front of the villa shall have a view over the landscape, "where nature seems as good as the garden made by art".'[67]

In the same way, the landscaped vale of Tempe in the garden of Hadrian's villa at Tivoli 'served as a link between the ordered beauty of the formal gardens and the wild mountainous landscape of the Tiburtine hills'.[68] Statius, in his praise of the villa of Pollius Felix at Sorrento, makes particular mention of the fact that each room has a different view of the surrounding landscape.[69] This consciousness of the room with a view, the confidence in the beyond, the turning outward rather than inward, are all aspects of a Roman world view which is in sharp contrast to the medieval distrust of natural reality, and which will not be found again, in garden design at least, until the Tuscan gardens of the late fifteenth century.

The Odyssey Landscapes, which have often been regarded as typical of Hellenistic landscape painting, are perhaps a special case (Plate 4). They are a series of prospect pictures, discovered during excavations in the Via Graziosa in 1848, and now preserved in the Vatican library. They date from the first century AD, and represent seven scenes from books X and XI of the *Odyssey*: four of the land of the Laestrygonians, one of the meeting with Circe, and two of the underworld. They show a strong sense of perspective in depth, and anticipate Alberti's window simile for the concept of perspective, as Panofsky points out, in that 'a continuous stretch of scenery is viewed through a framework of simulated pilasters'.[70] The scenes are mostly of rocky coasts with sea views, and with Hellenistic personifications of mountains and rivers (a relic of classical concentration on the human figure) scattered around. The interest in space composition has led to a vivid observation of light effects, as in the way the light of the outer world shines in under the arch of the cliff on to the shadow realm of ghosts in the underworld, and to an illusionistic blurring of line and rendering of form by colour contrast in accord with the distant point of view. Human figures are sketchy, and completely subordinated to the landscape in and out of which they move. The shadowy presence of humanity, the misty skies and melting horizons, the lack of compositional unity, the 'unreal, almost spectral quality'[71] of the sense of space, all contribute to the creation of a unique impressionistic effect. The vision of landscape in these paintings escapes from the lucidity and stability of pastoral into pure romanticism.

The Pompeiian manner survived well into the third century, according to the descriptions by Philostratus of his gallery at Naples. Representation of landscape and of atmospheric effects aims at a consistent illusionism, in a moonlight scene, for instance, or in the Memnon, where the Colossus is reddened by the rays of the rising sun.[72] There was also elaborately realistic development of the 'broken terrace' landscape, horizontal rocky slabs broken by vertical fissures, as in the famous mosaic from Hadrian's villa of the *Battle of the Centaurs and Leopards* (Plate 5), or the *Pastoral Landscape with Goats*, with their strong sense of light and shade and colour harmony. But neither the comfortable syntax of Hellenistic pastoral, nor the classical rationalism in which it played a minor part, could survive intact the turbulence and ideological crisis of third- and fourth-century Rome. Auerbach finds evidence as early as Seneca and Tacitus of the dark realism of the fourth-century Ammianus Marcellinus, where 'the sensory, the perceivable runs riot', where 'with glittering words and pompously distorted constructions language begins to depict the distorted, gory, and spectral reality of the age',[73] and hints of a like disturbance of the placid Hellenistic manner can be found in the passionately declamatory *Trojan Horse* from Pompeii.[74] The

Barberini Mosaic at Palestrina, probably from the time of Hadrian, shows tendencies of a different kind (Plate 7). Though clearly related to the Campanian pastoral and harbour scenes described by Vitruvius, it seems ambitious to emulate the comprehensiveness of Roman monumental sculpture, and the result is a massive but fragmented anthology, a 'storied framework',[75] a unified idea rather than a unified space. The artist seems desirous of 'composing' a scene, but is defied by the richness of his material, and takes refuge in some fairly obvious horizontal segmentation and varied point perspective. It is the significant achievement of late Roman painting that it turns this embarrassment to advantage, abandoning fixed point perspective in favour of planar presentation, and historical narrative in favour of a thematic organization of picture space which is at times startling in its anticipation of medieval principles. The major monument of this late Roman style is the fourth-century villa of Piazza Armerina in Sicily, whose mosaic floors demonstrate its varied potential, from the richly allusive grandeur and vitality of *The Corridor of the Great Hunt* (Plate 6) to the emotional expressiveness of *The Stricken Giants* in the Trilobate Hall.[76] But the abandonment of unified perspective and of narrative organization leaves this kind of painting prone to yield to a purely decorative magnificence, as in the work of the Court Master at the Piazza Armerina, or the mosaics of the Constantinian villa of Daphne-Harbie at Antioch. The existence of a late Roman *koine* could well be admitted,[77] and the ease with which Christian artists took over its main characteristics. But perhaps it might be said that fourth-century Rome, having created a style, had nothing to celebrate in it but a dying mythology, and therefore handed over a form suitably empty of content to the new religion, just as the exhausted rhetoric of late classical antiquity was taken over and revived by Christian apologists and scholars.

The assumptions of Hellenistic landscape, pushed to one side in the late Roman style, were now to be totally undermined by an Eastern religion which had little respect for the realities of the outer world, and which was to concentrate in its art on the moral and typological identity of its figures, less and less on their surroundings. The first Christian art, that of the Catacombs, adapts to its use many of the Hellenistic motifs, but is already beginning to invest them with symbolic significance, as in the portrayal of *The Good Shepherd* in a mountainous landscape in the catacomb of Domitilla,[78] or in the unusual application of the Alexandrian *stele* in the background of *The Raising of Lazarus* in the catacomb of the Via Latina.[79] When Christian painting emerges above ground, in the fourth century, it employs a varied vocabulary for its landscape backgrounds, sometimes full of Hellenistic memories, sometimes responsive to the late Roman style, but always

I *The Four Evangelists*, from the Aachen Gospels. Aachen Cathedral Treasury, Codex Aureus, f. 13r. Early ninth century. Photo: Ann Münchow.

tending to flatten perspective and project symbolic meaning. The mosaic pavements of the Basilica of Theodore at Aquileia include a panoramic seascape, embodying the story of Jonah, which is a perfect demonstration of the 'paratactic vision' of the Piazza Armerina, with the whole scene transposed to the surface of a single foreground plane.[80] Yet its source is in the exotic Nile riverscapes which had long been popular in fashionable Alexandrian art. They appear again, probably the work of an artist trained in secular decoration, in the (now lost) mosaic wall decoration of the Mausoleum of Constantina (S. Costanza) in Rome, but the most significant work here is in the two lunettes by a later Christian artist, the *Traditio clavium* and the *Traditio legis*, figures set against a landscape background which is already beginning to take on an unearthly symbolic quality, 'where ancient vestiges of late Alexandrian pastorals lose themselves in delicate surfaces of celestial meadows, spangled with flowers, branches, stars and crosses.[81] Similar lunettes in the chapel of S. Aquilino in Milan (*c.* 400) seem at first richer in Hellenistic memories, but it is possible to see how mountain backgrounds, running water and foreground flowers are growing more stylized and schematic as the subject figures take on a greater emotional charge.[82]

The mosaics of S. Maria Maggiore in Rome (432–40), however, are the most extended example of the Christian reinterpretation of older landscape styles. They are the first to offer a systematic historical representation of Old Testament scenes and, whatever the origin of the new iconography, whether it is in manuscript illustration being done for the Greek translation of the Old Testament (the Septuagint) or in sequences like those of the synagogue at Dura-Europos, it is clear that within it Hellenistic landscape could be preserved only as a relic. The mosaics still show figures and groups moving in skilfully suggested space, with landscapes of red, blue and green hills, houses and cities, under a sky dappled with fantastically coloured clouds. The picture of *The Parting of Lot and Abraham* has a diagonal temple-like structure with a tree beside it, recalling familiar features of Hellenistic landscape, and in the representation of *Abraham entertaining the Angels* the same temple and tree do duty for Abraham's tent and the oak of Mamre.[83] But in other scenes the gold ground has already taken the place of sky, the mountains have become stylized swirls, and the remnants of illusionism in perspective and highlighting cannot disguise the fact that landscape has become two-dimensional, a screen or backdrop to place the figures against.

Similar remnants can be seen in the mosaic in the apse of S. Cosmas and S. Damian (526–30), with its blue sky broken with variegated cloud, but the artistic centre had shifted by now from Rome to Ravenna, and landscape was even further subdued to dogmatic purposes. There is no immediate break with tradition: the mosaic of *The Good Shepherd* (Plate 8) in the Mausoleum of Galla Placidia (*c.* 450) has a charming, if fragmented, pastoral setting, though the figure of the shepherd itself is heavily symbolic, with nimbus, cross for crook, and patrician robes, which in turn invests the landscape with paradisal overtones.[84] Morey compares Roman statuettes of realistic shepherds, with lambs over their shoulders, 'to measure the Christian shift from Hellenistic naturalism, wherein the allegory never transcends the physical, to an arbitrary rearrangement of nature in the interest of transcendental truth'.[85] The sixth-century mosaics of S. Vitale show a similar continuity with Hellenistic tradition (Plate 9), in the Abraham and Abel scenes, for instance, with suggestions of sky in cloud-dotted blue or many-coloured striations, hints of perspective in a foreshortened colonnade, and the ever-present Alexandrian tree. But the broken terrace has now become stylized, proliferates fantastically, and slopes to fit the curvature of the lunette, so that the picture seems designed to fill a frame rather than represent a space. The rocky backgrounds of the Evangelist portraits are likewise piled up from top to bottom of the picture, with the Evangelists in an indeterminate floating position in front of them.[86] Landscape plays a larger part in S. Vitale than in other Ravenna mosaics, but the lack of relation of figure and background, the frontal pose and open-eyed stare of the figures, all point to fundamentally non-spatial and symbolic concepts. The full consequences of this are seen in the Justinian and Theodora groups in the same basilica, with their gold backgrounds and anatomical impossibilities, and also in the purely arbitrary, decorative and symbolic disposition of trees, flowers, animals and clouds in the mosaics of S. Apollinare in Classe. Pictures now reflect theology and theological dispute; they have a dogmatic point, to uphold an orthodoxy of the intellect, not to minister to the illusion of reality. Vitruvius had said, 'Pictures cannot be approved which do not resemble reality';[87] but Plotinus is the arbiter of the new order, and for him the appearances of reality, the visual laws of which he fully understands, must be dematerialized by the 'inner eye', which alone can penetrate to the intelligible truth.[88] So Ravenna moves away from even the limited representationalism of historically reconstructed biblical scenes, towards the symbolic schemes of the Byzantine manner, with their specific purpose, 'ce fut d'exprimer sur les murailles le dogme dont l'église apparaissait comme la figure visible'.[89]

Yet the hardening of this Byzantine style, which may seem to be complete in the metropolitan mosaic programmes of Ravenna and Constantinople, is never totally monolithic. Byzantine artists are always susceptible to a breakthrough from their Hellenistic inheritance, and it is to waves of this 'perennial Hellenism',[90] rather than to historical events such as the dispersal of Greek artists at the start of the Iconoclast movement in 726, that we might attribute the occasional appearance of antique landscapes in painting and mosaic of the seventh and eighth centuries. There are fragmentary evidences of Hellenistic style in the murals of S. Maria Antiqua in Rome; and in the mosaics formerly in S. Demetrius in Salonica two of the panels open up surprisingly into a picturesque Alexandrian landscape, with trees, mountains, even the ubiquitous pillar, surmounted by a vase. The best evidence, however, comes from the extraordinary frescoes of S. Maria di Castelseprio, near Milan, discovered in 1944. This Nativity cycle, painted perhaps about 700, is almost Pompeiian in manner, with mountain backgrounds, flat-topped rocks, pillars, receding arcades and distant architecture to give a sense of space, and illusionistic light effects such as the cast shadows of the Magi.[91] The donkey in *The Flight into Egypt* is of a kind that we shall not see again for six centuries.

The employment of Greek-trained artists may help to explain a similar revival of classical landscape in some manuscript illumination of the same period, though, since manuscripts are mostly copied directly from earlier models, such changes of fashion are necessarily blurred. Earlier book illustration, of secular works, such as the fifth-century Milan *Iliad* and the Vatican Virgil (*c.* 400), is in the Alexandrian tradition, with impressionistic highlighting, graduated skies, and a strong sense of space. But the compositions are beginning to lose coherence, and in another Vatican Virgil, the *Codex Romanus*, 'locus classicus for the disintegration of the illusionistic ensemble into its component details',[92] this tendency is still more pronounced. The well-known pictures of *Dido and Aeneas sheltering from the Storm*, or of *Shepherds Tending their Flocks* (Plate 10), show no sense of spatial relations in their landscape background, but scatter trees, animals and figures indiscriminately to fill the picture area and bring every detail forward on to the picture surface. Individual features such as leaves are carefully and accurately drawn, but this kind of fragmented realism has more to do with Dorigo's late Roman style than with classical landscape tradition. We shall find it throughout the Middle Ages, in the exotic flora and fauna of the Ashburnham Pentateuch (*c.* 600) as well as in medical treatises and encyclopaedias.

The Vienna Genesis (*c.* 500) shows the Alexandrian tradition in somewhat less debilitated form, perhaps because it is based on the illustrated Greek Septuagints, but it is the work of several artists, some of whom misunderstood Hellenistic perspective completely. The more intelligent copiers can portray 'Alexandrian' mountains, architectural perspectives, the inevitable *stele* with tree. But Wickhoff's remarks about the rendering of atmospheric effects, of the sky in various moods, of the sun piercing through morning mists,[93] are fanciful at best. The figures are awkward, and the careful stylized trees show a tendency to fill space rather than to grow. The illustrators of the Gospel Book of Rossano, the *Codex Rossanensis* (sixth century), found a happier solution in discarding altogether the paraphernalia of illusionism. The Codex is written in silver letters on purple vellum, is probably from Constantinople or even further East, and lacks the Hellenistic models that Old Testament illustrators had in the Greek Septuagints. As a result, the two-dimensional character of the page is frankly accepted, buildings are shown in both frontal and side elevation, as opposed to the Alexandrian diagonals, space is dissolved into narrative, line into magnificence of colour. Certain scenes, such as *The Entry into Jerusalem* or *The Agony in the Garden*, are here given the iconographical structures which were to remain fixed for centuries in Byzantine art, up to and beyond Duccio.

There was, however, a last Alexandrian intrusion before the Byzantine style hardened, which may have been due to the dispersal already mentioned, or to the further dispersals of the Iconoclastic period. The Joshua Rotulus and the Paris Psalter are both tenth-century texts, with earlier illustration, variously dated (*c.* 700–*c.* 900), based on still earlier models. The most famous miniature in the latter is that of *David the Harper* (Plate 11), a remarkable copy of some Alexandrian original, with deep perspective, distant architecture, *stele* and tree, carefully brought-out light and shade, betraying its ancestry only in some ill-drawn detail such as that of the bronze vase on the pillar. It could almost be from Pompeii. The Joshua Roll, a sequence of scenes from the book of Joshua, is more laboured in its imitation of naturalistic landscape, but the idyllic picturesqueness of the Alexandrian style still comes through: 'Buildings in the distance thrust their silhouettes above the shoulders of the hills; the cities of Ai and Jericho are rendered with the same broad impressionism as the walls of Troy in the Iliad of Milan, or the seashore villas of Campanian landscapes'.[94]

The metamorphosis of Hellenistic landscape in Carolingian and Byzantine tradition we must leave for a moment, to turn to the development of landscape description in poetry. Here there is eventually the same tendency towards the schematization and fossilization of classical style that we have seen in mosaic and book illustration. But first there is a spectacular flourishing of ornamental landscape in late Roman poetry, which we can set beside the late sophistication of the Alexandrian style, and see being cut off from its sources of nourishment, in Roman realism, in the same way. Virgil had integrated landscape into a comprehensive epic vision, and Ovid and Statius, despite their tendency to the bravura interlude, still subordinate landscape to narrative. But the fourth century sees the ornamental landscape, the *locus amoenus*, achieve independent poetic existence, as in the elaborate poem by Tiberianus quoted by Curtius,[95] where the wealth of detail is already being organized into systematic patterns:

> 'Ales amnis aura lucus flos et umbra iuverat.'
> ('Bird and river, breeze and woodland, flower and shade brought ravishment.')

A little poem by Claudian, *Est in conspectu longe locus*, isolates the Virgilian harbour into an independent vignette:

> 'Est procul ingenti regio summota recessu,
> insula qua resides fluctus mitescere cogit
> in longum producta latus, fractasque per undas
> ardua tranquillo curvantur brachia portu.'[96]

('There is a place deep buried in a huge bay where an island, stretching far out into the sea, stills the rough waves to quiet, and steep cliffs, jutting out into the broken water, curve themselves into a peaceful harbourage.')

Claudian is also responsible for some of the most extended and influential developments of ornamental landscape, as in the Sicilian fields of the *De Raptu Proserpinae*, a studied blending of favourite motifs. Here is Zephyrus 'painting' the flowers; the mixed forest, and catalogue of trees;[97] the lake of Pergus, with its pellucid depths; and the enveloping shaded and well-watered meadowland.[98] The comparative restraint of this description, with its sense of epic precedent, should be measured against the overblown luxuriance of the mountain in Cyprus, consecrate to pleasure and Venus, in the *Epithalamium de Nuptiis Honorii Augusti*. Eternal spring reigns here, ever flowering; the very leaves live for love, and the trees are under love's sway, palm bending to mate with palm, poplar with poplar. Cupid dips his arrows in two fountains, one bitter, the other sweet, and many personified abstractions roam the enclosed country, encircled by its hedge of gold— Licence, Anger, Pallor, Fear, and Youth, who has shut out Age. In the midst is the palace of Venus, built of gold and gems. In this poem, with its many anticipations of the *Roman de la Rose*, we may say the Middle Ages begin: landscape is invaded by allegory, and deliberately reconstructed to embody an erotic ideal. There is even the sense of artificial enclosure ('aurea saepes') inseparable from the medieval ideal landscape.

The same subordination of landscape to erotic sentiment is seen in the probably contemporary *Pervigilium Veneris*, a rapturous celebration of spring as the festival day of Venus, the reawakening of nature and love:

> 'Cras amet qui nunquam amavit quique amavit cras amet;
> ver novum, ver iam canorum, ver renatus orbis est;

vere concordant amores, vere nubunt alites,
et nemus comam resolvit de maritis imbribus.
cras amet qui nunquam amavit quique amavit cras amet.'[99]
('Tomorrow shall be love for the loveless, and for the lover tomorrow shall be love. Spring is young, spring now is singing, spring is the world reborn. In spring the loves make accord, in spring the birds mate, and the woodland loosens her tresses under nuptial showers. Tomorrow, etc.')

The countryside quickens with love's delight, Dione paints the crimsoning year with flowery jewels (IV), the dew unfolds virginal buds from their wet sheaths (V). The imagery is strongly erotic, suggestive of virginal awakening, moistening, and spring itself is Danaë-like:

'ut pater totum crearet veris annum nubibus
in sinum maritus imber fluxit almae coniugis.'
(XV)
('To quicken the whole year from the clouds of spring, the bridegroom-shower has flowed into the lap of his fair bride.')

This rhapsodic sexual interpretation of nature is quite alien to the objectivity of pastoral, where the countryside may echo or mock the lover's moods but not embody them. It is, however, in more discreet form, an important element in the medieval landscape of love, as we shall see in Gottfried's *Tristan*, where the outer realities of nature are reconstituted according to the inner realities of human passion. In Virgil, by contrast, landscape retains its objective reality, the peacefulness of a night scene which provides a dramatically contrasting background for Dido's anguish, or the noontide heat when all creatures rest except the unhappy lover.[100]

A subjectivity similar to that of the *Pervigilium* is present in the fourth-century poem *De Rosis Nascentibus*, formerly attributed to both Virgil and Ausonius. The poet here takes an early morning walk in spring, in a garden laid out with flowers, vegetables, rose bushes, and divided by paths, when the air was still sharp from the frost, 'round drops rolling together upon the cabbage-leaves'.[101] He sees the roses, some in bud, some just flecked with colour, some opening at the tip, some with leaves unfurling, some fully open, others blown. Such is life, he reflects, and therefore:

'collige, virgo, rosas, dum flos novus et nova pubes,
et memor esto aevum sic properare tuum.'
(49–50)
('Then, maidens, gather roses, while blooms are fresh and youth is fresh, and be mindful that so your life-time hastes away.')

A high degree of naturalistic precision is combined here with a fundamentally subjective and symbolic view of nature which is no different aesthetically from the biblical and patristic imagery of the fading flower.

Ausonius himself represents a stage in the disintegration of classical landscape which may be compared with the Virgilian *Codex Romanus*. His *Mosella*, a descriptive eulogy of the river Moselle, has moments of close and keen observation, as when he imitates Ovid in gazing into the limpid depths of the water:

> 'quod sulcata levi crispatur harena meatu,
> inclinata tremunt viridi quod gramina fundo:
> usque sub ingenuis agitatae fontibus herbae
> vibrantes patiuntur aquas lucetque latetque
> calculus et viridem distinguit glarea muscum.'[102]

('How the furrowed sand is rippled by the light current, how the bowed watergrasses quiver in the green bed; down beneath their native streams the tossing plants endure the water's buffeting, pebbles gleam and are hid, and gravel picks out patches of green moss.')

Or when he develops the Virgilian motif of reflection in the water, of boats sailing through the reflected foliage (189–99). Elsewhere he shows a taste for the picturesque and a sense of perspective, describing the vineyard-clad slopes of the river valley as a 'natural theatre' (156), or the country seats perched on the summits of the rocks overlooking the river, their sites chosen for height and a 'rich outlook' (326). The reminiscences of Virgil's eulogy of Italy in *Georgics II* are there, but all this is mixed with mythological excursuses, lists of fish, and descriptions of fishing. The eye is unsteady, and wavers from the object; other things, one of them rhetorical ostentation, are more important than the reality of landscape. As in the *Codex Romanus*, each feature is presented independently, with no sense of coherence and, in the end, no sense.

Sidonius, too, is still scraping amongst the orts and relics of Roman tradition. In his prose *Epistle to Domitius* (II, 2) he describes his own villa at Avitacum in Gaul, with its summer rooms lying open, in the Roman fashion, to the lake and to the sounds and sights of a pastoral landscape. But the barbarians were already closing in, and the age is more truly reflected in the poem on the castle (*burgus*) of Pontius Leontius.[103] This rhetorical exercise is modelled explicitly on the villa descriptions of the *Silvae*, but the spacious villa is now battlemented to withstand siege warfare. By the sixth century, Ausonius' lush Moselle landscape has also changed, and Venantius Fortunatus now celebrates the castle of Bishop Nicetius, towering as a ward of defence above the river:

'Here we see the vast frowning fortress, with the river below; the mighty towers contrasting with the peace of field and vineyard; the threatening ballista and the fruitful orchards.'[104]

The villa has given way to the castle, and castle and church both turn their back on landscape, so ushering in the Middle Ages.

Chapter Two

THE EARLY MIDDLE AGES

Classical landscape passes down to the Middle Ages in stylized and denuded form in Carolingian and Byzantine manuscripts, and in the rhetorical elaboration of the *locus amoenus* in the Latin schools. There was little interest in observation of the natural world of reality, or in the development of new motifs of landscape portrayal. The eye was turned from the illusory shadows of the outer to the pressing concerns of the inner world. The mythological personifications of Hellenistic painting, designed to express and control man's vision of his relation with the natural world, are replaced by the allegorical personifications of Prudentius and his illustrators, the teeming psychomachia uncovered by the Christian inward eye. The new eschatology raises the stakes of existence, so that the delight of the senses in the pleasures of landscape may come to seem not merely an irrelevance but a positive distraction from the all-compelling battle for salvation. Earlier patristic writers like St Augustine or St Gregory of Nyssa,[1] still under the influence of the classical vision, had paid some respect to the world of sensory experience, but the high spirituality of the eleventh and twelfth centuries regarded it with contempt, and St Bernard would have agreed with St Anselm, who concluded that 'the delight of the senses is rarely good, mostly bad'.[2]

In art, there is a profound distrust of the natural eye, and the *Libri Carolini*, the official statement of Carolingian art policy, are extremely dubious about the value of religious art and give only a grudging acceptance to paintings in churches.[3] Where the language of concepts had to be spoken in picture, it was made plain by the use of a fixed iconography, which laid down the composition of a particular biblical or other scene, so that the artist, free from the clutter of sense impressions and the compulsions of imitation, could concentrate on the spiritual significance of figures and events. The high Middle Ages codified this view of the artist as a spiritual teacher, insisting on a particular iconographic content, especially stressing the typological harmony of Old and New Testaments, and on a hieratic non-individual style. Even the colours to be used are set down, as in the twelfth-century treatise *De Diversis Artibus:*

'Tree-trunks are painted with a mixture of viridian and yellow ochre with the addition of a little black and sap green. With this colour one also paints the earth and mountains.'[4]

Figures are distorted, backgrounds stylized, as if deliberately to break up the primary world of perception so as to disclose the world of Christian truth. The characteristic setting of figures against a gold ground isolates them in the same way, emphasizing the transcendental reality of their existence. There is little attempt to convey a sense of perspective or of spatial relations: in group scenes, the heads of those behind are placed above, filling the picture space rather than suggesting depth, and the law of 'inverse perspective' operates, according to which objects are larger or smaller according to their importance and not according to their supposed distance from the observer. Settings are unimportant, serving only to identify a figure or explain an action, as a tree, for instance, indicates an outdoor scene. Recognition, not illusion, is the aim. It is important that the locus of the action should be identifiable—a river for the Baptism, the rocky 'garden' of Gethsemane, the mount of the Transfiguration—but not that it should be represented. Illusionistic representation of landscape in mural implies the desire to look through the walls into the reality of the outside world. But Christian art throws everything up on to the surface of the wall—or the page, which was ideal for Christian purposes, since by its very nature it defied the more obvious kind of illusionism—making clear that the reality is in what figures and objects stand for, not in what they appear to be.

The preoccupations of Christian artists and the consequent conceptualization of landscape coincided with obvious changes in social environment. It might be a viable generalization that all developed landscape art is urban pastoral, and certainly Hellenistic landscape and its Italian descendants are the product of city cultures, in Alexandria, Rome and Pompeii. Medieval civilization, however, was a predominantly rural one in the West. In the ninth and tenth centuries, 'la campagne est tout. De vastes contrées, l'Angleterre, la Germanie presque toute entière, sont absolument sans villes', and the ones that there are 'sont des agglomérations dérisoires', whose inhabitants 'vivent profondément engagées dans la campagne'.[5] These, as contemporary critics of Wordsworth pointed out, are not the conditions that produce a taste for landscape. One might say further that it is when cities again begin to assume prime importance, detaching themselves from the rural environment and subduing it to their own concerns, that pastoral begins to reappear. The phenomenal development of landscape in French book illustration of the late fourteenth century may be part of this urbanizing process, accelerated by the

Black Death and, in France particularly, by the flight to the towns which followed on the continuous warfare of the 1350s and 1360s.[6]

In a wilderness dotted with castles and churches, therefore, the love of natural landscape, where it finds expression, is narrowed to the confines of the garden; and the point of growth in these four centuries, from 800 to 1200, is the development of the enclosed garden, with its symbolic attributes, both spiritual and erotic. The association of the garden with paradise, which was the powerful motive behind the development, began early. The *atrium* or porticoed garden court of the early Christian basilica was often called *paradisus*, and the twelfth-century plan of the monastery of St Gall shows a semi-circular place at either end of the church similarly labelled.[7] Monastery gardens were by far the most elaborately developed of this period, both for use and pleasure, and the cloister garden, a grass-plot with flowers and trees, was sometimes called a paradise. Writers on gardens, though they include some authentic detail,[8] concentrate on their symbolic significance, and Hraban Maur, in the chapter on 'Gardens' in his encyclopaedic *De Universo*, 'compares the garden with Holy Church, which bears so many diverse fruits of the spirit, under the protection of God. . . . The garden signifies the inner-most joys of Paradise'.[9] Castle gardens were insignificant during the early part of this period, but with the development of a more ordered and leisured society in the twelfth century, and the growth of a doctrine of secular love which had its own notions of paradise, the way was open for a new kind of paradise garden. Ultimately focused and passed on to subsequent generations of poets in the *Roman de la Rose*, the garden of love accommodated the classical traditions of the *locus amoenus*, still an active part of rhetorical teaching, to the nascent realities of the castle walled-garden and to the symbolic paradise of love, and established itself as the dominant motif in medieval landscape description.[10]

The landscape of medieval Christian art is presented in perhaps its most characteristic form in Byzantine miniatures. Byzantine fresco and mosaic were frozen early, as we have seen, into a marmoreal symmetry, apart from isolated throwbacks like the frescoes of S. Demetrius in Salonica. Whatever resurgence of naturalism there was during the Iconoclastic period (726–842) was subsequently obliterated. The great monuments of Byzantine mosaic work, such as those in the monastery of Daphni, have little or nothing to do with study of landscape. The iconographic schemes of church decoration were exclusively symbolic, the Old Testament, for instance, being represented not in narrative scenes, but through the relation of the Prophets to the dominating figure of Christ. But the manuscript illuminators always had before them models, in copies many times removed, based on the Greek Septuagints with their 'Alexandrian' landscape backgrounds. Out of the combination of these models with strict ecclesiastical prescription grew the formalized mountain-and-tree backgrounds of Byzantine manuscripts in the golden age of the Macedonian and Comnenian dynasties (867–1204):

'The most characteristic features of Byzantine landscape are hills symmetrically disposed in pairs, with a conventional vegetation of trees or plants, the smaller of which are sometimes dotted over the surface in such a way as to resemble a continuous pattern. The hills are composed of prism-shaped rocks, the tops of which form sloping or horizontal planes, and are strongly lighted, contrasting with the vertical sides remaining in deep shadow. The trees which cling to the barren ground are mere schematic forms of the 'mushroom' and other types, copied and recopied until all connexion with nature is lost: only cypresses, palms and dead trunks faithfully suggest the vegetation of the actual world. In the foreground a formal band of green is diapered with conventional flowers. The architecture is composed of colonnades, porticoes, and artificial units fantastically but symmetrically arranged, though here there is more observation of nature than in the case of natural objects.'[11]

Some of the manuscripts described in the previous chapter, such as the Paris Psalter, are of Byzantine origin, and it is sometimes difficult to draw sharp distinctions between their freer imitations of classical landscape and the gradual 'embalming' of this landscape in developed Byzantine style. A copy of the Homilies of St Gregory Nazianzenus, the most popular of Greek patristic writers, from the reign of Basil I (867–86), shows close connections with the Paris Psalter, or with some common model, and perhaps a more naturalistic sense of colour. But Morey's comparison of the two scenes of *David anointed by Samuel* shows the later artist's preference for a flattened perspective, and a distorted sense of scale which reflects the significance of figures and not their relation to objects in space.[12] The Bible of Leo the Patrician, from the early tenth century, is also closely associated with the Paris Psalter, and the illustrations of *Moses on Mount Sinai*, for instance, would seem to be from a common source. The Psalter scene (Plate 12) has something of the serenity and harmony of its fourth- or fifth-century ancestors, but in the Leo Bible (Plate 13) there is a kind of frenzy or intoxication about Moses' posture, and dominating all a superbly extended 'broken terrace' landscape, with ledges and conical mountains rearing up in extravagant profusion. There is some sense of depth, of foreground and background, but an air of unreality has crept in.

At the same period, there are still strong Hellenistic suggestions in the backgrounds of a secular manuscript such as the *Theriaca* of Nicander, a medical treatise, particularly in the portrayal of a Grecian figure walking amongst broadly impressionistic trees.[13] Even as late as the eleventh century, non-aristocratic psalters such as the Theodore Psalter,[14] distinguished by their use of marginal illustration in place of the sumptuous miniatures of imperial or aristocratic psalters, show reminiscences of picturesque style. This particular manuscript goes back to models of the immediate post-Iconoclast period, and the illustration contains a good deal of satiric reference to iconoclasm, to which the monks of Studion, where the manuscript was copied, had been openly opposed. There are no landscape backgrounds, but some naturalistic marginalia, with lively rabbits, birds, sheep, goats and wolves, trees of palmate foliage, and pastoral scenes of digging, reaping and fruit picking. Hellenistic river personifications appear frequently.

But constant repetition in the more careful and formal style of the miniature had already crystallized the characteristic Byzantine landscape described by Dalton, as in the Menologion of Basil II, dated 979–84, with its 430 miniatures of saints and martyrdoms set in landscapes of extraordinary uniformity (Plate 14). Here are the rounded conical peaks with terraced tops which are the signature of Byzantine style in landscape, the decorative disposal of vegetation, the invariable gold sky, the total unrealism which portrays the drapery of reclining figures according to the conventions of standing figures. There is no *sense* of landscape, of space or air, and the backgrounds are no different, as backgrounds, from the draped walls which appear in other miniatures. The contemporary Venice Psalter of Basil II, with only two illustrations, has more vigour, especially in the six scene page of *The Life of David*, with its well-drawn animals. But the toppling and spiralling peaks are formally disposed and the lack of scale and perspective is well illustrated in the way the soldiers loom over the shoulder of the hill in the scene of *David and Goliath*.[15]

Further systematization of the Byzantine landscape is seen in the five illustrated Octateuchs of the twelfth century (Plate 15), the final working out of the archetypal Septuagint tradition, where the horizontal tops of the abbreviated hummocks which now do duty for mountains have developed into independently drawn and coloured swirls; and in the early twelfth-century copy of Simeon Metaphrastes' *Lives of Saints* for September in the British Museum,[16] which is an anthology of Byzantine motifs. Pairs of conical terrace-topped mountains frame the pictures of saints and martyr-doms, occasionally curling round to fit a circular panel, as in *The Martyrdom of S. Anthimus* (f. 44b), and coloured according to an arbitrary decorative scheme, in pink, purple, brown, slate, ochre or green. The 'foreground' is a linear section of hummocky ground with leafy vegetation in the hollows and figures tiptoeing precariously on or above it, effectively a border rather than a foreground. Architecture is perched on pinnacles, as in *The Martyrdom of S. Callistratus*, where the figure of the executioner floats between heaven and earth (f. 209b), or juts out from one side with partially understood diagonal perspective (f. 242b). Foliage is sparsely scattered, often in the form of little plants with curlicue tendrils, which creep up the crevices of the mountains, but more notably in the form of tiny trees, parasol cedar and stylized palm. This reflects a characteristic medieval tendency to picture nature in terms of identifiable 'things' rather than in broad impressions of scenery. The eye refuses the large panorama of sky and mountain and vegetation, and concentrates instead on detail, often fragmentarily realistic but usually formalized, of sun and star, rocky outcrop and dwarf tree. Even in the Trecento, Cennini advised those who wished to paint mountains to take stones as their models.[17]

These motifs of landscape portrayal are widely recognizable in medieval art. The hummocky foreground reappears frozen into immobility in the solid domes of some Ottonian and English illumination,[18] though the immediate sources here are Carolingian rather than Byzantine. Perhaps the most striking survival, and one worthy of brief digression, is the 'broken terrace' rocky landscape, a feature of landscape backgrounds from early classical times to the fifteenth century, and for long periods the only distinct tradition of landscape painting. The broken terrace backgrounds of Pompeiian and Roman paintings may be a naturalistic imitation of the Apennine landscape behind Rome and Naples, which in outcrops shows a bedded structure of limestone in horizontal strata, with jointing along lines of weakness, forming quadrangular blocks;[19] or they may be derived from Anatolian models. The more arid climate of Mediterranean regions sharpens the angles of this structure: similar outcrops in Pennine limestone, as at Malham cove, are softened in outline by the action of water. The imitation of this terraced form in classical landscape was a painter's delight, since the effect of receding shelving solved many of the problems of spatial representation, while the sharply defined verticals and horizontals gave obvious opportunities for light contrasts and highlighting. Subsequently, artists used these same contrasts, shaded slopes and brightly-lit horizontal facets cleft with dark vertical fissures, in more and more stylized form as a kind of shorthand for 'mountains', easy to draw and readily recognizable. The mosaics of S. Vitale show one line of development, Byzantine illumination another, in which the terracing is gradually confined to the tops of domed or conical peaks. When landscape reappears in Western painting after the canopied and diapered backgrounds of the twelfth and thirteenth centuries, it is from these Byzantine sources that it draws, gradually restoring a natural geological reality to the artificiality of the stepped and broken terrace.

An early stage in this development is illustrated in the early thirteenth-century frescoes of S. Jacopo at Grissiano, in the north Italian mountains of the upper Adige. A rustic copyist has here produced not only blue skies and suggestions of white cloud, but also an extraordinary mountain landscape, in the *Abraham and Isaac* scene, of flat-topped pinnacles with steep sides and a sliced-off appearance. This naïve variation on the Byzantine terrace-topped peak has been greeted with rapture by some writers, as an 'entirely new phase of European painting', and even Otto Demus speaks of the rocky background as 'an improbable but unmistakable attempt to represent the local Dolomite scenery'.[20] But one can look too hard for naturalism, and what we have at S. Jacopo is probably a freakish variation of style rather than a new directness of observation. A century later, Duccio and Giotto, in opening up a new world of space and actuality, took little interest in landscape, and are content with the usual rocky outcrops. The backgrounds of Duccio's *Lamentation* and of *The Maries at the Sepulchre* from the Maestà are constructed according to familiar Byzantine principles, sloping planes with jagged-edged table tops and strongly emphasized verticals: the two backgrounds are almost identical, and have no relationship with foreground figures. The Byzantine convention is more subtly interpreted in *The Agony in the Garden* from the same panel, and further refinements are introduced by Giotto. In the Arena Chapel paintings of the *Dream of Joachim*, *The Flight into Egypt* (Plate 53) and *The Deposition*, the sharp outlines are smoothed and blurred, and the rocky slopes are scattered with sensible but precariously perched trees. There is not much integration of foreground and background, but there is a sense of composition, perhaps derived from Byzantine models,[21] in which the rocky hills echo the rhythm of the figures, especially in *The Flight into Egypt*. The fresco of *St Francis and the Poor Man* (Plate 54) in the Upper Church of S. Francesco at Assisi, whether it is Giotto's or not, is still more interesting. Solidly three-dimensional hillsides recede here into a skilfully suggested space, with carefully foreshortened diagonal architecture; but still the hillsides are formally cleft and highlighted, and the recession begins at some unidentified point behind the foreground figures.

Giotto had prepared a space for landscape, one might say, without caring to develop its implications, and later painters, in the fourteenth and well into the fifteenth centuries, went on filling this space with variations on the broken terrace structure, even after Masaccio, in his *Tribute Money*, had experimented successfully with naturalistic bare hills, shattered trees, and a convincing aerial perspective. In about 1460 that great Italian practitioner of the International Style, Benozzo Gozzoli, was still performing elaborate arabesques on terrace structure in his *The Adoration of the Magi* (Plate 60), especially the right panel, with its elegantly fluted cliffs and sculpted ledges, calcified bone or carved alabaster rather than limestone. Earlier, in France, the Dijon Triptych of Melchior Broederlam shows a similar elegance and fantasy. The mountain terraces of *The Visitation* and *The Flight into Egypt* are rounded and softened, with some attention to rocky texture and colouring, but the mountains themselves rear up dizzily to fantastic overhangs, and the light and shadow contrasts are almost melodramatic. The juxtaposition of this extravagance with the rustic Joseph in the *Flight*, with his famous footwear and drinking gourd, is characteristic of the International Style about 1400. Many other instances could be quoted, from both panel painting and manuscript illumination, of the universal sway of the broken terrace in mountain backgrounds during this period, an extraordinary continuity of tradition ended only in the local realism of Flemish landscape and, more strikingly, in Italian painting, in the naturalistic imitation of the very rock formations from which the broken terrace had originally been derived. Mantegna's *Gethsemane* is perhaps too much like a geological exercise, the sharp angularity of the platform on which Christ kneels being rather monotonous and diagrammatic, and contrasting oddly with the spiralling purgatorial cone in the background. The final resolution can better be seen in the corresponding platform in Giovanni Bellini's *Gethsemane* (Colour plate VIII), an austere reality transfigured by light, or in the terraced structures of *St Francis in Ecstasy* (Plate 64), where the stratification and faulting of rock layers, and the blending of rock into soil vegetation, are all minutely observed. The cross-section into rock and turf in the foreground of his *Transfiguration* (Plate 66) shows a concern, like Leonardo's, for the relation of surface to core, an interest which corresponds, in its attempt to penetrate the reality of reality, to the figure painter's interest in anatomy.

We could hardly be further from the abstraction of Byzantine tradition, where the reality of landscape lay in its iconographic association with a particular symbolic scene, in a conceptual rather than a visual scheme. Before turning to Carolingian landscapes, we might perhaps restore the high medieval perspective by glancing at what is often considered the most lavish efflorescence of Byzantine tradition, the mosaics of Norman Sicily. The Norman kings, especially Roger II and William II, vying openly with the Eastern emperors, commissioned vast projects of decoration, above all in the chapel of the Royal Palace at Palermo (1129–43) and in the cathedral of Monreale (1174–82), where Byzantine models were reproduced with great magnificence and a more elaborate scenario. The mountain backgrounds and stylized trees of these mosaics, glittering against the brilliant gold 'sky', represent perhaps the ultimate subjugation of natural reality to a decorative

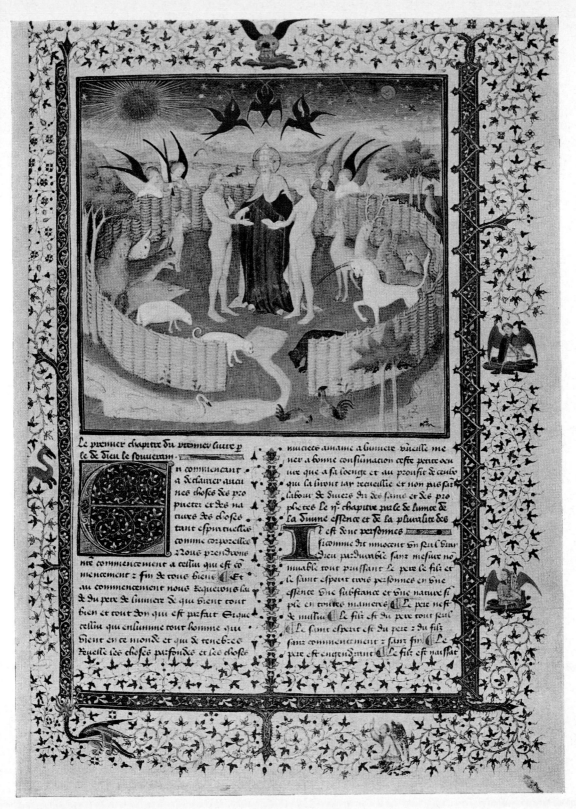

II *God Presenting Eve to Adam*, from *Le Livre de la Propriété des Choses*.
Fitzwilliam Museum, Cambridge, MS 251, f. 16. Early fifteenth century.

scheme, though the disposition of the landscape is not without a sense of rhythmical composition in relation to the figures, especially at Monreale.[22] Trees are shaped into decorative and symmetrical patterns and often, as in the Monreale Creation sequence, the foliage is framed in a dark outline so that it gives the impression of a single entity, a gigantic leaf, as if the untidiness of nature were intolerable (which it was, in mosaic). Every effort seems to have been made to dispute the evidence of the eye and to reinforce the sense of the artificiality of the construct. The basaltic columns which crown the tops of mountains, a characteristic and universal stylization of broken terrace structure in these mosaics, often have tops which look like hammered metal, as far as possible from the 'living rock', as in the Palatine *Lazarus* and *Entry into Jerusalem*. Depth and scale are totally disregarded, especially in this last mosaic, where the 'hill' down which Christ rides is merely an excuse for a colour change, 'a purely flat subdivision of the picture plane',[23] and where the feet of the apostle and the donkey are inextricably intertwined. The beast steps delicately in mid-air, as if he at least thought there were ground there, a pretence which he cannot maintain in the corresponding scene in Queen Melissenda's Psalter (executed by Western artists from Byzantine models about the same time in the Latin kingdom of Jerusalem), where Christ and the donkey actually float in front of the other figures, defying gravity and space alike.

Sicily is also the home of the best surviving secular mosaic work, especially in the Sala Normanna, from the same period, also in the Royal Palace at Palermo. Here, in a series of hunting scenes, centaurs, leopards and peacocks confront each other in heraldic rigidity with decoratively styled palms and cedars between. This characteristic grouping, and the fondness for floral and geometric abstraction, betray the strong Arabic influence which was at work in Sicily, only recently under Saracen sway, and should remind us of the potential presence of oriental non-representationalism in all Eastern Christian art. Byzantium preserved Hellenistic figure art for Christian purposes against the pervasive abstraction and decorative symmetry of the East; it also preserved the dried remnants of classical landscape tradition for later revival.

Classical landscape was under similar pressure in the West, from barbaric art, and again it was the copying of classical models, in the Carolingian Renaissance, that preserved any sort of landscape tradition, though even that was short-lived and contained from the start the seeds of its own supersession. Irish and Hiberno-Saxon manuscript illumination certainly has no place at all for landscape: it is totally non-naturalistic, and is characterized by the development of initial decoration, unknown to the ancients, a decorative and symbolic act of worship to and within the Word. Animals and plants appear in the Irish initials, fish, especially, in the cruder Merovingian illustrations, but as elements in a geometric design only, distorted and convoluted, not as natural objects. It is interesting that Irish illumination of this period, in the Book of Durrow and the Book of Kells, should contrast so strongly, in its geometrical and abstract character, with Irish nature poetry of a slightly later date (ninth and tenth centuries), where there is a degree of naturalism, of cool and unforced observation:

> 'The woodland thicket overtops me,
> the blackbird sings me a lay, praise I will not conceal:
> above my lined little booklet
> the trilling of birds sings to me.
>
> The clear cuckoo sings to me, lovely discourse,
> in its grey cloak from the crest of the bushes;
> truly—may the Lord protect me!—
> well do I write under the forest wood.'

not without its moments of astringency:

> 'I have tidings for you;
> the stag bells,
> winter snows,
> summer has gone.
>
> Wind high and cold,
> the sun low,
> short its course,
> the sea running high.
>
> Crimson the bracken,
> it has lost its shape,
> the wild goose has raised
> its accustomed cry.
>
> Cold has seized
> the birds' wings,
> season of ice,
> these are my tidings'.[24]

Some extravagant claims have been made for this poetry, particularly for what Jackson identifies as 'hermit poetry', in terms of its intimate communion with nature, its 'acute awareness of external things . . . fresh wonder . . . sincerity'.[25] One might be tempted to draw, on this interpretation, a distinction between poetry as a 'private' and personally expressive medium and art as a 'public' medium.[26] But post-romantic enthusiasms are a will-o'-the-wisp here: this nature poetry takes its inspiration from motives a good deal more complex than a simple 'love of nature', and most of it has a readily discernible literary ancestry. There is much seasons poetry and physical catechism, catalogues of natural features and their attributes, trees, birds—in part a naming ritual, in part a kind of gnomic science. In the hermit poetry, the core of Jackson's argument, the dominant motive is an enraptured celebration of God's creation manifest in the world of nature:

> 'That I may see its heavy waves
> over the glittering ocean
> as they chant a melody to their Father
> on their eternal course.'[27]

And, more specifically, of the plentiful sustenance that nature provides for the simple-living hermit. From time to time in all this poetry there is a remarkable independence and acuteness of individual perception, 'a blackbird from a yellow-heaped branch', 'small-nutted branching greenhazels',[28] but it is no different in kind, no more important within the larger programme of motive, than the equally acute and equally fragmentary naturalism that is displayed in leaf and flower drawings in manuscript from time to time throughout the medieval period, or, indeed, in some contemporary Latin pastoral of the ninth and tenth centuries.[29] Nowhere is there evidence of a sustained contemplation of nature's forms, or of any attempt to compose those forms into landscape, as Kuno Meyer admits:

'In none of them do we get an elaborate or sustained description of any scene or scenery, but rather a succession of pictures and images, which the poet, like an impressionist, calls up before us by light and skilful touches.'[30]

And if we admit the significance of this distinction between fragmentary impressionism and 'sustained description', then the notion of an early Celtic nature poetry must seem in many ways a modern invention, and one which has to draw on genres of elegiac and gnomic poetry in which nature is simply a storehouse of exemplary forms. And if Jackson's case rests on the hermit poetry, then it is slim indeed, a handful of poems at most, rooted in religious motives of a familiar kind. His comparison with the Alexandrian poets, with Theocritus, 'so convincing and so unartificially artificial', is much influenced by the idea that these Irish monks and hermits lived out their pastoral, where 'the Greeks stopped short of the wilderness' (p. 108). But this argument is circular:

'It cannot be doubted that the poems were really written by monks and hermits, for their tone is far too sincere to be anything but the genuine expression of men who felt intimately and personally what they wrote about.' (p. 96)

It is much undermined by evidence such as Murphy's that the first poem Jackson quotes, *The Ivy Bower*, is in fact a parody of the form, the madman Suibne's version of the simple life in the wilderness.[31] In the end, one would need little persuasion to believe that the hermit poetry is working Irish variations on the pastoral, that the poets are well acquainted with Latin models, and that it was here that they differed from the early Irish illuminators who, working in independent and remote monastic ateliers, reproduced the art of primitive goldsmiths and metalworkers. Only a poem like the little one quoted above, *The Scribe in the Woods*, would linger in one's mind to disturb, perhaps, the comfortable generalization that a 'sense of landscape' is always the product of a sophisticated culture and is by no means a natural or basic human property.

It hardly came naturally to Carolingian illuminators who, working from a variety of Italian and Byzantine models, reproduce features of Hellenistic background conscientiously, but with a growing sense of alienation. Atmospherically gradated skies are transformed into skeins of colour which are purely ornamental in function and have no reference to nature, and Oakeshott's juxtaposition of two scenes of *Moses Speaking to the Israelites* from ninth-century bibles of the School of Tours shows neatly how the coffered ceilings of classical models, at first carefully imitated in the Grandval (or 'Alcuin') Bible, are then patterned into a flat trellis, with total lack of vanishing point perspective, in the Vivien Bible.[32] The St Paul scenes in the latter show a similar flattening of Hellenistic diagonal architecture, a total loss of scale, and a colonnade which is so much on a plane with the figures that it is impossible to tell, except from the crudest evidence, whether they are in front of or behind it.[33] Yet the trees in these bibles, and in the Bible of S. Callisto, from the later School of St Denis, are surprisingly naturalistic, evidence that the Carolingian illuminators could copy accurately the impressionism of their models when that impressionism could be subdued to an overall decorative effect, even though they had little interest in depth or spatial relations. The eclectic and academic nature of such backgrounds, which we may relate to medieval handling of the literary *locus amoenus*, is analysed by Hinks in his comments on the Jerome scenes of the S. Callisto Bible:

'We find bird's-eye views of towns and walled enclosures, horizon-seascapes cheek by jowl with stepped hills in the *coulisse*-tradition, mushroom-topped trees like those in the Vienna Genesis, baldacchino-interiors, illusionist groves, and scalloped foregrounds: in other words, the whole repertory of antique landscape-motifs jumbled together into a completely irrational synthesis. It is clear that the artist has no interest whatever in the representation of space as such; he uses spatial metaphors merely as links to connect one narrative episode with another.'[34]

In one school of Carolingian illumination, however, that of Reims, there took place a unique fusion of classical landscape modelling with the linear excitement derived from Northern art, to produce, in one manuscript at least, a landscape of unparalleled vivacity. The prototype of the style can be found in the Aachen and Vienna Gospels, where the former shows *The Four Evangelists* grouped in a rocky landscape (Colour plate 1). The picture is really in two storeys, a pair of Evangelists in each, without differentiation of scale, and reminiscent of the vertical assembly of the S. Vitale mosaics of the Evangelists. But the two 'scenes' themselves have a ghostly sense of space, partly produced by an adaptation of Hellenistic mountain backgrounds in terms of interlocking flat planes, like the 'flats' of theatrical scenery, what Hinks calls '*coulisse*-landscape'.[35] The effect is clearly seen in the interlocking slopes of the upper scene, with a spectral space suggested beyond, a distant foretaste of the favourite fifteenth-century device for indicating recession in depth, the winding river with crossing diagonals of hillsides. There are also hints of three-dimensional modelling in the shading and highlighting of the rocky slopes, and one of the rare appearances in Carolingian art, beneath St John, of the broken terrace. While Byzantine art, even at its most formal, preserved the plastic values of Hellenistic landscape enshrined in the terrace and the basaltic column, Carolingian art, with its strong linear inheritance, tended to convert the recession of planes into a series of ground lines. Even this picture of the Evangelists in the Aachen Gospels, which is exceptional in its sense of landscape depth, uses the skyline as a perch for all its sketchy plant life. At least two of the Evangelists' symbols, supposedly looking out from behind rocky ledges, seem simply to have been cut off at the waist. The further consequences of this Carolingian emphasis on line are seen in the later Ebbo Gospels (Plate 16), where the breathtaking vitality of figures and drapery in the Evangelist portraits, done in the style of the *frissonnant*, has pushed the rocky background almost out of the top of the picture.

Impressionistically shaded slopes rise to a skyline on which are perched 'trees' and jocular little allusions to Hellenistic diagonal architecture.

The great masterpiece of the Reims School, however, and one of the most miraculous productions of the Middle Ages, is the Utrecht Psalter (*c.* 830), which may trace its ancestry back to early Christian models of the fourth century or earlier, or which may be, as Wormald says, a deliberate and eclectic 'pastiche in the antique manner'.[36] Every one of the psalms is illustrated in a composite drawing, in pen and ink without frame, which alludes to the text of the psalm often with a witty fantasy and a charade-like literalness. 'I was a beast before thee' (Psalm 73:22) appears in a touching picture of mare and foal; 'I have hated them that regard lying vanities' (31:6) in a large crowd surrounding an acrobatic troupe and a dancing bear; while the illustration of Psalm 23 shows not only goats, cattle and sheep grazing among the 'green pastures', and a 'table' prepared beside 'still waters' but even 'mine enemies' shooting arrows at the psalmist from the other side of the stream.[37] The buoyant confidence and free spatial illusion of these pictures, done by more than one illustrator, have led critics to speak of a *renovatio* of a classical pastoral, even of a return to the Odyssey Landscapes. They are not that, but Panofsky clearly identifies the reminiscences they evoke:

'These airy landscapes, organised in depth by undulating mountain-ranges, dotted with buildings all'antica and feathery, light-dissolved trees, alive with bucolic or ferocious animals and teeming with classical personifications, are reminiscent of the wall-paintings and stucco reliefs in Roman villas and palaces.'[38]

The differences, however, should be made clear too—a restless and inexhaustible inventiveness, a total neglect of composition, and a quivering instability in which landscape heaves and rolls as if in the throes of a perpetual earthquake, as if not merely space were being opened up, but infinitude. The non-naturalistic quality of Northern illumination is present, in a paradoxical way, even in these illusionistic spaces. The swirling rocky outcrops are derived ultimately from the same sources as the columnar terrace tops of Byzantine painting, but have undergone a curious metamorphosis, so that a rock formation like that on the right of the illustration of Psalm 6 (Plate 17) can momentarily have the appearance of a gigantic gnarled hand grasping a tree, complete with finger nails, relics of the old terrace tops.

The Utrecht Psalter has a further importance in art history, beyond its intrinsic quality, for by the late tenth century it had found its way to the monastic atelier at Christ Church, Canterbury, and there it provided a model for successive generations of illustrators, so that the whole history of style for these four centuries from 800 to 1200 can almost be written from an analysis of the Utrecht Psalter and its copies. The first copy was made in the early eleventh century (MS Harley 603), and reproduces with remarkable accuracy the vigorous linear style of the original (Plate 18). The drawings are still unframed, but a concession has already been made to non-naturalistic decoration in the addition of a coloured outline to the plain brown ink of the Utrecht, the colour being chosen arbitrarily for its decorative effect.

'The monochrome lines and contours in Carolingian art, which in spite of their expressive emphasis had yet created a certain naturalistic illusion and, by means of light and shade, had suggested a visual pictorial unity of object and space, became increasingly abstract and hardened, and were more and more used as ornamental patterns. But what is lost in optical function and naturalistic illusion is gained in linear definition of form and rhythmical structure.'[39]

The landscape is still very close to its model, but some signs of change can be detected, as for instance in the illustrations to Psalms 6 and 7. The free delineation of folded hills is giving way to more careful formal swirls; the impressionistic rendering of tree foliage is giving way to a systematized impressionism, with parallel lines of scribble in a pyramid shape; and the fading of page into picture is being replaced by a linear 'foreground' upon which figures stand. In the midst of the landscape, where the Utrecht figures are placed halfway up a slope, in the copy they stand on lines provided for them.

In a later copy, the Eadwine Psalter (in Trinity College, Cambridge) of about 1146, though the strong influence of the original is still recognizable, especially in comparison with the mature Romanesque of contemporary work like the Lambeth or Dover Bibles, the hardening of line into a solid, heavy stroke, with decorative colour shadowing, is immediately apparent (Plate 19). The drawings are now framed, the figures are frozen, landscape conventionalized to a regular curly outline, not far from the crozier-heads which do duty for 'ground' in contemporary Byzantine-influenced manuscripts,[40] and trees wrought into symmetrical or mushroom shapes derived from metalwork, ivory carving or mosaic, indeed anything but nature. The curlicue relics of *coulisse*-recession, which in the Utrecht Psalter gave a sense of spatial continuity to the whole scene, are now used frankly to divide the picture space into a series of independently contrived scenes. The final monumentalization of style takes place in the Paris Psalter (Bibl. Nat. 8846) of about 1200. The compositions are still recognizable as based on the Utrecht, but the sense of landscape is now totally lost in the splendour of opaque pigments and burnished gold backgrounds (Plate 20). Richly decorated and diapered architecture and statuesque sculpted figures dominate the picture space, the surface of which is partitioned by broad ribbons of colour, which are all that remains of the curves which previously indicated hilly terrain. The pressure of Christian symbolism has overtaken natural reality altogether, and the trees are now even more like mushrooms or candelabra than ever, with gigantic stylized leaves symmetrically arranged and shoots emerging from the characteristic draped sockets. The effect is of some artefact in metal or copperwork, and this indeed is both the origin and purpose of such painting.

What we see developing in these copies of the Utrecht Psalter are in fact the characteristics of high Romanesque. In Ottonian illumination of the Reichenau School, for instance, gold grounds are universal, and the visual phenomena of spatial recession, when they are imitated, are used as a form of painterly decoration and not to indicate perspective. Oakeshott juxtaposes two astrological portrayals of Andromeda and shows clearly how the rocks, stylized and columnar enough in the Carolingian model, but with sharp highlights, become mere swirls in the Ottonian copy.[41] All that remains of landscape in much illumination of the period, whether from England, Germany or Spain, are the trees, and these take the strangest forms. The illuminator of the Joshua initial in the Winchester Bible (*c.* 1160) shows a taste for fungoid growths with decorated bell-shaped tops, and also for pine cone finials, while the Morgan Leaf, of the same date, has curling tendrils and metallic shoots emerging from the draped sockets.[42] A somewhat earlier psalter of the same school (MS Arundel 60), has a scene of the Crucifixion with two trees flanking and echoing the curve of the body, their leafage represented by 'solid blue ovals patterned with foliage and red flowerets' and perched on top of pink trunks and branches.[43] The 'ground' from which the trees grow consists of a series of blue and red discs, representing the ultimate formalization of the scallop-line foreground. It may be compared with the scene of *The Agony in the Garden* in the St Alban's Psalter (*c.* 1130), one of the most important documents in the history of pictorial narrative, where Jesus kneels on a hill of solid crozier-heads and where one starkly columnar tree actually has capitals at the head of the trunk.[44] Where the narrative demands other natural features, they are portrayed in an equally non-naturalistic manner, the waters of the Baptism, for instance, in the Benedictional of St Aethelwold, being indicated by a curtain of drapery to waist height, with a purely planar existence.[45] Outside the strict traditions of monastic illumination, there is, in mural painting, with its even more exclusively and overwhelmingly didactic function,[46] a similar reluctance to portray landscape backgrounds. Apart from some isolated relics of classical influence in Italy (which of course always had physical evidences lacking elsewhere in Europe) among the frescoes of S. Pietro al Monte at Civate, and here and there in the mosaics of S. Clemente at Rome and S. Marco at Venice, the whole tendency is towards schematic abstraction in the backgrounds—golden skies, decoratively disposed one-plane architecture and simplified tree forms. Where classical features such as the graduated skies of aerial perspective are imitated, they are formalized into sharply differentiated bands of colour:

'The painters seem to have forgotten the actual significance of the convention and used it merely decoratively, as the sequence of colors has no relation to anything that exists in nature.'[47]

The ossification of classical landscape in Byzantine, Carolingian and Romanesque painting may be compared, it has been suggested, with the formalization of the *locus amoenus* in the Latin poetry of the period. The insignificance of landscape, in any form, in the native vernaculars reinforces the generalization about the sophisticated and particular provenance of a taste for landscape. There is no 'taste for landscape' in Old English poetry, for instance, and no 'feeling for nature', though there is an awareness of its grim realities. When those realities are evoked, as in the *Wanderer*:

'ðonne onwæcneð eft   wineleas guma
gesihð him biforan   fealwe wegas,
baþian brimfuglas   brædan feþra,
hreosan hrim ond snaw   hagle gemenged.'[48]

('Then the friendless man wakes again, sees before him the dark waves, the sea-birds bathing, spreading their feathers; frost and snow falling mingled with hail.')

or in the *Seafarer*:

'þæt se mon ne wat
þe him on foldan   fægrost limpeð,
hu ic earmcearig   iscealdne sæ
winter wunade   wræccan lastum,
winemægum bidroren
bihongen hrimgicelum;   hægl scurum fleag.
Þær ic ne gehyrde   butan hlimman sæ,
iscaldne wæg . . .
Nap nihtscua,   norþan sniwde,
hrim hrusan bond,   hægl feol on eorþan,
corna caldast.'[49]

('The man who fares most prosperously on land knows not how I, careworn, have spent a winter as an exile on the ice-cold sea, cut off from kinsmen, hung round with icicles. The hail flew in showers. I heard nought then save the sea booming, the ice-cold billow ... The shadow of night grew dark, snow came from the north, frost bound the earth; hail fell on the ground, coldest of grain.')

it is the bitterness of exile that they image forth. There is observation here, and fidelity to nature of a kind, but the striking attachment of Anglo-Saxon poets to these winter seascapes is due to their effectiveness as images of exile, and of the harsh penitential discipline of the life of the *peregrinus*. Natural phenomena such as the 'hrimcealde sæ' provide the rhetoric of misery and sorrow: it is not the call of the sea, but the sea answering the call of an effective poetic expression. As Stanley says, referring to Wordsworth's 'meanest flower', that gives 'thoughts that do often lie too deep for tears',

'Few will deny that with the old poets the processes of nature may be symbols of their moods: but it is not the flower that gives the thought: with the Old English poets it is the thought that gives the flower. And the flower that is born of the mood may take on sufficient concreteness to appear capable of existence without and outside the mood.'[50]

The passage from the *Seafarer*, particularly, can thus achieve a degree of realism which seems autonomous, and which can tempt 'romantic' interpretations in the style of *Sea Fever*. Such interpretations are clearly mistaken, and yet one would not wish to deny the reality of the poet's vision by insisting on a purely allegorical reading. Perhaps the answer is to see the realism as 'typological', as that term is used in biblical exegesis;[51] in other words, the poet's description of the winter seas is valid in terms of natural reality and personal experience, but that validity is subsumed in a larger purpose which concerns itself with spiritual and conceptual truths. These priorities are important, for they operate in most medieval descriptions of nature. If we can say that in Virgil the reality of landscape is an integral aspect of the interpretation of reality as a whole, for the Middle Ages we must say that natural phenomena are available, in more or less stereotyped form, as a mode of expression for an interpretation of reality which transcends or even denies those phenomena.

'Nis þeos woruld na ure eðel, ac is ure wræcsið.'[52]
('This world is not our homeland, but our place of exile.')

The fluctuations between allegorical, symbolic and typological landscape depend on the immediate pressures of that interpretation. They depend also on the nature of the poem: the *Wanderer* and the *Seafarer*, which use the wintry landscape as part of an individually controlled poetic whole, convince us of two kinds of truth. But in *Andreas*, the similar emphasis on cold and ice in the description of Andrew's imprisonment in Mermedonia (1253ff) is purely symbolic, a rhetorical amplification of the saint's state of mind which has nothing to do with the reality of the narrative context.

Natural description is thus always ready to dissolve into symbol, or into rhetorical decoration. The very use of kennings, in Old English and Old Icelandic poetry, argues a stronger interest in verbal ingenuity and enigma than in descriptive accuracy. To call the sun 'woruld-candel' or the ocean 'hron-rad' is not 'descriptive', though admittedly such terms do not defy visualization as do some skaldic kennings, such as 'Amlóða kvern' ('Hamlet's churn') for 'sea'.

The great set-piece symbolic landscape of Old English poetry is the description of Grendel's mere in *Beowulf*:

> 'Hie dygel lond
> warigeað wulfhleoþu,   windige næssas,
> frecne fengelad,   ðær fyrgenstream
> under næssa genipu   niþer gewiteð,
> flod under foldan.   Nis þæt feor heonon
> milgemearces,   þæt se mere standeð;
> ofer þæm hongiað   hrinde bearwas,
> wudu wyrtum fæst   wæter oferhelmað.
> Þær mæg nihta gehwæm   niðwundor seon,
> fyr on flode.   No þæs frod leofað
> gumena bearna,   þæt þone grund wite.
> ðeah þe hæðstapa   hundum geswenced,
> heorot hornum trum   holtwudu sece,
> feorran geflymed,   ær he feorh seleð,
> aldor on ofre,   ær he in wille,
> hafelan beorgan;   nis þæt heoru stow!
> Þonon yðgeblond   up astigeð
> won to wolcnum,   þonne wind styreþ
> lað gewidru,   oð þæt lyft drysmaþ,
> roderas reotað.'[53]

('They possess unknown land, wolf-cliffs, windy crags, a dangerous fen path, where the mountain stream falls down under the darkness of the rocks, a flood under the earth. That is not a mile hence where the mere stands; over it hang rime-covered groves; the wood firm-rooted overshadows the water. There each night a baleful wonder may be seen, a fire on the flood. There is none so wise of the children of men who knows those depths. Though the heath-stepper hard pressed by the hounds, the hart strong in antlers, should seek the forest after a long chase, rather does he yield up his life, his spirit on the shore, than hide his head there. That is an eerie place. Thence the surge of waves mounts up dark to the clouds, when the wind stirs up hostile storms till the air darkens, the skies weep.')

It is impossible to organize the details of this description into a coherent visual 'scene', because no such scene was intended. The intention—and it is dramatically reinforced, being part of Hrothgar's discourse, to which Beowulf will make suitably undeterred reply—is to arouse horror, and every detail is charged with symbolic power. The imagery of frost reappears in 'hrinde bearwas', and there is a strong sense of reversal of nature in the paradoxes of 'flod under foldan' and 'fyr on flode', and in the unnatural behaviour of the hart. It is an extraordinarily powerful and evocative description, and to deny its factual existence, which we must, even to call it 'a gallimaufry of devices',[54] is not to undervalue that power. That the bare facts of the description recall the tree-shaded waters of classical poets is curious, but irrelevant, for the real associations of the passage are with the hell landscape of Christian homilists. Specific analogies with one of the Blickling Homilies have been seen, and the poet is undeniably aware of the tradition.[55] There is thus already present in Old English literature the medieval Christian tendency to polarize all landscape into symbols of heaven and hell.[56]

All these examples of consciously symbolic landscape have a strong Christian colouring. It may be thought that the exigencies of secular narrative will often produce descriptive accuracy in neutral contexts, much as the illustrators of treatises on hunting and botany can often present accurate pictures of beasts and plants. But there seems little evidence in Old English poetry to support such a thesis. The topography of the *Battle of Maldon* is extremely casual, and only careful detective work has identified the site, which the poet indubitably knew at first hand: perhaps he and his audience knew it too well to bother. But, even so, the fragmentary nature of his observations about the 'scene' argues that he had other things on his mind than the visual coherence of things. Natural description in *Beowulf* is always charged with dramatic force, is always the symbol of some pattern of thought or feeling, whether it is the sea cliffs that shine for Beowulf's arrival in Denmark, or the fetters of ice that bind the waves in echo of Hengest's mood in the Finn episode.[57] Our momentary sense that we have in the 'fealwe stræte' ('streets of brown sand'), along which Hrothgar's men course their horses, the sort of casual and neutral visual accuracy which to us seems fundamental to observation itself is probably mistaken, depending as it does on a modern interpretation of a notoriously difficult epithet. To the poet, the phrase probably connoted 'ideally suited to horse racing'.

44

The landscape of the Old Icelandic sagas is, by contrast, compellingly real. A thousand details of hill and harbour and grazing slope, of Icelandic nights and winters, build up an unmistakable authenticity of background. Biorn's landfall in Iceland[58] can still be followed, detail by detail: there can be no other national literature where the topographical pilgrimage is so romantically rewarding. But the romance, let us be clear, is ours, for the sagas have the Homeric sense of *land* not the Virgilian sense of landscape. No saga writer ever stops to describe a natural scene, unless it is vital to the understanding of the narrative, and then the account is precise, familiar, casual:

'There is some marsh-land stretching away from the ridge with much grass-land, where Thorbjorn had made a quantity of hay which was just dry . . .'[59]

Land is described according to its use, not its beauty:

'A little farther up than Höskuldstadir lies, on the north of the Laxá river, there had been cut a clearing in the woodland, which lay near to the grazing-grounds...'[60]

The description of the cave under the waterfall to which Grettir tracks the troll woman, in an episode closely related to Beowulf's adventures with Grendel's mother, lacks all the symbolic charge of the mere: we are told, in the coolest terms, simply what we need to know in order to understand Grettir's problem:

'When they reached the falls they saw a cave up under the rock. The cliff was there so abrupt that no one could climb it, and nearly ten fathoms down to the water. . . . Grettir dived beneath the fall. It was very difficult swimming because of the currents, and he had to dive to the bottom to get behind the fall. There was a rock where he came up, and a great cave under the fall in front of which the water poured. He went into the cave. . . .'[61]

Egil's journey into the snowy wilderness of Vermaland, with its steep rocks and crags,[62] could likewise be compared with Gawain's journey beyond Wirral in *Sir Gawain and the Green Knight*. Again it lacks the moral and emotional overtones of the Christian poet's vision, which sees landscape as a rhetorical expression of a state of mind. For Egil and his party, it is a matter of digging the horses out of snow drifts and pressing on, the blunt realities of exhaustion and dogged persistence replacing the rhetoric of terror and privation. Perhaps on only one occasion does a saga character pause to contemplate the beauty of natural scenery, and that is the marvellous moment in *Njal's Saga* when Gunnar, travelling into exile, turns and looks back on his home and the slopes of Hlidarend:

' "How lovely the slopes are," he said, "more lovely than they have ever seemed to me before, golden cornfields and new-mown hay. I am going back home, and I will not go away." '[63]

Even here it is the farmer who speaks, whose sense of beauty is a pride in use, as in the garden of Alcinous.

The epic naturalism of the Icelandic sagas, though it plays no large part in the economy of the narratives as a whole, is exceptional in the Middle Ages. (It differs significantly from the naturalistic impressionism of Irish saga, which is traditionally enclosed within the speech poems woven into such stories as those of Suibne and Fionn.)[64] If we return to the great epic literature of the Christian West, that of the French *chansons de geste*, we find ourselves nearer to *Beowulf* than to *Njal*. The landscape of the Pyrenees in the *Chanson de Roland*, though there is nothing unreal about it, looms and lowers,

'Halt sunt li pui e tenebrus e grant,
li val parfunt e les ewes curant.'[65]
('Huge are the hills and shadowy and high,
Deep in the vales the living streams run by.')

and the formulaic repetition through the tragic climax of the phrase 'Halt sunt li pui' builds up a symbolism of gloomy grandeur in which nature matches the mood of the poem. The land of France is likewise rent with earthquake and tempest as Roland's death draws near.[66] It is possible to talk of this interpretation of nature as 'romantic',[67] in contrast with the naturalism of primary epic, and in so far as it prepares for the landscape of romance, where nature is used to reflect both psychological mood and social assumptions.

But another influence is already beginning to intervene, even in *Roland*. Charlemagne holds his council of war:

'Suz un lorer ki est enmi un camp.'(2651)

and, as Curtius points out, the laurel is no accident, since it is the tree designated in the *rota Virgilii* as appropriate to the high or epic style.[68] From here on, the landscapes of the rhetorical tradition begin to play a larger and larger part, especially the *locus amoenus*, and their dissemination into the vernacular, in *chanson de geste*, in lyric, and in romance, foreshadows the emergence in the *Roman de la Rose* of the fully-developed medieval garden landscape.

Precept for *descriptio loci* is clear in rhetorical theory, and abundantly fortified in the practice of classical poets well known to the Middle Ages. It came down through the traditional teaching of the schools by a number of routes. First of all, it had a part in topical theory as one of the attributes of actions: propositions in forensic oratory were to be supported by argument drawn from various sources, or *loci communes*, among them place, time, occasion, manner and facilities:

'In considering the place where the act was performed, account is taken of what opportunity the place seems to have afforded for its performance. Opportunity, moreover, is a question of the size of the place, its distance from other places, i.e. whether remote or near at hand, whether it is a solitary spot or one much frequented, and finally it is a question of the nature of the place, of the actual site (*natura ipsius loci*) . . . .'[69]

This may seem a long way from poetry, or even poetic theory, but the decay of forensic oratory in late Roman times, and the wholesale transfer of its teaching to the arts of poetry, meant that a twelfth-century rhetorician like Matthew of Vendôme could use the whole theory of attributes to expand his account of *descriptio*, which he clearly considers to be the major ornament of poetic discourse. Thus his *descriptio quatuor temporum anni* and *descriptio loci* appear among the *attributa negotii*,[70] and, whether they profited or not from the spurious claim to thematic function, they are typical set-piece models for the transmission of classical landscape description to the later Middle Ages. One fourteenth-century reader of the *Roman de la Rose* showed his awareness of this debt in a comment that he wrote beside line 78 of that poem:

'Totum istud punctum Matheus Vindocinensis de loci placidi descriptione.'[71]

though the matter is probably more complex than that.

Further precedent for landscape description came from *epideixis*, the oratory of panegyric and invective, which often included topics such as the praise of a garden or the praise of spring among its set themes. Curtius reminds us, in analysing a tenth-century poem on the swallow, how profoundly this affects the treatment of nature in poetry, and how small a part experience and observation are likely to play.[72] It is not difficult, too, to see how such practice, adumbrated in Statius' eulogy of the country retreats of his friends or Ovid's vilification of Tomis, would crystallize, as a matter of formal technique, the polarized attitudes to landscape already strong in Christian symbolism. Medieval poets are unlikely ever to see much beauty in winter, any more than the simple paradox for lovers of April as 'the cruellest month'.

A third channel of communication for landscape description in rhetorical theory is through the position of *descriptio* as one of the figures of thought. The figures are the staple of rhetorical teaching, and in the *Rhetorica ad Herennium*, the classical treatise best-known to the Middle Ages (it was attributed to Cicero), description already appears prominently, both as *descriptio* and as *demonstratio* (ocular demonstration).[73] It is Quintilian, however, who develops the latter most forcefully and eloquently as an aspect of the ornate style, calling it *enargeia* or *evidentia*, the vivid word picture which brings a scene immediately to the eyes.[74] He discusses *evidentia* further in the next book, paying particular attention to *locorum dilucida et significans descriptio*, which others call *topographia*.[75] The last is a well-known term: it is used by Matthew to introduce his *descriptio loci*, and was still being used by sixteenth-century rhetoricians.

It was thus possible for classical landscape conventions, the idealized spring landscape in particular, to be passed down to the Middle Ages as part of a systematic body of rhetorical teaching, and in conveniently codified form. This codification, already under way in late classical poets, was made more absolute in the teaching of professional rhetoricians such as the fourth-century Libanius, whose *Descriptio Veris* became a model of its kind, and the close relation, detail by detail, of medieval spring landscapes to classical literary tradition proves its effectiveness.[76] The full consequences of such a scholarly inheritance can be seen in Matthew of Vendôme's own *descriptio loci*, an anthology of classical motifs which bears comparison for its eclecticism with the Carolingian manuscripts described by Hinks,[77] and for its iron schematization with contemporary Byzantine miniatures. A lacuna near the beginning of the 62-line *descriptio* was probably occupied with a catalogue of trees, such as we find elsewhere in Ovid, Statius, Joseph of Exeter, Boccaccio, Chaucer and Spenser;[78] it is followed by a catalogue of birds with their characteristic song, another favourite device, beautifully developed in one of the 'Cambridge Songs', *Vestiunt silve*.[79] In the last fourteen lines Matthew comes into his own:

> 'Flos sapit, herba viret, parit arbor, fructus abundat,
>   Garrit avis, rivus murmurat, aura tepet.
> Voce placent volucres, umbra nemus, aura tepore,
>   Fons potu, rivus murmure, flore solum.
> Gratum murmur aquae, volucrum vox consona, florum
>   Suavis odor, rivus frigidus, aura tepens.
> Sensus quinque loci praedicti gratia pascit,

III *The Virgin and Unicorn in an Enclosed Garden.* Fitzwilliam Museum, Cambridge, MS 99, f. 11v. Early sixteenth century.

Si collative quaeque notata notes.
Unda juvat tactum, gustum sapor, auris amica
Est volucris, visus gratia, naris odor.
Non elementa vacant, quia tellus concipit, aer
Blanditur, fervor suscitat, humor alit.
Praedicti sibi fontis aquam, sibi floris amicat
Blanditias, genii virgo, studentis opus.'[80]

('The flower gives off scent, the grass is green, the tree bears fruit, the fruit grows in abundance, the bird twitters, the brook murmurs, the breeze blows warm. The birds give pleasure by their voices, the grove by its shade, the breeze by its gentle warmth, the spring by its cooling drink, the brook by its murmuring, the earth by its flower. Pleasing is the murmur of the waters, harmonious the voice of the birds, sweet the scent of flowers, cooling the stream, warm the breeze. The pleasures of the place I have described nourish all five senses, if you observe together all that I have noted. Water pleases the sense of touch, its flavour the sense of taste, the bird is the friend of the ear, beauty to the sight, the scent to the nose. No element is lacking, for the earth gives birth, the air caresses, heat quickens, moisture nourishes. The spirit of the place which I have described infuses itself through the water of the spring, the caresses of the flowers, (and to describe this is) the task of the student (of nature).')

This 'school exercise in grammatical permutation', as Curtius calls it,[81] is itself an impoverished example of the medieval *locus amoenus*, but it is at least a witness to the ubiquity of the form and the stability of its content.

Its metamorphoses are to be seen everywhere. In Alan of Lille's *Anti-claudianus*, for instance, an important ancestor of the *Roman de la Rose*, it provides a skeleton for the encyclopaedic and richly allegorical garden of Nature:

'quicquid depascit oculos, vel inebriat aures,
seducit gustus, nares suspendit odore,
demulcet tactum, retinet locus iste locorum.'[82]

('Whatever captivates the eyes, or intoxicates the ears, charms the taste, makes delirious the nostrils with its smell, caresses the sense of touch, was contained in that place of places.')

In love lyric, Latin, Provençal, French and German, the spring opening is *de rigueur*, whether it is part of the celebration of love's reawakening, as in the song *Letabundus rediit* from the *Carmina Burana*,[83] or simply a setting or form of introduction, as in many Provençal lyrics:

'Pus vezem de novel florir
pratz e vergiers reverdezir,

49

> rius e fontanas esclarzir
> auras e vens,
> ben deu quascus lo joy jauzir
> don es jauzens.'[84]

('Since we see meadows flowering and gardens growing green anew, and breezes and winds purifying rivers and springs, let everyone take delight in the *joi* which is his.')

There is remarkably little originality or local realism in these spring scenes, and often they are reduced to mere stylized gestures: flowers are frequently mentioned, for instance, in the German *Minnelieder*, but almost always it is the conventional rose and lily, both exotic to the climate.[85] The Latin lyrics are on the whole more elaborate, with a wider range of classical allusion, and some variations on the theme of spring and love. Spring sometimes reawakens the pain of love, or its joys can be contrasted with the sorrows of lovers parting, as Geoffrey of Vinsauf advises in his *Poetria Nova*;[86] or else winter is described, to contrast with the ardour of the lover's passion; or the lover will declare his independence of the weather. But there is little attempt to renew the content of the universal spring landscape:

> 'Erat arbor hec in prato
> Quovis flore picturato,
> Herba, fonte, situ grato,
> Sed et umbra, flatu dato.
> Stilo non pinxisset Plato
> Loca graciora.'[87]

('This tree was in a field where grew
Vivid flowers of every hue,
Grass, a fount with waters blue,
Shade too and a welcome breeze.
More delightful scenes than these
Plato ne'er portrayed.')

Here are the six 'charms of landscape' again (Philomela follows in the next stanza), so summarily recapitulated that there can be no question of a response to the scene as a scene, but rather a recognition of its formal identity—much as in the landscape backgrounds of Romanesque illumination. Even where a whole poem is devoted to the 'scene', as in *Musa venit carmine* from the *Carmina Burana*,[88] it is recognizably embroidery of a theme, not individually observed reality. The same is true of the French *reverdies*, where the embroidery is often quite subtle.

A longer Latin poem, the debate *De Phillide et Flora* (concerning whether *clercs* or *chevaliers* make better lovers), shows how the traditional *locus amoenus* was enriched from other literary sources. Here, in the garden of the God of Love, there are musical instruments and scents of myrrh and cinnamon in addition to the usual flowers and trees and birdsong, and similarly in the *verger* of *Floire et Blanceflor*, with its precious stones, artificial birds, and magical fountains, or the garden of Mabonagrain in Chrétien's *Erec*, closed in its curtains of air. Faral[89] traces these new influences, which are part of the complex derivation of the developed landscape of the *Roman de la Rose*, to various sources: to oriental and Byzantine motifs, to Christian concepts of the *paradis terrestre*, to renewed classical influence through the revamping into romance of the stories of Troy, Thebes, Aeneas and Alexander; and perhaps not least, to encyclopaedias like those of Isidore and his growing army of imitators, for it is often the catalogue, the accumulation of rich and rare names, that dominates these descriptions, what Curtius calls 'Luxus der Nomenklatur'.[90]

The *locus amoenus* plays its part in the literature of romance, usually in attenuated and symbolic form as an expression of the ideal values of chivalric society. The recurring pattern of romance is of a journey through a wild forest or undifferentiated wilderness, broken here and there by pockets of idealized garden or meadow landscape with paradisal associations. *Huon de Bordeaux* and the Grail romances are good examples of the developed use of this symbolic landscape, though its lineaments are already clear in Chrétien de Troyes. Yvain sets forth, and the early stages of his journey are those which every romance hero has to pass:

> 'Mes sire Yvains ne sejorna
> Puis qu'armez fu ne tant ne quant,
> Einçois erra chascun jor tant
> Par montaingnes et par valees
> Et par forez longues et lees,
> Par leus estranges et sauvages,
> Et passa mainz felons passages
> Et maint peril et maint destroit
> Tant qu'il vint au santier tot droit . . . .'[91]

('My lord Yvain made no delay after putting on his arms, but hastily made his way each day over the mountains and through the valleys, through the forests long and wide, through strange and wild country, passing through many gruesome spots, many a danger and many a strait, until he came directly to the path . . . .')

The clearing, when he comes to it, as described in the earlier recital of Calogrenant, has a magnificent pine tree beside a fountain, and birds which flock to the tree to sing a joyous *servise* (472). Certain features of the description are derived from the other-world landscapes of Celtic legend,[92] another rich source of material for the increasingly complex literary landscape tradition. The best-known garden landscape in Chrétien, that of the *Joie de la Cort* episode in *Erec*, has an inverted symbolism to suit the theme of the romance, the claustrophobic delights of the garden representing the perils of an exclusive devotion to women.

Where landscape has no symbolic purpose to fulfil, it hardly exists, except as a series of glimpses caught by the knight from the road, or the lady from the castle window—mown meadows, or a neat beech grove with greensward beneath.[93] The view is arcaded, distanced, as remote from the realities of the romance situation as the occupations of the peasants in earlier Calendar pictures of the labours of the months. Landscape features are called into existence from nowhere to provide occasions for romantic action, and are as indefinite as the article which designates them—a forest, a fountain, a meadow. When Lancelot meets an assailant in a narrow place, the forest suddenly opens up into a bright, level, clearly-lit meadow for the joust which must follow. Everywhere the castle dominates the surrounding countryside, much as in the *Très Riches Heures* Calendar pictures:

> 'Au desbuschier del pleisseiz
> Troverent un pont torneiz
> Par devant une haute tor,
> Qui close estoit de mur an tor
> Et de fossé le et parfont.'[94]

('After emerging from the hedged enclosure they came upon a drawbridge before a high tower, which was all closed about with a wall and a broad and deep moat.')

And often there is nothing between one castle and the next. More attention seems to be devoted to description of nature as part of some human artefact than to nature itself, so that flowers and birds are elaborately pictured in descriptions of clothes, and a whole landscape of mountains, plains, rivers and forests in the flaps of Adrastus' pavilion in the *Roman de Thèbes*.[95] This short-circuiting of phenomenal experience is characteristic of the Middle Ages, which will always subdue images of nature to images of human sway and human beauty.

The forest, which is to be distinguished from the grove (Curtius' 'mixed forest'), is perhaps the most striking aspect of romance landscape, though its precise features are dissolved in symbol. It is a place of mystery, a place of testing, and always potentially evil, 'a locus apart from society where the hero participating in adventures is liable to undergo supernatural ordeals'.[96] Hell in Dante is approached through a 'selva oscura'. Even where the forest appears to be a place of refuge, its harshness and alien nature makes it into a form of expiation or redemption through suffering, as it is for the arrogant and exiled hero in *Girart de Roussillon*. The escape of the lovers in Béroul's *Tristan* into the forest of Morrois is likewise symbolic of their exile from society:

'The life the lovers lead in the forest is one of physical and mental suffering. Not only do they have to endure the hardships arising out of the rigours of their new environment, but they must also forgo all the advantages of birth and rank which they have hitherto enjoyed. They are free from the constraints which society has imposed upon them . . . but their isolation, while it brings with it immunity from moral sanctions, implies alienation from their fellows and from God.'[97]

In Gottfried von Strassburg's version of the story, which is later, more 'romantic', more concerned with the celebration of a self-transcending love than with social morality, the lovers find in the heart of the wilderness a shaded hillside, with birds, breezes, greensward and flowers, and an explicitly allegorical grotto in which their love is sacramentalized.[98]

The view of the forest which prevails in high medieval romance is a reflection, albeit somewhat dated, of physical reality. In an age when forest still covered most of Western Europe, the 'wild wood' could retain something of its horror and mystery, and could be an apt symbol, therefore, of the alien wilderness. But by the late twelfth century, it is clear, the situation was changing. A rapidly expanding economy meant an increased demand for timber (Abbot Suger had difficulty finding hardwood for his building programme) and for the caste privileges of the chase, and the forests began to recede. From being a constant reminder of the fragile presence of man in a hostile environment, they became precious preserves for exploitation,[99] and the proliferation of rules concerning rights and usages, protection and reservation, and especially the forest laws of the reign of Henry II, were bound to make a difference to the symbolism of the wild wood. Exploitation of the forest was well-organized by the late thirteenth century, and perhaps we can see in the growth of the Robin Hood story, or in the early fourteenth-century *Tale of Gamelyn*, where the hero similarly sees no terrible hardship in a temporary forest exile,[100] a reflection of these changes.

Two points should be emphasized at the conclusion of this chapter. One is the close association between the developing *plesaunce* landscape and concepts of secular love. It is not always a direct association; in other words, the delights of the landscape do not always correspond to the legitimate delights of love, but it remains true nevertheless that landscape is brought into existence in order to provide a natural imagery or rhetoric of love. As a final example of this subordination of natural phenomena to human love, we can take Gottfried von Strassburg's description of the Maytime festivities at Tintagel, where the landscape embodies the hopes and joys of lovers:

'Charming, gentle spring had busied himself about it with a sweet assiduousness. Of little wood-birds (fit delight for the ear), flowers, grasses, leaves, and blossoms and all that soothes the eye and gladdens noble hearts, that summer-meadow was full. Of all that May should bring, one found whatever one wished there: shade together with sunshine, lime-trees by the fountain, tender, gentle breezes regaling Mark's company each according to its nature. The bright flowers smiled up from the dewy grass. May's friend the greensward had donned a summer smock of flowers so lovely that they shone again from the dear guest's eyes. The delightful blossom on the trees smiled out at one so pleasantly that one's heart and all one's soul went out to it through eyes that shone, and gave back all its smiles. The soft, sweet, lovely singing of the birds, that often assuages ears and soul, filled hills and valleys. The heavenly nightingale, that enchanting little bird—may its sweetness abide with it for ever!—was trilling among the blossoms so wantonly that many a noble heart took joy and zest from it.'[101]

The second point is equally important in the development of the characteristic landscape of the later Middle Ages and of the *Roman de la Rose* tradition in particular, and that is the strong sense of enclosure. The classical mind could tolerate open vistas, in which garden merged into surrounding landscape, but the Middle Ages tend to close off the view and to hedge round the garden. The walled garden is nothing more nor less than the etymology of paradise (from Persian *pairidaeza*, a walled enclosure), and in this it reflects both medieval idealism and medieval 'inwardness'. This subduing of natural landscape to the humane and artificial control of the garden is well illustrated in the medieval treatment of the episode of Hypsiphyle from the *Thebaid*. Statius, describing the journey of the Argives to Thebes, shows them passing through a drought-parched land which merges imperceptibly and in the most natural manner into the wooded slopes of a river valley and its shaded waters.[102] In the *Roman de Thèbes* the travellers are one minute in a wilderness, the next, abruptly, in an enclosed paradise garden:

'Mout chevauchoent a grant peine,
Quant aventure les ameine
A un vergier que mout ert genz,
Que onc espice ne pimenz
Que hon peüst trover ne dire
De cel vergier ne fu a dire.

54

Mout esteit bien enclos li jarz
De forz paliz de totes parz.'[103]

('They rode for miles through difficult country, until at last by chance they came upon a beautiful garden, in which was to be found every kind of spice and exotic flowering plant known to man. The garden was enclosed on all sides with a strong palisade.')

The displacement is automatic and irrational and all to no purpose, since the sole function of this paradise garden is to provide a poisonous snake to sting the child Hypsiphyle is nursing.

Chapter Three

THE LANDSCAPE OF PARADISE

Quid est paradisus? ... locus amoenissimus in Oriente.[1]

Many versions of paradise were offered to medieval man; its landscape was variously described by theologians, poets, artists and travel writers. Lying so provocatively between fact and concept, religious and secular experience, the real and the ideal, it focused quite naturally both faith and imagination. By turns, it engaged, transmuted and rejected the evidence of the senses. As the beginning and the end of man's quest for perfection, as Eden and as the Celestial Paradise, it spanned all human history. In more limited forms, tangible or intangible, it measured man's constant desire to approximate to perfection. The gardens of lyric, romance and allegory, the gardens of early Christian churches, of monasteries and of palaces are all paradisal reflections, whether clear, dim or distorted. Few medieval authors used the word 'paradise' without some active sense of its full potential of meaning; even in the most profane contexts it could suddenly become spiritually resonant. If the ideal gardens and landscapes of classical and oriental literature were often plundered for medieval purposes, the nature and significance of the Paradise garden of Genesis were never long neglected.

In certain paintings of the very end of the Middle Ages it may sometimes seem that the subject of the earthly paradise was only an opportunity for urgent acknowledgement of the substantial beauty and power of the natural world. In a *Paradise* picture by Herri met de Bles (active 1480–1550), the poignant story of man's creation and fall is set in a wooded countryside, robustly familiar (Plate 22). At the moment of temptation, Adam and Eve are surrounded by their animals, some apparently alert and tense to danger, some preoccupied with the search for food. Beyond the delusive security of the wood lie bare promontories, and misty reeded lakes; over all, the clouded skies of northern Europe, crossed and recrossed by migrating birds. But even here, in what is virtually a landscape study, we have something more than naturalism. The painting demonstrates the richness and delicacy of late medieval vision, its quickness to realize eternal events in moving images of

56

terrestrial reality. So, also, the descent of the Virgin and Child from the high austere thrones of the twelfth century on to the flowered meadows or into the walled gardens of the fourteenth and fifteenth centuries was in part at least an admission of the unique and moving qualities of tree and flower; but it was also a conviction that they might contribute uniquely to statements of religious truth. In fact, the green gardens of these painters, and of poets contemporary with them, are very rarely presented as unqualified celebrations of earthly beauty. They more often mirror a beauty which transcends them:

> 'I passed thurgh a gardyn grene.
> I fond an herber made ful newe;
> A semelier sight I have not sene—
> On ilke tree song a turtel trewe.'[2]

The 'bright maiden' of this fifteenth-century English poem, singing in a garden of Christ's nativity, and the thoughtful Madonna of the Frankfurt *Garden of Paradise*, painted in the Rhineland during the same years, are crowned and completed by natural forms of sensuous colour, potent in themselves, and as symbols of perfection (Plate 21).

The pressing need of the Middle Ages to be assured of 'some imperishable bliss' was abundantly answered. There was the plain fact, supported by theologians and repeated by geographers and voyagers, that the original garden of Eden, 'spun bud of the world', still existed, although closed to all men by thunderous waters, a high wall and a gate of flame. The anonymous fourteenth-century compiler of *Mandeville's Travels* summed up the conflicting emotions of his age when he described the approaches to 'Paradise Terrestrial'; cast out of Paradise and recognizing exile, man would still restlessly search for a way back:

'Ye shall understand that no man that is mortal ne may not approach to that Paradise. For by land no man may go for wild beasts that be in the deserts and for the high mountains . . . and by the rivers may no man go, for the water runneth so rudely and so sharply . . . Many great lords have assayed with great will for to pass by these rivers towards Paradise, but they might not speed in their voyage.'[3]

The legends of Alexander the Great and his unsuccessful attempt to enter the Earthly Paradise neatly allegorized both the pride and the pity of human longing:

'In all this world I have won nothing unless I win a part in this delight . . . .'[4]

Some had won such a part: the prophets Enoch and Elias, snatched away before death to 'dwell in the green garden of Paradise and eat of the sweet bread from the starry heaven'.[5] And if it was presumptuous to imagine that this Paradise was accessible 'without special grace of God',[6] it was not presumptuous to imagine what might lie within those walls. To exercise the imagination in such a way was not simply to exercise literary skills in the descriptive convention of the *locus amoenus*.[7] It was, in addition, to confirm that benediction had not been quite withdrawn from created things, that man and his dying world were ultimately redeemable. Significantly, for poets and artists, 'all the sweet waters of the world take their beginning of the well of Paradise'.[8] The streams of Paradise flowed out through earthly regions, and gave some faint intimations of immortality, in life as in art. The twelfth-century French poet who wrote the romance *Floire et Blancheflor* knew that the Euphrates, which bordered the orchard of the sultan of Babylon, rose as one of the four rivers of Paradise (Genesis 2:14). And the precious stones in its depths spoke of their rare origin:

> 'De l'autre part, cou m'est a vis,
> Court uns flueves de paradis,
> Qui Eufrates est apelés . . .
> En icele eve, demanieres
> Truevé on precïeuses pieres:
> Saffirs i a et calcidoines,
> Boines jagonses et sardoines,
> Rubis, et jaspes, et cristaus,
> Et topasses, et boins esmaus.'[9]

Many gardens of medieval poetry, secular and religious, were watered by jewelled streams and fountains; they were fed, however remotely, from Paradise. So, even the twin crystals, seen in the fountain of Narcissus by the lover of the *Roman de la Rose*, reflect a lover's understanding of 'Paradise'; they literally reflect the enclosed garden of love:

> 'Si n'i a si petite chose . . .
> Don demonstrance n'i soit faite,
> Con s'ele iert es cristaus portraite.'[10]
> ('For ther is noon so litil thing . . .
> That it ne is sene, as though it were
> Peyntid in the cristal there.')

And the glittering stones seen by the dreamer in the fourteenth-century English poem *Pearl* warn him clearly of his approach to the Earthly Paradise itself:

'In the founce ther stonden stones stepe, *founce*, bottom; *stepe*, bright
As glente thurgh glas that glowed and glyght . . .
For uche a pobbel in pole ther pyght *pyght*, set
Was emerad, saffer other gemme gente,
That al the loghe lemed of lyght.'[11] *loghe*, pool

The rich sound and colour of this passage are remarkable. But remarkable too is the fact that in the context of the poem the deeper significance of the features described is finely indicated. Without any dimming of sensuous power, it becomes evident that the light refracted is spiritual, that the water is also sacramental. The rays of the sun are dark compared with this light, the water separates the dreamer from Paradise.[12]

The poet of *Pearl* takes his own way to reconcile medieval beliefs about the nature of Paradise: the belief, on the one hand, that the garden of Eden existed, and was miraculously preserved, beyond the reach of the Flood waters, as the Terrestrial Paradise, and the belief, on the other hand, that Eden was the mystical prefiguration of other, and greater Paradises. Not only did it prefigure the Paradise of the Blessed, in Heaven, into which St Paul had visionary sight ('raptus est in Paradisum et audivit arcana verba', II Cor. 12:4), not only that of the Christian Church, with Christ as the Tree or Fountain of Life, set among the other trees of the Just ('et erit tamquam lignum, quod plantatum est secus decursus aquarum', Psalm 1:3), but also the Paradise of the Christian soul, planted with the trees of the virtues and tended by Christ, divine Gardener. If we explained all this as an allegorization of the narrative of Genesis, and of other biblical accounts of gardens, we should underestimate the wealthy complexities of the medieval situation. The teaching of the Church on Paradise provided writers and artists, as it did preachers and students of theology, with a range of alternatives, rather than with a straightforward choice between literal and spiritual truth, between history and exegesis. Above all, it provided for the simultaneous holding of beliefs which to later ages might seem mutually exclusive.

For although it was open to the medieval Christian to view the text of Scriptures as only a means of expressing a deeper reality, and its historical sense, therefore, a matter of comparative indifference, he was also encouraged, by authorities from Augustine onwards, to think that 'what Scripture gives as history is historically true, even if it is also a type of the higher reality that exists in the world of eternity'.[13] We may wish to formulate these approaches, using, for convenience, descriptive terms such as 'allegorical' and 'typological' or 'figural' to record the differences between them. What is more important for our present purposes, however, is the recognition that the garden of Genesis, first described so boldly in the phrasing of the

Vulgate—'Plantaverat autem Dominus Deus paradisum voluptatis a principio' (Gen. 2:8)—was, from the beginning of Christian commentary, interpreted and presented in the widest variety of ways. We can see how writers moved among non-literal treatments of it, as a moral or psychological allegory, and treatments in which the Garden Paradise was preserved as a historical and enduring fact, but was also seen as revelatory of another Paradise. This Paradise had been foretold by the prophets as an event at the end of time, but had been 'realized' for man in the present as well as in the future by Christ himself: 'Hodie mecum eris in paradiso'.[14]

The concept of the *paradisus voluptatis* was rich enough to attract all modes of Christian thinking—the 'allegorical', with its elaborately developed system of layered spiritual meanings, or the 'typological', with its double or triple vision of paradisal correspondences in human and divine history. And here theology underscored literature: if theologians, from St Augustine to St Thomas Aquinas, could insist upon the 'veritas historiae' of Paradise, there was more than one reason for poets and artists to speculate imaginatively upon the nature of that 'voluptas' with which it had been divinely endowed, and even, eventually, to associate it with the familiar beauty of known gardens and clement landscapes.

It is not entirely satisfactory to order this into a neat chronological sequence. Certainly, many of the best-known allegorical expositions of Paradise come from earlier Christian centuries, and many of the most striking concrete descriptions from the close of the medieval period. But such was the structure of medieval thought that at any point during the period a great number of resolutions was possible. The landscape of Paradise could be austerely drawn in the fourteenth century, sensuously imagined in the ninth. An indefinite number of gradations could be managed in the delicate adjustment of the real to the ideal, the real to the supra-real. Historical accident—country of origin, working conditions, availability of materials, pressure of patron or convention—was influential. No one would deny that the landscape details in the *Paradise* of Herri met de Bles are particular products of late Flemish descriptive naturalism or that the flower-filled settings of many northern European paradise gardens of the fifteenth century are specifically indebted to Italian botanical studies of the preceding decades. They are datable and definable versions of realism. But there are encounters and contacts with the 'real', less easily definable but equally significant, in treatments of Paradise throughout the centuries: the relationship of literal and spiritual truth was most variously interpreted in art and literature.

Even the sermons and treatises of the Fathers of the early Church, for instance, take up markedly different attitudes to the 'reality' of the garden of God. Although none can be said to be interested in representational fidelity, some, convinced of the historical existence of the Genesis garden, work to draw out a more substantial symbolism, while others are concerned only with the possibilities it offers for psychological analysis. Philo, the Jewish exegete of first-century Alexandria, saw primarily an allegory of man's inner conflicts in the Genesis narrative: Adam represented understanding, Eve sensation, the serpent pleasure. As for Paradise, Philo is scornful of those who 'fancied that Paradise was a garden'. He is quite clear that 'virtue is called a Paradise metaphorically, and the appropriate place for the Paradise is Eden . . . The plantation of this Paradise is represented in the east; for right reason never sets and is never extinguished, but it is its nature to be always rising'.[15] Whenever possible, the story is emptied of literal meaning: 'The word Paradise if literally taken . . . means a place thickly crowded with every kind of tree; but symbolically taken, it means wisdom, intelligence both human and divine, and the proper comprehension of the causes of things'. In such a setting every tree is a virtue, and 'the best and wisest authorities have considered that by the tree of life is indicated the best of all the virtues of man—piety'.[16] This allegorizing of Paradise as the interior of the soul was adopted by a succession of Christian theologians and became a permanent part of Western tradition, expressed in Latin, and in the vernacular languages. The *De Paradiso* of St Ambrose, with its meticulous setting-out of the landscape of Paradise as 'anima fecunda', Adam as 'nous', Eve as 'sensus', the beasts and birds of the garden as 'nostri irrationabiles motus' and 'inanes cogitationes', the four rivers of Paradise as the four cardinal virtues, confirmed this psychological drama for later centuries.[17] In many important respects, this is the lineage of the 'garden of man's heart' in *Piers Plowman* (B. XVI), which is a setting for a re-enactment of the Temptation and the Fall as they affect all classes of mankind. And this is substantially the lineage, too, of the 'fair garden', the 'paradis right delitable', described in the thirteenth-century French treatise *Somme le Roi*, translated many times into English during the next century:

'Thes thinges doth the Holy Gost to the herte, and he maketh hit as a paradis right delitable, ful of goode trees and precious.'[18]

The 'paradis the God sett in the holy soule' needed to make only the lightest reference to the delineation of Paradise in the Genesis story; the literal account could be dissolved, and re-set into acceptable shapes of Christian morality. But different in its literary and artistic potential is the attitude of many early Christian thinkers who were less interested in the dissolution of the biblical text than in its transmutation, or even in its transfiguration. For them, the 'reality' of Paradise was at least two-fold; far from being simply 'the symbolical name for virtue', it was the Genesis garden, rich in material and sacramental truth. Early liturgical hymns, such as the *Odes of Solomon*, present a paradisal world which is as sensuous as it is spiritual:

'My lips were touched with clear water, coming straight from the Lord; my nostrils enjoyed the pleasant fragrance of the Lord: and he carried me to his Paradise, where is the abundance of the Pleasure of the Lord.'[19]

St Gregory of Nyssa attends to biblical detail not only because of a conviction that it is in the 'East, where God has planted his Paradise', but also because of an equally strong conviction that the 'blissful locality' is in a sacramental sense, through Christ and baptism, open once more to man.[20] If this should, in theory, sound as much a 'spiritual' reading of the bible as that of the allegorical paradise of the soul, we must, in practice, observe the very real distinctions between the two. It is true that much of the character of Gregory's writing on Paradise depends upon his repudiation of some established physical features; by virtue of baptism, 'the garden of Paradise, and indeed heaven itself, is once again accessible to man . . . the sword of flame no longer prevents his approach'. By a bold denial of the total power of matter, he easily disposes of those ominous wastelands which daunted all Paradise seekers of the later Middle Ages. If it was a fact, for them, that 'many died for weariness of rowing against those strong waves', Gregory stresses the more significant fact that the baptismal water of the river Jordan, flowing from Paradise, can bring man easily back to his original home. But this semi-mystical solution of a material problem is expressed in language of sensuous and dramatic strength; the Genesis garden, its beauty and its terror, springs to life in Gregory's triumphant words:

'Thou didst banish us from Paradise and didst recall us; thou didst strip off the fig leaves, an unseemly covering, and put upon us a costly garment. No longer shall Adam hide himself, cowering in the thicket of Paradise.'[21]

Even when he dwells upon the idea of man's inner nature as a 'paradise', he draws heavily upon texts which provide him with a full range of garden and pastoral imagery, and does not deny their sensory appeal in a spiritual context. The association of the Genesis 'paradisus voluptatis' with the *hortus conclusus* of Canticles 4:12, and with the various trees and animals of the psalms and prophetic books is particularly fruitful; in place of the sword of flame is the protective wall of the Ten Commandments, and, fortified by obedience, the garden prospers:

'*A garden enclosed is my sister, my spouse* . . . he must become a flourishing garden, having within himself the beauty of all kinds of trees. There must be the sweet fig, the fruitful olive, the lofty palm, the blossoming vine. He must have no thorn bush or fleabane; these must be replaced by the cypress and the myrtle. . . . In addition, our garden is enclosed in on all sides by the fence of the Commandments, so that no thief or wild beast can gain entrance to it. . . . It cannot be reached by the solitary wild boar or *the boar out of the wood.*'[22]

Poets and painters were to find the enclosed garden their favourite paradisal form, and the Canticles one of their finest sources for garden detail. Here, in Gregory's *Commentary*, words that so excited later centuries are delicately manipulated between the sensuous and the spiritual. As Gregory observed, 'there is a correspondence between the movements of the soul and the sense organs of the body',[23] and so he uses the corporeal senses to conduct and prompt spiritual understanding. His treatment of the 'paradise of the pomegranates' (Cant. 4:13) typically combines sharp and subtle observation with abstract interpretation. We are not dealing with that paradise in the lavish terms of late medieval visual realism—the glimmering fruits which spread like summer lanterns above the captive unicorn in the seventh and last of the tapestries made for the marriage of Anne of Brittany in 1499.[24] Yet summer ripeness is strongly suggested as Gregory explores the 'meaning' of the text:

'But when the season allows us to enjoy it, the pomegranate offers us the combined pleasure of every kind of fruit. And the taste is not like that of peaches or dates . . . but all sorts of different kinds of perfumes are found in its fruit.'[25]

A window of the scholar's study is open upon the real world—the sounds and scents of summer, the labours of autumn; for Gregory's 'enclosed garden of paradise' does not shut out the activity of the countryside—the 'fruitful olive tree' (Ps. 51:10) reminds him of 'the bounty we receive by the cultivation of the olive. At first, in the autumn, it contains a sharp and bitter juice. But later, by proper care and maturation, it is transformed into the true olive.'[26]

It is, indeed, clear that many early Christians were encouraged to envisage Paradise—both the earthly and its heavenly counterpart—in the form of gardens and groves and pastoral landscapes already familiar to them from nature and art. Gregory's comment, 'a grove that is thickly planted with trees is accustomed to be called a paradise',[27] returns us to the 'paradises' of Eastern princes and noblemen, to the origin of the word and the hunting parks of Persia which it first signified.[28] The pastoral imagery of early Christian mosaics and wall-paintings and that of contemporary vision literature, with its four rivers of Paradise, and its shepherd-gardener in his landscape, have the same kind of 'double' appeal to belief in irreducible facts, and in the spiritual significance of those facts—the baptismal re-entry of man into Paradise, the redemptive care of Christ for man, the eternal assertion of 'hodie'. The garden in the third-century *Vision* of the martyr Perpetua:

'an enormous garden, and in the middle of it a man with white hair, sitting down and dressed as a shepherd, tall and engaged in milking his flock. He raised his head and said to me, "You have come through very well".'[29]

is substantially the same as the garden in the apse of the Mausoleum of Galla Placidia in Ravenna.[30] The fifth-century mosaic also places Christ, 'the new Adam', in an immediate context of natural objects and activities: the original garden of Eden has been redeemed, sanctified and preserved. But the eye is led to it along a great expanse of stars and roundels, backed by a deep vibrating blue (Plate 8). There is the strong sense, as in the *Vision of Perpetua*, that this is a vision of both earthly and heavenly Paradises, the Paradise of Adam, of Enoch and of Christ; that, indeed, man has 'come through' very well. There is also the sense, in the mosaic, that this Paradise lies high in a rocky setting—a reference perhaps to Christian tradition, 'whence not even the waters of the flood could reach it'.[31] But there may also be a reference here to classical traditions of ideal landscape, which stress mountainous surroundings—the heights of Olympus, of Ida, of Parnassus.[32] Here we recognize the wealth of materials available to writers and artists of the early Christian centuries—their geographical and cultural contacts with the worlds of the classical and oriental past were, so to speak, given a proper meaning in a Christian world which saw history as a series of divine intimations and fulfilments, and reality as historical, sacramental and spiritual.

So, the ideal landscapes of classical poetry, with their perfected versions of Mediterranean scenery, often envisaged as part of a vanished 'Golden Age', could easily be adapted to Christian purposes. Their 'spiritualization' could be achieved not by any denial of the substance of their earthly beauty, but by relating it more explicitly to detail from the gardens of Genesis and the Canticles. The absorption of the *locus amoenus* of Greek and Latin poetry into the Terrestrial Paradise of Christian tradition is more than a simple instance of 'classical influence'. It is a more important kind of transmutation, dependent upon typological views of reality. Dante, writing in a country where the

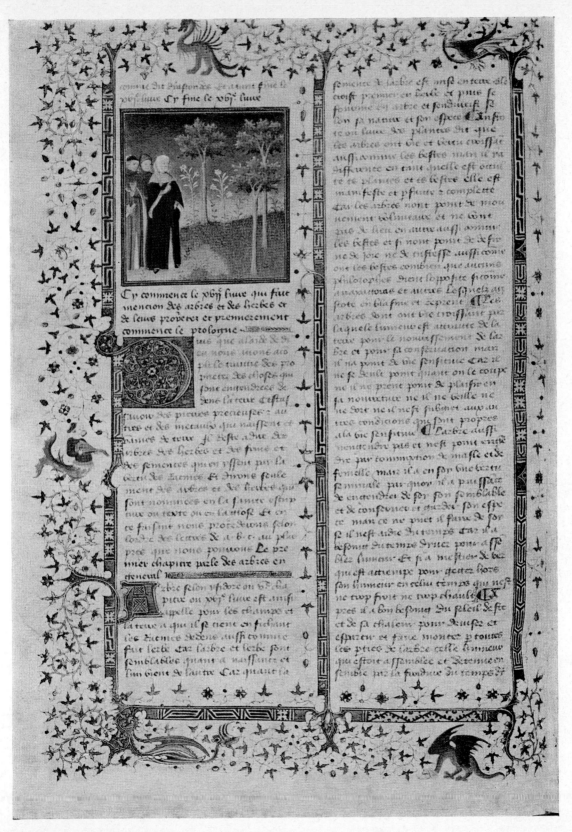

IV *Figures in a Landscape*, from *Le Livre de la Propriété des Choses*. Fitzwilliam Museum, Cambridge, MS 251, f. 251v. Early fifteenth century.

influence of classical civilization had always been strong and close, and at a time when it was possible both to reaffirm and look critically at that influence, gives full and clear expression to this. The lady Matilda accounts for pre-Christian descriptions of the Golden Age with its terrain of unfading beauty as dim recollections of Paradise before the Fall: they are imperfect but acceptable testimonies to the literal reality of that place in which the poet now, miraculously, is permitted to stand:

> 'Quelli che anticamenti poetaro
> l'età dell'oro e suo stato felice,
> forse in Parnaso esto loco sognaro.
> Qui fu innocente l'umana radice;
> qui primavera sempre ed ogni frutto;'[33]
> ('Those men of yore who sang the golden time
> And all its happy state—maybe indeed
> They on Parnassus dreamed of this fair clime.
> Here was the innocent root of all man's seed;
> Here spring is endless, here all fruits are.')

Nothing, then, in the art and literature of the past need be irrelevant to the Christian celebration of the earthly and heavenly paradise, which completes and fulfils all earlier tentative descriptions by putting them in deep spiritual perspective. So the mosaics in the Christian basilica, the Catacomb paintings, many of the hymns, poems and vision treatises of the earlier Christian centuries can legitimately picture Christ as a shepherd-Orpheus figure, in his idealized (but not allegorical) landscape of trees, grass, rocks and sheep. And so, too, the English poet of the eighth century, who adapted the late classical *Carmen de Ave Phoenice* of Lactantius for his own Christian purposes, can benefit from the Latin account of the paradise in which the phoenix lives—a place such as Dante might have had in mind when he wrote of clouded paradisal memories:

> 'Est locus in primo felix oriente remotus . . .
> Hic Solis nemus est et consitus arbore multa
> Lucus . . .
> Sed fons in medio est, quem 'vivum' nomine dicunt.'[34]
> ('There is a happy place, far distant in the east . . . there lies the grove of the Sun, and a wood thick with many a tree. . . . But a fountain rises at its centre, called "the living spring".')

A place, too, of perceptual, almost tangible delights, even in their idealized form: the fountain is 'perspicuus, lenis, dulcibus uber aquis' (line 26); the dawn reddens, the stars fade:

'Lutea cum primum surgens Aurora rubescit,
Cum primum rosea sidera luce fugat.'

(35–6)

The whole setting for the life, death and resurrection of this marvellous and strange bird is redolent with spices and luminous with colour:

'Cinnamon hic auramque procul spirantis amomi
Congerit et mixto balsama cum folio ...
Albicat insignis mixto viridante zmaragdo
Et puro cornu gemmea cuspis hiat.'

(83–4, 135–6)

(Here cinnamon mixes with the distant breath of scented amomum and balsam-leaf. ... Its crest is white, streaked with emerald green, and its polished beak shines, inside and out, like a gem.)

Not all of this detail did the English poet use, but he based his more complex treatment of the Phoenix story upon the concept of a *locus felix*, a concentration of all forms of sensuous beauty in a stabilized, eternalized state. Thus, although his ultimate aim in the poem is to 'interpret' the Phoenix legend as an allegory of the resurrection of Christ, and of man, he is very much concerned in his treatment of the *locus felix* to remind his readers of the contrast between the two worlds of the senses, the one perfectly adjusted to man's needs, and bestowed upon him by God, the other jarring and inclement—his 'terram confusionis et ariditatis', 'land of confusion and sterility'.[35] So, before turning to allegory, and acting upon suggestions in the Latin poem, he compares the harsh landscapes and weathers of the North with the temperate pleasures of the land of the phoenix in a way which moves subtly between the real, the ideal and the spiritual.[36] Clearly, this paradisal country is both terrestrial and heavenly; the doors of heaven are often opened to it, and the singing of the angelic chorus is heard by the blessed who inhabit it. Appropriately, it is often described in such non-specific but emotive terms as 'wynsum' ('joyful') for both its appearance and significance. But its waters are 'brimcald' ('cold as the sea'), its groves and plains are green, and the ocean beyond it flows with 'sealte streamas' ('salt currents'). And clearly, too, the features of the other country, 'swa her mid us' ('as in our region'), are no less real, and registered with some feeling, because they are symbolic of the uncomfortable exile of man, always longing for the garden which

'afyrred is
þurh Meotudes meaht manfremmendum.' (5-6)
('distanced from human beings by the might of the Lord.')

Not again until the early fifteenth century did painters of the *Expulsion from Eden* seriously attempt to convey the unwelcoming prospect of the world outside Eden; even then, in the Bedford Hours of 1423 (Plate 23b), a rougher tree or two, a stylized crag, a barer strip of ground serve, economically. Here, in the eighth-century poem, great vistas of mountainous countryside, in the grip of winter, are evoked and contrasted with the level unchanging beauties of Paradise. Well into the fifteenth century, a frieze or cluster of formalized peaks satisfied artists as concise notation for the chaos of man's life outside Paradise: they form a narrow border to the *Expulsion* scene in the *Très Riches Heures* made for Jean de Berry (Plate 23a), before 1416.[37] But here, in *The Phoenix*, they are invested with power to terrify; although we are given a visual impression rather than a description, the sinister hinterlands of Paradise are real enough:

'Beorgas þær ne muntas
steape ne stonda ð, ne stanclifu
heah hlifia ð, swa her mid us,
ne dene ne dalu ne dunscrafu,
hlæwas ne hlincas . . .'
(21–5)

('There no mountains or crags rise steeply, nor do high stony cliffs menace, as here in our region, nor are there passes, valleys, ravines, nor mounds nor hills. . .')

We may be persuaded that these are images of human stress, as well as solid objects of vision—'the mind, mind has mountains, cliffs of fall/Sheer, no-man-fathomed'—just as we may be persuaded that the 'changing weather, fierce under the heavens' ('wedra gebregd, hreoh under heofenum'), which brings frost, and rime, windy clouds, rain from a sullen sky, is also an image of mutability. But some treaty has been made with sensuous perception; here, and in the 'happy land' of the phoenix, shapes and substances and textures are not immediately allegorized out of their earthly existence, but given a significant, though limited, part to play in conveying the whole message of the poem.[38]

Comparable but not identical kinds of adjustment are made in the Old English *Genesis*, a highly dramatic verse rendering of the Fall of the Angels and the Fall of Man, written, probably, between the seventh and the ninth centuries. The sole manuscript in which it occurs (Bodleian MS Junius XI), has illustrative drawings dating from the tenth or eleventh centuries

(Plate 24a).[39] Both drawings and poetry take some interest in the substance of Paradise and its environs, but the poets (it is of composite authorship) are far more directly concerned not only with biblical geography but also with weather:

> 'Heoldon forðryne
> eastreamas heora   æðele feower
> of þam niwan   neorxnawonge ...
> Þæra anne hata ð ylde,   eorðbuende,
> Fison folcweras;   se foldan dæl
> brade bebugeð   beorhtum streamum
> Hebeleac utan.   On þære eðyltyrf
> niððas findað   nean and feorran
> gold and gymcynn,   gumþeoda bearn ...[40]

('Four fair rivers hold their course,
Flowing from the new Paradise ...
One is named Phison by dwellers on earth;
The broad lands of Hevilath it compasses round
With its bright waters.
Throughout its soil, the children of men
Find gold and gems ...')

Adam's lament for the changed conditions of life after the Fall:

> 'cymeð hægles scur   hefone getenge,
> færeð forst on gemang,   se byð fyrnum ceald
> (808–9)
> ('The hailstorm beats down from heaven,
> Frost strikes, strangely cold')

and his reconciliation with a 'realm less rich in blessings', but still watched over by God:

> 'Hyrstedne hrof   halgum tunglum'
> (956)
> ('the sky set with holy stars')

present a version of a real world, full of terrors and consolations.

The artists, on the other hand, show the strongest tendencies to reduce the landscape elements to functional symbols or decorative patterns. The trees of Paradise, rooted stoutly in recognizable ground, develop into fleshy scrolls, osmetimes into plaited abstract designs, reminiscent of late Viking metal and woodwork. Realism is encountered not so much in landscape, but in the light active figures which inhabit it. The traditions which lie behind the

Junius drawings are classical, and therefore based, at many removes, upon a perceptual outlook: these medieval artists, however, are drawn towards the conceptual.[41] Although it might be over-fanciful to see, in the heavy drooping fronds of the paradisal trees which shelter Adam and Eve from the wrath of God, a reference to sin and contrition, there is a possibility that the illustrations are taking a slightly allegorical turn. These trees of Paradise remind us, even though faintly, of the allegorical trees of vices and virtues so popular in moral treatises from the eleventh century onwards.[42]

The movement towards the conceptualizing of Paradise and its terrain was strong throughout the Middle Ages. The author of the *Phoenix* proceeded to allegory in the second part of the poem, and there is no doubt that the severe beauty of this particular kind of answer to the irritable questionings of the exiled flesh was attractive to a wide range of writers and artists. Its refusal to deal in compromises recommended it to them: as they found in works such as the *De Paradiso* of St Ambrose, its searching of the biblical text for lavish significances and its almost total neglect of appearances was an advantage, a release of spiritual invention made possible by the curbing of the visual imagination. For whether Paradise was 'interpreted' as the interior man or as the Christian Church, as the microcosm or the macrocosm, as the Virgin Mary or as Christ, in this mode of thought it was a paradise of scriptural colour and sweetness only. To St Jerome, in the fourth century, the Virgin is the 'true garden of delights, in which are sown all kinds of flowers and spice plants of the virtues'.[43] To Honorius of Autun, in the twelfth century, the Church is Paradise; it real delights are the sacred scriptures and Christ, who is both fountain and tree of life:

'Per Paradysum qui *hortus deliciarum* dicitur, Ecclesia accipitur, in qua sunt Scriptuarum deliciae et quae est vocata ad domum Dei ubi sunt gloria et divitiae. In tali paradyso fons oritur, dum Christus, fons omnium bonorum, de casta virgine nascitur. Quatuor flumina quae inde oriuntur, quatuor evangelistae intelliguntur.'[44]

('By Paradise, which is said to be a garden of delights, we should understand "the Church": here are the delights of the scriptures; it is called the house of God, full of glories and riches. In such a paradise a fountain rises—just as Christ, fountain of all good things, springs from a chaste virgin. The four rivers which flow thence signify the four Evangelists.')

In these accounts all sense of location, all sense of substance is dissolved, as the tree of life becomes the tree of the Cross, bearing its sacred fruit in Paradise, and linking man to heaven through love:

'Arbor crucis est lignum vitae in paradiso, id est, in Ecclesia. Hujus arboris fructus est Christus in ea pendens.'[45]

It is to this type of concept of the paradise garden that the twelfth-century nun, Herrad of Landsperg, referred when she called her treatise *Hortus Deliciarum*—a work which covers all significant parts of man's moral history.[46] The garden from which Herrad picked her flowers was that of the writings of the Church:

'ex diversis sacrae et philosophiae scripturae floribus quasi apicula deo inspirante comportavi.' (p. 23)

And as if to underline the dangers of valuing, even of envisaging, any garden save this perdurable ground of salvation, Herrad has an illustration of the fate of the hermit who falls from the ladder to true Paradise because his eyes are fixed upon an earthly garden:

'Hortum suum excolens . . . plantationi suae intendens . . . dulcedine sequestratur.'[47]

('cultivating his own garden . . . intent upon his own plot . . . he is shut out of bliss')

The seductive arbour is sketched in with a few herbs and grasses: the economical little drawing tersely expresses its contempt for garden imagery, as well as for gardens in general.

The special qualities of this literature, and of the art which frequently accompanies it, are clarity and comprehensiveness: its symmetries are those of dogma, its flowerings those of faith. Here the relationship of word and picture can be very close. In many of the manuscript copies of the twelfth-century *Speculum Virginum*, by Conrad of Hirschau, a description of the nature of Paradise is confirmed by a drawing, in formalized rose shape (Plate 24b). Reminiscences of leaf, petal and stem are present, but slight: at the centre of this spiritual flower is Christ, clasped by the Virgin. From him flow the four rivers of Paradise, channelled into symbolic river god figures who hold medallions with representations of the Evangelists' symbols and the Doctors of the Church. The trees of Paradise are flat bushes, surmounted by the Virtues. This is an anatomy of spiritual relationships, expressed in graphic terms, with the merest concessions to 'natural' appearances. Here is the structure of Paradise, conceived as the Church, radial to Christ. The stylized mode of indicating human and vegetable forms, suggesting nothing in the way of illusion, but a good deal in the way of comprehension, and the simple colour range—in the Arundel manuscript, for instance, only brown ink, and a pale green colour wash—proclaim the strongly cerebral and didactic intent of the writer and artist.[48] The perspective is literally shallow, but intellectually and spiritually deep. Art, here, perfectly responds to the demands of literature, and it is appropriateness rather than literal beauty or drama that the nun, Theodora, for whom the treatise was written, is encouraged to expect. She, and her companions, should 'drink from the springs of the Gospels or the teachings of the Church',[49] which, in their turn, derive from the original spring of Paradise, Christ. This is a picture of Paradise as valid as that of Herri met de Bles, but concerned with theological, not representational truth, with a garden of which St Bernard had written— 'non pedibus in hunc hortum, sed affectibus introitur'.[50] And in fact, over the medieval period, the gradual growth of interest in that very representation of truth would often prove inimical to the perfect balance of literature and art which we must admire in texts such as the *Speculum Virginum*.

A case in point is the *Somme le Roi*,[51] which very early on established a set of pictures appropriate to its subject matter, but which continued to receive illustration well into the fifteenth century. The earlier type of picture which accompanied the description of the allegorical Paradise (Plate 25a) followed the words of the treatise exactly, portraying Christ simply as a larger central tree:

'But right as God sett ertheli paradis ful of goode trees and fruyght, and in the myddel sett the tree of lif . . . right so doth gostly to the herte the good gardyner, that is God the fadre, for he sett the tree of vertue and in the myddel the tree of lif, that is Jhesu Crist.'[52]

In the fifteenth century, the illustration to an English version introduces a 'realistic' scene of active gardening, with Christ as both tree and divine gardener (Plate 25b). He appears to be grafting new stock upon old, the garden of the heart is a convincing walled enclosure, the trees are burgeoning and sinuous. But the allegorical equivalents are not so clearly expressed: it is not clear, for instance, whether the artist intends us to understand Christ or God as the 'good gardyner', or man and tree as a double representation of the 'tree of lif'. There are similar occasions when an enthusiastic welcome to realism disturbs the equilibrium of this art and literature, disturbs the cool speculative certainties they proclaim. The invasion of one mode by another, always interesting, was not always a spiritually enriching process, and the surest triumphs were most often won by artists and poets working confidently within the bounds of one chosen mode, whether it was that of representational realism, typological or figural realism, or abstraction.

From the purely imaginative point of view, the second mode probably always offered widest scope to those who sought to evoke paradisal states and landscapes. Transfusing 'the real' with 'the spiritual', they were able to call upon many different kinds of material without risking domination by any one. Dante's description of the Earthly and Heavenly Paradises illustrates this perfectly. The Earthly Paradise is a realization, in fully material terms, of a wooded countryside, part reminiscent of classical grove, part of scented pinewood near Ravenna, and part of biblical garden—'this holy plain' which 'teems with seeds of everything/And in its womb breeds fruits ne'er plucked of men'. But it is also realized as an 'earnest of eternal peace' (*Purg.* XXVIII.93), a pledge to be fulfilled only by the Heavenly Paradise. So Adam speaks to Dante of the 'earthly Paradise/Where apt for this ascent thy soul did grow' (*Par.* XXVI.110–11). The Earthly Paradise, lovely in itself, looks to the greater: its beauty presages true heavenly beauty. The subtlety with which Dante presents, links and distinguishes the two Paradises is remarkable. Both are referred to as 'gardens'—by Adam, who calls the Earthly Paradise 'eccelso giardino' (*Par.* XXVI.110), and by Beatrice and St Bernard, who direct Dante's attention towards the 'bel giardino', no ordinary rose garden but the garden which is the 'rosa sempiterna' of God's love and which lies at the very rim of the vision of the Infinite.[53] Yet in differentiating between the two, Dante is not tempted to over-materialize the Earthly Paradise: with propriety, he carries some of his description in simile, so that this Paradise is never identified, but only associated with a recognizable type of fourteenth-century Italian landscape:

> 'tal qual di ramo in ramo si raccoglie
> per la pineta in sul lito di Chiassi,
> quand'Eolo Scirocco fuor discioglie.'
> (*Purg.* XXVIII.19–21)
> ('So, in Chiassi's pinewood by the sea,
> From bough to bough the gathering murmurs swell
> When Aeolus has set Scirocco free.')

And, with propriety, all particularized forms of natural beauty—the 'thick and leafy tent' of the sacred wood, the stream which flowed 'bending the grasses on the edge of it' (*Purg.* XXVIII.2,27)—are reserved for the Earthly, as opposed to the Heavenly Paradise. For the Heavenly Paradise, as Dante admits, the poet has to take 'adventurous ways' (Parad. XXIII.68) in order to convey something of its irradiated beauty. Its flowers are the Virgin and Apostles, growing in the light and warmth of the true sun:

> 'bel giardino
> che sotto i raggi di Cristo s'infiora . . .
> Quivi è la Rosa in che il Verbo divino
> carne si fece: e quivi son li gigli

al cui odor si prese il buon cammino.'
(Par. XXIII.71-5)

('the garden bright

Shone on by Christ, and flowering in his rays . . .
There blooms the rose wherein God's word was dight
With flesh, and there the lilies blow whose scent
Wooed man to take the road that runs aright.')

Its essential nature is best described in terms of light—'intellectual light, fulfilled with love', 'luce intelletual, piena d'amore' (*Par.* XXX.40)—but as a concession to the limited power of human understanding it is presented in terms of a spring landscape, with river, glittering river bed, and flowered banks. Such a landscape is never to be mistaken for the familiar 'ideal garden' of the Earthly Paradise: Beatrice stresses to Dante that what he sees are 'shadow-prefaces', 'umbriferi prefazii' (*Par.* XXX.78), of the final truth. And, indeed, this is made clear in the details of the description: the river sparkles with jewelled spray, which mingles with the flowers; the springtime is 'wondrous':

'E vidi lume in forma di rivera
fulvido di fulgore, intra due rive
dipinte di mirabil primavera.
Di tal fiumana usciàn faville vive,
e d'ogni parte si mettean nei fiori
quasi rubin che oro circonscrive.'

(*Par.* XXX.61-6)

('Light I beheld which as a river flowed,
Fulgid with splendour; and on either shore,
The colours of a wondrous spring-time showed.
And from the stream arose a glittering store
Of living sparks which, winging mid the blooms,
To rubies set in gold resemblance bore.')

The full meaning of these phenomena is revealed to Dante when, before his eyes, they are transmuted into a vision of the courts of heaven:

'così mi si cambiaro in maggior feste
li fiori e le faville, sì ch'io vidi
ambo le corti del ciel manifeste.'

(*Par.* XXX. 94-6)

('So, as I looked, to greater joyances
The gems and flowers were changed, and I beheld
Both courts of Heaven in true appearances.')

73

Without the garden imagery ever being totally relinquished, the company of the Blessed is ultimately seen as a 'golden rose', bathed in everlasting spring sunlight:

> 'che si dilata ed ingrada e redole
> odor di lode al Sol che sempre verna.'
> *(Par.* XXX. 125–6)

as Dante raises it, stage by stage, to new and enhanced significance. And so, all gardens are resolved and sanctified in the last great paradise garden, of God: the flawed landscapes of Adam's garden of banishment,

> 'Le fronde onde s'infronda tutto l'orto
> dell' Ortolano eterno, am'io cotanto
> quanto da lui a lor di bene è porto.'
> *(Par.* XXVI. 64–6)
> ('And through the garden of the world I rove
> Enamoured of its leaves in measure solely
> As God the Gardener nurtures them above.')

the 'level meadows', 'campagna lento' *(Purg.* XXVIII.5), of the Earthly Paradise, and the dancing waters of the Heavenly.

Such felicitous accord of vision and communication is more rarely matched by medieval painters of similar subjects who tended increasingly to express Earthly and Heavenly Paradise in decorative renderings of natural or cultivated beauty. Giovanni di Paolo's version of the Heavenly *Paradise*, for instance, with Beatrice floating in a golden haze of light—a direct reference to those lines in the *Paradiso* which describe how 'on mine eyes her light at first so blazed,/They could not bear the beauty and the burning' *(Par.* III.128–9)—takes a far simpler path than that of Dante (Plate 26). Here, the tree, flower and grass detail of Dante's Earthly Paradise is formalized as an elaborate background for the grave and joyful reunion of the Blessed. There is nothing in this setting, delicate, refined and moving as it is—the trees a thin tracery against an egg-shell sky, the turf starred with flowers of an Italian spring—to distinguish the garden from any earthly garden, literary or real. Only the luminous Beatrice speaks to the beholder of Heaven.

Indeed, it needed a painter of the intellectual and visionary range of Hieronymus Bosch to find visual symbols of similar power for the two paradisal states. Even then, the garden is transcended, rather than transmuted: the imagery is not held in suspension, as it is in Dante. Two of the four panels from the Ducal Palace in Venice picture the *Garden of Eden* and the *Ascent to the Empyrean* (Plate 27). In the *Garden* panel, the Elect, visited by angels, look longingly towards the Fountain of Life, just as the Christian soul, in the 'Paradise of the Church', looks towards Christ. The scene is fully expressed as a garden of delights, with a deep landscape stretching towards the horizon: it is also fully significant as an expression of delights which are only prefatory, 'umbriferi prefazii'. The yearning of the Elect is satisfied in the *Empyrean* panel; gardens are left far behind as the Blessed are drawn irresistibly down a narrowing but brightening tunnel of light, towards God. The concepts which lie behind such a picture are those of Dante's 'ciel, ch'è pura luce', Ruysbroek's 'immense effusion of celestial light which encircles and attracts us': it was more difficult for painters than for poets to envisage—or if they envisaged, to describe—a state in which 'the fire and the rose are one'.

Chapter Four

THE ENCLOSED
GARDEN

*Hortus conclusus soror mea sponsa, hortus
conclusus* (Cant. 4:12)
The gardyn is enclosed al aboute... (Merch. Tale)

Adam's sober words to Dante[1] about the proper limitations of human attachment to the natural beauty of the world recall, although they do not endorse, a whole area of medieval literature and art concerned with the Earthly Paradise not as a stage in a spiritual drama of ascent to the Empyrean but as a complete embodiment of sensuous delight, a refuge of earthly love and happiness, a solace for mortal pain. The twelfth century is rich in Latin and vernacular poetry which explores its themes of human love in paradisal settings of opulent or fragile detail, as much dependent on biblical as secular sources.[2] Latin love debates seek their answers in groves furnished from Genesis as well as Virgil, and the troubadour lyrics of Provence often enclose their private moralities of passion in orchards or secluded gardens more than a little reminiscent of those of the 'Song of Songs'.[3] In fact, it was the *hortus conclusus* which early became the specific and dominant version of the paradise garden of profane as well as divine love. In the romance of *Cligès*, by Chrétien de Troyes, the lovers Fenice and Cligès have a walled garden, opening off the tower in which they have taken refuge from the persecution of family and society. It is, indeed, their 'paradise', and all outside is ugly and hostile:

'Fenice passed out through the door into the garden ... In the middle stood a grafted tree, loaded with blossoms and leaves.... Beneath the tree the turf is very pleasant and fine, and at noon, when it is hot, the sun will never be high enough to penetrate there.... There they taste of joy and delight. And the garden is enclosed about with a high wall connected with the tower, so that nothing can enter there without first passing through the tower.'[4]

No, doubt, in these lyrics, debates and romances we encounter something of actuality;[5] the gardens they describe had their material counterparts in the seigneurial life so familiar to poets and patrons—walled plots of civilized and private pleasure-ground, contrasting with the wild or roughly practical countryside beyond the castle gates, and offering respite from the noisy communal life of the hall. In 1250 Henry III gave orders for a queen's garden at Woodstock which could have served lyric or romance:

'To make two good high walls around the garden of the queen so that no-one may be able to enter, with a becoming and pleasant herbary near the king's fish pond in which the same queen may be able to amuse herself . . . and with a gate from the herbary . . . into the aforesaid garden.'[6]

But the interplay of life and art during these medieval centuries is as much concealed as revealed by the records offered to us: did courtly gardens attempt to mirror the gardens of poetry, or were those literary paradises based on humbler but real enclosures? The mixture of fact and imaginative fiction is complex. In the case of monastery gardens, for instance, we know that flowers were grown and enjoyed for their symbolism, as well as for their beauty—Walafrid Strabo's *Hortulus* poem, from ninth-century Reichenau, praises the rose and the lily in the abbot's varied garden, for their message of blood and milk, passion and purity. But they are also the flowers of the Song of Songs: literature and life join in metaphor.

Historians have insisted that, as far as the practical business of gardening is concerned, the walled orchards and gardens of medieval Europe were modelled upon Eastern, and ultimately Persian, example—upon gardens first revealed to Western eyes during the Crusades, and constantly accessible to travellers in Sicily and Moslem Spain.[7] And it may be that such an influence was more widely operative. In the poetry, decorative arts and courtly rituals of Persia, for instance, gardens and garden imagery play a significant part. The antiquity and the elaborate beauty of Persian gardens and hunting parks had been famous from the days of Xenophon:

'Their name is Paradise, and they are full of all things fair and good that the earth can bring forth.'[8]

A sophisticated relationship between gardens and garden art was already displayed in the 'winter-carpet or the spring-garden' of Chosroes I (531–79)— a vast woven pleasure garden, formal as the real gardens of a Persian monarch and able to remind the king of summer in winter:

'The ground was yellowish, to look like earth, and it was worked in gold. The edges of the streams were worked in stripes, and between them stones bright as crystal gave the illusion of water.'[9]

This double image, of the artefact in nature, and nature in the artefact, is a striking feature of Persian garden scenes, as they come to us first from the poetry of the tenth century, and, later, from miniature painting. The poet Firdausi describes the laying of flowered carpets upon flowered turf, at royal feasts, and what the poet describes, the miniaturists of the fourteenth and fifteenth centuries illustrated—princes seated in walled gardens, where nature's luxuriance is brought to a fine point of comparison with the skill of the weaver or textile worker.[10]

We cannot help but be taken by the similarity of concept which seems to inform the descriptive language of much garden art in the medieval West. Poets, from the twelfth to the fifteenth centuries, 'clothe' the earth with embroidered 'fabric' in spring.[11] Tapestries of the *millefiore* variety, the painted foregrounds to studies of saints and madonnas in meditation, or to scenes of hunting and courtship, seek to formalize natural detail into richly textured designs. But it is not easy to trace the precise ways in which Eastern poetry and painting, on garden themes, affected those of the West. It is not enough to point to those vaguely oriental references in garden poems, Latin or vernacular, of the twelfth and thirteenth centuries—the trees which were brought 'fro the lande of Alexandryn' for the garden of love in the *Roman de la Rose*.[12] We know that one Islamic account of the prophet Muhammad's visit to the gardens of Paradise, the *Kitāb al-mi'rāj*, was available to European writers in the fourteenth century, through Spanish and French intermediaries. As the *Liber Scalae*, it may have provided Dante and the English '*Pearl* poet' with some descriptive imagery.[13] In painting, the accessibility of Eastern exemplars is even more open to interested speculation. Many of the finest Persian garden pictures come from the fifteenth century, and are therefore too late to have affected Western art. But it is now clear that, by the last decades of the fourteenth century, Persian miniaturists had developed a mature style for treating garden subjects, and it is hard to believe, on the evidence of the works they produced, that northern Italian painters of the early fifteenth century, as well as some from the lower Rhineland, did not have contact with Persian material, either at one or two removes. The anonymous northern Italian artist who illustrated the Cocharelli manuscript, in the later fourteenth century, had some such access to Persian models, as he had, also, access to types of paradise garden motifs, themselves of Eastern origin, but transmitted through Sicilian mosaic.[14] The rôle of Sicily and Venice was probably crucial in this East-West process. It has been suggested that the Madonna-in-a-garden pictures were first developed, as a distinct art form, in Venice:[15] to that city, throughout the Middle Ages, European merchants came to buy spices, dyes and textiles, brought from the East by Venetian galleys. The trade routes of the period make out a pattern which could begin to account for the remarkable likenesses between garden pictures from southern Germany, Verona and and Herat over the years 1390–1430. Juxtaposition of Italian and Persian paintings can reveal startling likenesses, of both a general and a detailed nature. Stefano da Zevio's *Madonna in the Rose Garden* (Plate 32a), from Verona, suspends its subject in an enclosed flower-studded area with the same disregard for spatial illusion, and the same enthusiasm for overall decorative effect, as Persian miniatures of lovers meeting in palace gardens. Beyond the high wall of the Frankfurt *Garden of Paradise* lies that same vibrating blue background which gives Persian garden paintings their paradisal context—whether that paradise is heavenly or terrestrial. (Plate 29)[16]

Most interesting is the imaginative use made of the walled garden by Persian poets and prose writers, working in both secular and religious contexts. In the spiritualized, but still powerfully sensuous, *Haft Paikar*, or *Seven Beauties*, by the twelfth-century poet, Nizāmī, a story is told in which the hero has a garden:

'The earth with scent of roses was perfumed: its fruits were like the fruits of paradise . . . therein a fountain of life's water flowed . . . all hearts were centred in its pomegranates: its roses had no mediating thorns.'[17]

It is said to be another earthly paradise, its four high walls 'towering to the moon' and protecting it from 'the evil eye'. Such an enclosed garden is probably as much indebted to the Song of Songs as to the poet's heightened appreciation of real gardens: he knows the difference between this and the 'rose-garden whose rose is only as the thorn, whose thorn is sharp'.[18] The lovers who are described and painted in palace gardens are seen, after death, in settings only a shade more ravishing than those they knew in life:

'He saw, within a rosy glade,
Beneath a palm's exclusive shade,
A throne, amazing to behold,
Studded with glittering gems and gold;
Celestial carpets near it spread,
Close where a lucid streamlet strayed;
Upon that throne, in blissful state,
The long-divided lovers sate.'[19]

The soul is pictured, allegorically, in exile from a garden 'which, through all the four seasons, never lacked for fragrant herbs, verdant grasses and joyous pleasances; great waters therein flowed . . .'.[20] Though it cannot properly remember its 'garden kingdom', it has stirrings and restless longings 'whenever a breeze blew and the scent of the flowers and the trees, the roses and violets and jasmine and fragrant herbs wafted'. The blending of natural growth and artefact, of fact and invention, of secular passion and spiritual aspiration, is characteristic of the Persian garden as it comes to us in historical record, art and literature. The garden was an approximation to Heaven, with its constant striving to improve upon nature—palm trees plated in gilt copper, exotic graftings of rose upon almond—[21] but Heaven itself could be expressed as a concentration of all sensuous delights in a perpetual garden. Muhammad, ascending to Paradise, was seen by the poet Nizāmī as 'rose of that exalted garden of Paradise', 'fairest hyacinth in the garden of glory': the image threads through his eulogies of the Prophet—'Thy dust is itself the garden of my soul. Thy garden is my soul and my world'.[22] The *hortus conclusus* was a reality and a dream of perfection, a secular and a religious paradise in life as in death: 'Abandon the crow for the tail of the peacock: remain in the garden with the song of the nightingale'.[23]

But whereas in the East all of these varied facts and concepts seem to have co-existed peacefully, in the Christian West they were sometimes uneasily combined, or used as the basis for ironic and penetrating debate. It is true that the *hortus conclusus* was widely and successfully adopted as the earthly paradise of human love. Definitions of paradise, in totally profane terms, often confidently and naturally combine imagery from the Song of Songs and Genesis with other kinds of descriptive material, naturalistic and literary. A fifteenth-century prince such as Lorenzo de' Medici has this to say about man's paradise of beauty and love:

'For "paradise". . . means nothing more than a most pleasant garden, abundant with all pleasing and delightful things, of trees, apples, flowers, vivid running waters, song of birds and in effect, all the amenities dreamed of by the heart of man; and by this one can affirm that paradise was where there was a beautiful woman, for here was a copy of every amenity and sweetness that a kind heart might desire.'[24]

The apparent total reversal of religious values, the independence of the concepts, first strike the reader: in this secular paradise, woman is the crown of beauty, not the symbol of sensual weakness. She creates paradise, and is no exile from bliss. Yet even on this point such a passage can still remind us of the biblical *hortus conclusus*—of the inescapably erotic language of the Song of Songs, and of the clear connection of the *hortus* image with the physical reality of the beloved. It was possible for this particular text to provide rich substance not only for the exegete and for the religious poet but also for the medieval poet of secular love, who may or may not wish to stress the element

V *March*, a leaf from a Book of Hours. British Museum, London, Addit.
MS 18855, f. 108. Early sixteenth century.

of parody in his version. In spite of the seeming self-sufficiency of paradisal existence as it is presented in many a secular garden of love, there are probably few medieval poets who do not use the words 'paradise on earth' without some feeling for the ironies implicit in such a use. There are the half-cynical, half-melancholy lyrics of casual amours in a garden setting: their gross messages are conveyed, suggestively, through that very symbolism of grafting which was so powerful in a religious context:

'I have a newe gardyn,
   and newe is be-gunne;
swych an-other gardyn
   know I not under sunne.

In the myddis of my gardyn
   is a peryr set,   *pear-tree*
and it wele non per bern
   but a per Ienet.

The fayrest mayde of this toun
   preyid me
for to gryffyn her a gryf   *to graft upon her a shoot*
   of myn pery tree.

quan I hadde hem gryffid
   alle at her wille,
the wyn and the ale
   che dede in fille.

That day twelfus month,
   that mayde I mette:
che seyd it was a per robert
   but non per Ionet!'[25]

And there are the tales such as that of Simona and Pasquino, or of Andreuola and Gabriotto, from Boccaccio's *Decameron*, in which the idyllic, secret place, chosen by the lovers for their meeting, 'where they could be together more freely and with less suspicion . . .',[26] is also the place of death. Beneath sweet-smelling sage may lie poison, and ugliness—the venom of a toad; the roses gathered for love may only too quickly be strewn for sorrow. Indeed, the whole of the *Decameron* makes interesting comment upon the nature and significance of gardens. The retreat of the courtly company from the city of plague to the country estates of the rich is in itself a retreat from

death and the cruellest forms of mutability. The walled garden is set against
'the empty walls of our city',[27] and significantly, that garden to which the
courtiers journey on the third of their adventure is spoken of as a 'paradise':

'The sight of this garden, of its beautiful plan, of the plants and the fountain and
the little streams flowing from it, so much pleased the ladies and the three young
men that they said, if Paradise could be formed on earth, it could be given no
other form than that of this garden, nor could any further beauty be added to it.'[28]

The detailed description of this garden is as important to the history of
landscape gardening as it is to the history of ideas: the ingenuity of the
irrigation system, the almost mathematical precision of the planned alley-
ways, the careful concentration of colour and scent all point towards that
typical medieval concern to exploit and discipline natural beauty for the
greater pleasure and utility of man. It is striking that the fruit trees, citron
and orange, bear 'both ripe fruit and young fruit and flowers so that they
pleased the sense of smell as well as charmed the eyes with shade'.[29] This
yielding of extreme delight was unusual in the habitual cycles of natural
growth: man's rational dominance over nature is being used to sharpen
sensuous enjoyment. Paradisal echoes are strong in this garden—the central
fountain which does, indeed, give life to everything, the fruit trees, the shade
in the heat of the day, and the animals which roam the groves and lawns,
'about a hundred kinds, running gaily about as if they were tame'. It is no
surprise that Boccaccio pictures the company, in the garden, as a species of
the elect:

'They went along, garlanded with oak, carrying handfuls of flowers and scented
plants; and any person who met them would have said: "These people will not be
conquered by death, or at worst will die happy".'[30]

The ambiguities of this comment are many. The suspension of the courtiers
in a golden afternoon of summer scents and sounds is convincing: they do,
in fact, 'dwell in the green garden of Paradise'.[31] But their evasion of death
is temporary, as the last part of the statement admits. Even the Eden-like
tameness of the animals in the wood is by favour of death—'so free from
pursuit had they been owing to the plague'.

In the *Decameron*, Boccaccio plays delicately with themes of life and death,
garden and city, flower and toad. He hints at the impossibility of excluding
one kind of reality by withdrawing into another. If his courtiers escape the
plague, it is not at all certain that they will be safe from other mortal claims.

The world of their stories includes death in the garden, although their own world, as yet, does not.

To compare Boccaccio's handling of these themes with that of a painter contemporary with him—Traini, whose frescoes in the Camposanto, at Pisa, also tell of human reaction to the terror of plague[32]—is to move from the complex allegiances of a secular sensibility to the simpler and sterner values of a religious mind (Plate 28). Here, too, we have the dead bodies, from whom even the horses shrink, the ladies in their gardens, the courtiers at their unheeding tasks. But the arrangement of the frescoes makes it clear that the garden and grove are doomed; symbolic death figures advance from the sky upon them; the cavalcade is confronted by decay; only the hermit, praying among the bare rocks, has any hope of survival. And the painter forcefully contrasts the landscape of the hermit with that of the ladies: the garden with all its delights is reserved for death.

This primarily homiletic and negative approach to the problem did not, however, produce the most interesting poems and paintings of the Middle Ages, which deal, on the whole, with parallels between religious and secular concepts of a garden paradise. The parallels could be boldly or subtly drawn, and the audacity sometimes visual rather than conceptual— as in the northern French illustrations for Boccaccio's story of Andreuola and Gabriotto. Here the fifteenth-century French artists picture the death of Gabriotto in his lady's arms as a *Pietà* scene, backed by a trellis of roses; the dead body is carried from the garden in a stiff Entombment pose.[33] But the central idea—the imitation of the original Paradise garden, walled except to the elect, of the proximity of that elect to heavenly bliss, of the concentration of all beauty in one favoured place—was as attractive as it was daring. And since, in many cases, the authors of the poems in question were clerks, writing either for the sequestered pleasure of their own educated circle, or for the sophisticated pleasure of courtly patrons, it is not surprising that their tone is extremely variable, even perplexing to the modern reader.

This is eminently true of the most famous and influential of all garden poems of the Middle Ages—the thirteenth-century *Roman de la Rose*. In this particular work, all the descriptive conventions of the twelfth century, from whatever sources, medieval or directly classical, are gathered up, and re-expressed in an allegory of man and the enclosed garden which appears at first to have only a secular frame of reference. The original author, Guillaume de Lorris, about whom little is known except that he was extremely well-read, and familiar with both courtly literature and courtly life, produced, for his real or imagined lady, an account of the initiation and discipline of the devotee of love which is based upon the idea of a re-entry into a paradise garden—of love. This garden, it is true, approached in a dream, is not walled against a desert or a plague-ridden countryside; the dreamer comes to it through an earthly spring:

> 'Ou tens amoureus, plein de joie,
> Ou tens ou toute rien s'esgaie.'[34]
> ('In tyme of love and jolite,
> That al thyng gynneth waxen gaye.')

and through a dream landscape of vague paradisal lineage:

> 'Si vit tot covert e pavé
> Le fonz de l'eve de gravele.
> La praerie grant e bele
> Trés au pié de l'eve batoit.
> Clere e serie e bele estoit
> La matinee e atempree.'
>
> (120–5)
>
> ('Tho saugh I well
> The botme paved everydell
> With gravel, ful of stones shene.
> The medewe, softe, swote and grene,
> Beet right on the watir syde.
> Ful cler was then the morowtyde,
> And ful attempre . . .')
>
> (125–31)

But the garden wall, with its painted carved figures embodying concepts of exclusion, is already, subtly and skilfully, suggesting how this *hortus conclusus* is both a brilliant and a desperate replacement of one kind of Eden by another. The rejected figures of Poverty and Sorrow, of Envy, Covetousness and Hatred refer simply enough to the social and moral features of 'fin' amors', or 'amour courtois', which had, indeed, by the early thirteenth century, established its own code of ethics and its philosophy of paradise and perdition, of outcasts and elect, not so much by denials of Christian beliefs as by equivocations and substitutions of those beliefs. It is entirely fitting, therefore, that this garden of secular love should, like the original and re-made Earthly Paradise, refuse to countenance sins against charity such as Envy, Hatred and Covetousness. The perfect lover, like the perfect Christian lover, should be magnanimous, unselfish. It is also fitting, if we think of the pre-lapsarian state of Adam and Eve, of the state of the Christian elect, as well as of the happy and successful earthly lover, that sorrow should have no place in paradise. But the very confidence of the language is sometimes disturbing. That other Paradise, from which man was exiled to labour and to sadness, in an uncertain landscape, sometimes comes to mind, as the poet writes arrogantly of poor and sad men:

> 'Car povre chose, ou qu'ele soit,
> Est toz jorz honteuse e despite.
> L'eure puisse estre la maudite
> Que povres on fu conceüz!
> Qu'il ne sera ja bien peüz,
> Ne bien vestuz, ne bien chauciez;
> N'il n'est amez . . .'
>
> (456–62)
>
> ('For pover thing, whereso it be,
> Is shamefast and dispised ay.
> Accursed may wel be that day
> That povere man conceyved is:
> For, God wot, al to selde, iwys,
> Is ony povere man wel yfed,
> Or wel araied or wel cled,
> Or wel biloved . . .')
>
> (466–73)

It is also very much present as the poet describes the excluded figure of Old Age. True, Old Age has nothing to do with the passion and beauty of *amour courtois*, but Guillaume de Lorris writes rather too insistently about the power of Time for his speculations to remain limited to that small world:

> 'Li Tens qui envieilli noz peres,
> Qui vieillist rois e empereres
> E qui toz nos envieillira,
> Ou Morz nos desavancira.'
>
> (383–6)
>
> ('The tyme, that eldith our auncessours,
> And eldith kynges and emperours,
> And that us alle shal overcomen,
> Er that deth us shal have nomen.')
>
> (391–4)

Only one garden could, and in the Christian dispensation can, bar Time from its groves. The impossibility of dealing satisfactorily with a garden paradise of purely secular nature is finally indicated when the poet turns to the figure of the hypocrite, 'Papelardie', or, in the Chaucerian translation, 'Pope-Holy'. Again, it is proper for the inhabitants of a garden of love, not in any case regulated by orthodox Christian principles, to forbid entry to the false religious, whose strictures may be both destructive and despicable. But the paradise referred to by Guillaume de Lorris is, ambiguously, the Heavenly Paradise, as well as this quite different medieval paradise of love:

> 'A li e as siens iert la porte
> Devee de parevis;
> Car iceste gent font lor vis
> Amaigrir, ce dit l'Evangile,
> Por avoir los par mi la vile,
> E por un poi de gloire vaine,
> Qui lor toudra Deu e son reine.'
>
> (434–40)
>
> ('From hir the gate ay werned be
> Of paradys, that blisful place;
> For sich folk maketh lene her face,
> As Crist seith in his evangile,
> To gete hem prys in toun a while,
> And for a litel glorie veine,
> They lesen God, and eke his reigne.')
>
> (442–8)

The doubts that may have been raised in the reader as he stands, with poet and dreamer, surveying the walls, are, however, assuaged when once the gate of the garden is opened, by Idleness, and he steps inside this privileged, protected timeless world of refined sensuous pleasure. It would be ungrateful, perhaps, to make too much of the faint irony in the dreamer's praise of this 'terrestrial paradise':

> 'Il ne fait en nul parevis
> Si bon estre come il faisoit
> Ou vergier qui tant me plaisoit.'
>
> (640–2)
>
> ('Ther is no place in paradys
> So good inne for to dwelle or be
> As in that gardyn, thoughte me.')
>
> (652–4)

The visual and aural adornments of the garden, the pageant of noble participants in the 'dance of love' are presented with such excited admiration that only the self-sufficiency of life here, in this place, registers. Even the casual use of 'paradise' in the context of sexual passion is not more than momentarily surprising:

86

'Qu'il n'est nus graindres parevis
D'avoir amie a son devis.'
(1299–1300)
('For ther nys so good paradys
As to have a love at his devys.')
(1325–6)

And so dense, and yet so delicate is the description of the landscape that it is no wonder if the dreamer as well as reader is prepared to accept not only the existence but also the conditions of such a place. It is a landscape designed for man's delectation: its coverage is both complete and specific, as every succeeding 'garden poet' of the Middle Ages found. No pleasure of the senses is neglected: taste, touch, scent, hearing, sight are indulged[35]—deliberately, but with a formal grace that excludes grossness. The disciplining, as well as the concentration, of natural forms of beauty is a significant element in the garden. Nothing is rank or offensive: it is the very antithesis of Hamlet's 'unweeded garden, that grows to seed'. Sunlight is filtered through the trees:

'Mais li rain furent lonc e haut,
E, por le leu garder de chaut,
Furent si espès . . .'
(1369–71)
('But they were hye and great also,
And for to kepe out wel the sonne,
The croppes were so thicke yronne . . .')
(1394–6)

Fountains are clear, 'senz barbelotes e senz raines', 'without frogs and newts'; wild meadow has given place to lawn:

'Poignoit l'erbe bassette e drue:
Aussi i peüst l'en sa drue
Couchier come sor une coite.'
(1393–5)
('Sprang up the grass, as thicke yset
And softe as any veluët,
On which men myght his lemman leye,
As on a fetherbed, to pleye.')
(1419–22)

Above all, planned perfection: the garden is luxuriant with flowers and fruits, but they are selected for their efficacy as well as for their beauty.

Careful choices have been made, so that plants may satisfy as many sense requirements as possible. The regular spacing of the trees,

> 'Li uns fu loing de l'autre assis
> Plus de cinc toises ou de sis'
> >   (1367–8)
>
> ('Oon from another, in assyse,
> Fyve fadome or sixe.')
> >   (1392–3)

like the precise shaping of the garden's limits, 'toz de droite carreüre', 'right evene and square in compassing', points to the controlling principle here: the intensification of pleasure by design. The fact that the 'perfect square' may stir other kinds of paradisal memories—the 'four-square city, of the Revelations of St John—is probably just within the poet's calculation, but the reference, if indeed it can be so described, is brief. More deliberate, and more important for the immediate purpose of Guillaume de Lorris, is the naming, among other spice trees, of the 'graine de paradis novele', 'fresh grain of paradise'—a fitting emblem for a paradise of the senses, figuring as it did in many of the most elaborate culinary preparations of the Middle Ages.

As the poem, and the progress of the dreamer continues, it is with extraordinary finesse that the poet establishes both the delight and the peril of this paradise garden. Here man is hunted by his god—the god of love—like a beast; here the central fountain—the well of love—is both adored and feared; here the roses open and fall, although the grass is green, everlastingly. The magic crystals and silver gravel of the fountain promise the discovery of paradise, but it is, and is named, the death fountain of Narcissus. It is angled both to dazzle and to blind the dreamer:

> 'Cil miroers m'a deceü.
> Se j'eüsse avant coneü
> Queus sa force iert e sa vertuz,
> Ne m'i fusse ja embatuz.'
> >   (1609–12)
>
> ('That mirrour hath me now entriked.
> But hadde I first knowen in my wit
> The vertu and the strengthe of it,
> I nolde not have mused there.')
> >   (1642–5)

The dreamer is aware of fragility, even in what appears to be a paradisal and protected place:

> 'Les roses overtes e lees
> Sont en un jor toutes alees,
> Mais li bouton durent tuit frois
> A tot le moins deus jorz ou trois.'
>
> (1645–8)
>
> ('For brode roses and open also
> Ben passed in a day or two;
> But knoppes wille al freshe be   *buds*
> Two dayes, atte leest, or thre.')
>
> (1681–4)

The pensive, faintly melancholy note of 'atte leest' reminds us of Boccaccio's similar admission, that his garlanded courtiers 'at worst will die happy'.[36] The strands of pleasure and pain, security and strife, are constantly twisted; the god of this garden demands and receives complete dedication. But the folly of every curious and delighted step made by the dreamer in the garden is vigorously announced to him in the words of a visitor from another paradise, or at least one whose appearance convinces the dreamer of this:

> 'A son semblant e a son vis
> Pert qu'el fu faite en parevis.'
>
> (2985–6)

Reason's comments put the garden in an unsentimental perspective:

> 'Mar t'alas onques ombreier
> Ou vergier don Oiseuse porte
> La clef don el t'ovri la porte.'
>
> (3002–4)
>
> ('In yvell tyme thou wentist to see
> The gardyn, wherof Ydilnesse
> Bar the keye, and was maistresse.')
>
> (3224–6)

And, indeed, although her advice is firmly rejected by the devoted disciple of love, the instability of life in the garden is henceforward one of the poem's most pressing themes—the dreamer veers between happiness and misery. His successes in approaching and touching his Rose are followed by deprivations so sharp that

89

'Je sui en enfer cheoiz'
(3793)

or even more specifically in the Chaucerian translation:

'For I am fallen into helle
From paradys.'
(4136–7)

But if such dramatic reversals of fortune could still be seen and presented by Guillaume de Lorris as natural, even desirable elements in a philosophy of love dedicated to exquisite paradox, they were not viewed in this way by the continuator of the poem, the clerk Jean de Meun. If Reason had allowed Guillaume to hint that all was not well with the rose garden, Jean went much further in his analysis and exposure of this 'paradis li doulereus'. The spring landscape is spoilt by frost,

'Printens pleins de freit ivernage'
(4330)
('Pryme temps full of frostes whit.')
(4747)

The dancers and the birdsong fade, as dream and dreamer are called to reality:

'Les choses ici contenues,
Ce sont trufles e fanfelues.
Ci n'a chose qui seit estable,
Quanqu'il vit est corrompable.
Il vit queroles qui faillirent,
E faudront tuit cil qui les firent.'
(20351–6)
('Things here within the garden are deceits and fantasies; nothing is lasting. All he saw is subject to decay: dances and dancers alike will cease.')[37]

But not only does the 'insubstantial pageant' of the rose garden fade. It is replaced by another vision, of a perdurable enclosure—the 'parc' of the Good Shepherd, 'li fiz de la vierge berbiz'.[38] The distinctions between the two are very clear; De Meun refers to 'parc' and 'jardin' in entirely different terms, the one exclusively pastoral, with detail of classical and biblical significance—grass, hill, olive tree and triple fountain—the other formally catalogued in cultivated garden style:

'Erbes, arbres, bestes, oiseaus,
E ruisselez e fonteneles
Bruire e fremir par les graveles.'

(20342–4)

Both are enclosed, both exclude certain things, but de Meun's pastoral landscape reveals its essentially celestial nature by its exclusion not simply of ugliness, meanness and old age but of all material elements—the earth, with its ancient treasures, the sea and all its creatures, the air, the encircling fire, and the constellations. The 'parc' represents that stability which neither the dreamer nor, indeed, the poet could claim to find in the rose garden. It is the stability of divine purpose, from which all moving and corruptible parts of nature descend:

'For nature hath nat taken his bigynnynge
Of no partie or cantel of a thyng,
But of a thyng that parfit is and stable,
Descendynge so til it be corrumpable.'[39]

For the walled enclosure of the Good Shepherd, de Meun makes use of some natural landscape features. They are, however, of primarily conceptual importance: the olive tree, for instance, set beside the fountain, reminds us first of the biblical image of the olive as the righteous man in the house of God (Ps. 52:8), and when de Meun elaborates upon its miraculous growth, its reaching up into the sky, fed by the waters of the spring,

'Si devient si haute e si large
Qu'onques li pins qu'il vous conta
Si haut de terre ne monta.'

(20504–6)

('It becomes so tall and so broad that not even the pine the lover has described soars up so high from earth.')

we are reminded of the great cosmological trees of Christian tradition, which stretch from hell to heaven, and link man with God.[40] This association becomes a certainty in the words of the inscription hanging from the tree— we are looking at the fruit of salvation, fed by the fount of living waters:

'Ci cuert la fontaine de vie
Par desouz l'olive foillie
Qui porte le fruit de salu.'

(20521–3)

91

Behind such poetry lies the text of the psalms, and extensive medieval commentary upon it: 'Erit tanquam lignum quod plantatum est secus decursus aquarum, quod fructum suum dabit in tempore suo' (Ps. 1:3). The splendour of this heavenly paradise is most powerfully focused in the description of its constant noon and springtime:

> 'Car li solanz resplendissanz,
> Qui toujours leur est parissanz,
> Fait le jour en un point estable,
> Tel qu'onc en printens pardurable
> Si bel ne vit ne si pur nus.'
>
> (20027–31)

('For the glowing sun, always in sight, makes day stand still; none ever saw a lovelier, purer, everlasting spring.')

The issues presented by the two kinds of paradise are simply summed up: the rose garden intoxicates and is fatal, while the park revives and sustains life:

> 'Cele les vis de mort enivre,
> Mais cete fait les morz revivre.'
>
> (20625–6)

But it must be said that this lesson is placed into context in a way which is far from simple. The contrast between the 'park' and the garden is serious enough; what is more difficult to understand and define is its application and sequel. For, as it turns out, entry to the 'champ deliteus' where the Lamb promises everlasting life seems to depend primarily upon a willingness to serve Nature in rather limited ways—ensuring 'everlasting life' by drawing upon procreative energies.

> 'Penser de Nature enourer,
> Servez la par bien labourer.'
>
> (20637–8)

has here a very special and very crude sense, which the rest of the poem's narrative illustrates. The citadel of love is stormed, the lover plucks and possesses the rose with such ardour:

> Si que tout le boutonet tendre
> En fis eslargir e estendre.
>
> (21729–30)

('that the whole of this delicate bud became enlarged and distended')

A good deal can be—and has been—made of the fact that de Meun put his comparison of the parkland and garden into the mouth not of Reason but of Genius, a figure already well-established to represent the generative principle, and serving Nature, under God.[41] The rose garden of Guillaume de Lorris, dedicated, as was the whole doctrine of *amour courtois*, to the engendering of fine sensibilities rather than to the engendering of kind, could clearly be attacked by Christian apologists, and upon this very point— 'more for delit than kynde to multiplye'. But Genius is allowed by de Meun, and perhaps deliberately, to exceed his brief, not simply in his brash recommendation of what goes far beyond licensed procreativity, and amounts to sexual promiscuity, but also in his promise of the Good Shepherd's paradise to enthusiastic labourers in the most sensual of earthly vineyards. Does he intend to deride both the fastidious erotic philosophy of the rose garden and the traditional teaching of the Church on marriage? Both are turned to grotesque absurdity, as the rush to qualify for the park of the Good Shepherd, by storming the human citadels of Shame and Fear, begins:

> 'Don crient en l'ost plus de vint:
> "Or a l'assaut senz plus atendre!
> Qui bien set la sentence entendre,
> Mout sont nostre anemi grevé."
> Lors se sont tuit en piez levé,
> Prest de continuer la guerre,
> Pour tout prendre e metre par terre.'
>
> (20704–10)

('Then more than a score of the army shouted "To battle, without delay! If we read our brief aright, our enemies are as good as dead." Jumping to their feet, they were ready to get on with the battle, to take all, or raze to the ground.')

The amusing and fundamentally coarse description of the taking of the rose returns to the original garden for its setting. It is a garden barely recognizable—we see the tower first erected by Jealousy to protect the rose, but the flowers and arbours play no part, the streams are silent. Only the destructive words of Venus, threatening to burn down the enclosure, remind us that this was a place of rose trees and roses, lawns and meadows. The erasing of the landscape is achieved as ruthlessly as the taking of the rose, both garden and girl being violated by the 'fire' of Venus—'par tout le monde est alumée'.

No doubt the poem presented fewer medieval than modern readers with interpretative difficulties. Few poets, for instance, were deterred from borrowing the delicious garden detail for their own paradisal inventions by thought upon the fate of that garden. Many of the illustrators of the poem preferred to ignore the change of tone and climate brought about by de Meun, and pictured the winning of the rose as the logical outcome of that drama which began, so buoyantly, 'in tyme of love and jolitee'. The richly executed series of miniatures from MS Harley 4425, a late fifteenth-century Flemish production (Plates 30a and 30b), ends, as if nothing harsh had intervened, in that private world of trellised roses and turved benches which had first been opened to the dreamer by Oiseuse and Bel Acueil. In fact, although some artists made attempts to render, in visual terms, the curious ironies and antinomies of the text, very few were willing to disturb the mood of that last scene. The occasional use of two human beings instead of lover and 'rosier' is the most they will do to indicate what de Meun makes brutally clear about the final act in the garden.[42]

Taken as a consistent whole, the *Roman* should have spelt death to gardens of any but celestial nature. There is little to suggest, however, that it was 'taken as a whole' in quite that way. Not only in its descriptions of different kinds of garden but also in the placing of those descriptions it offered variety, certainty, ambiguity. Encyclopaedists made a virtue of necessity by calling it a 'vrai mappemonde de toutes choses humaines et devines';[43] theologians debated it; poets used it enthusiastically, finding in it rich descriptive and satiric material, and suggestively juxtaposed, even contraposed attitudes to subjects about which the imagination and the sensibility were reluctantly taught by reason. The poem was sufficiently wide and diffuse to allow for many kinds of reading. Chaucer's contemporary, Laurent de Premierfait, convinced himself that the 'livre de la Rose est souffisamment descript le Paradis des bons et l'enfer des mauvais'.[44]

What Geoffrey Chaucer, on the other hand, learnt from the *Roman* about gardens of paradise, heaven and hell, can partly be defined in terms of content, but more importantly in terms of complex, sometimes ironic presentation. This is particularly true of his *Parlement of Foules*: here the poet-dreamer's experience of a garden is phrased in a series of impressions, each qualifying or even contrasting with the other. Not only are the physical features of this walled park and garden taken freely from both rose garden and heavenly 'parc' of the *Roman* (often at one remove, via Boccaccio's *Teseida*), but the attitudes of the dreamer to what he encounters within the walls are varied and enigmatic. Enigma is present from the very beginning of the description, even in the slight detail of the colour of the walls—does 'wallid with grene ston' have no more than decorative or lapidary reference or is it meant to remind the reader (and the dreamer) of that legendary moment when Alexander first saw the walls of the Earthly Paradise, covered with green moss, 'The wallis war rouch, and all onreched with grene.'[45] Whatever the truth of this, the inscriptions over the gateway effectively remove certainty of significance from the dreamer's grasp. This is a garden of contraries: a 'paradisus voluptatis' which promises nothing but uncertainty, a 'welle of grace' and everlasting May with bare fruitless trees and dried-up streams. No real choice is offered to reader or dreamer. They are invited, simply, to subject themselves to the human condition, that of 'errour':

'No wit hadde I, for errour, for to chese.'

(146)

In fact, the relationship of the inscription to the garden and its contents becomes increasingly difficult to define except as it stresses the dilemma of man in search of gardens of felicity. Appearing to have arrived at the entrance to a particular kind of garden—the private garden of *amour courtois*, with its violent contraries of landscape experience, 'pryme temps full of frostes whit'—the dreamer soon finds that he has been admitted to a place more varied and significant, though not always more easily understandable, than the inscription suggests. Clearly this is no simple garden of love with fading roses: it is a garden of perpetual beauty. Although many of its characteristics are of the world of the senses, the world of Guillaume de Lorris— flowers and streams, green grass and 'bestis smale of gentil kynde'—they are given a paradisal context. It is the heavenly 'parc' of Jean de Meun which draws from Chaucer his most rapturous poetry:

'The eyr of that place so attempre was
That nevere was grevaunce of hot ne cold;
There wex ek every holsum spice and gras;
No man may waxe there sek ne old,
Yit was there ioye more a thousand fold
Than man can telle, ne nevere wolde it nyghte,
But ay cler day to ony manys syghte.'

(204–10)

This description has religious echoes, coming as it does after the deliberate reference to 'God, that makere is of all and lord' (199). The dreamer has walked into an earthly paradise, a garden of creation perfected and favoured by God. It is easy to accept this as an image of the divine stability from which all natural and renewable things descend, and to accept the goddess Nature as the proper 'vicayire of the almyghty lord' (379). The marriages over which she presides are, indeed, made in heaven.

95

But set into this peaceful enclosure is an area of unrest. Here, in the temple of Venus, and in the tableaux surrounding it, the theme is mutability, in love, in beauty, in desire. We might, for this section, be in the garden of de Lorris, for there is a similar sense of excitement tempered by fear, as the dreamer watches the rituals of passionate love acted out by allegorical and mythological figures, and reads, in art, the significance of all this. The tree, standing over the well of Cupid, is bound to be reminiscent of the oak tree over the well of Narcissus, in that earlier garden. And if this is the 'welle of grace' promised by the inscription, it is also the spring of pain, even perhaps of death: the arrows of desire, hardened in its water, serve

'Some for to sle, and some to wounde and kerve.'

(217)

It would not be right, however, to simplify the whole scene into a straightforward allegory of moral corruption. The dreamer's senses are captured by the power and elegance of what he sees, and while he recognizes pitiable, sometimes sinister implications, he is much more in the mood of Guillaume's dreamer, submitting to the exquisite terrors of the hunt of love, than in the mood of satirist or reformer. In the uncommented juxtaposition of:

'I saw Beute withoutyn any atyr
And Youthe ful of game and jolyte' (225-6)

some feeling for the limited life of both is conveyed, but it approaches the almost aesthetic sentiment of:

'She dwells with Beauty—Beauty that must die . . .'

There is nothing particularly advanced or unmedieval about such an attitude in Chaucer, or in his dreamer. The acceptance of 'the dredful joy, alwey that slit so yerne' was as much at the heart of *amour courtois* as the acceptance of 'Joy, whose hand is ever at his lips / Bidding adieu' was at the heart of early nineteenth-century romanticism.[46] Poets of both centuries perceived the inevitable melancholy of the temples of delight. Chaucer's dreamer, inside the temple of Venus, sees the sorrow of jealousy, the pain of supplicating love—'two yonge folk there cryede' (278). He sees the 'cloudy trophies', the painted records of those, Tristram, Iseut, Dido, Troilus, who did indeed taste the 'sadness of her might',

'And al here love, and in what plyt they dyde.'

(294)

VI *December*, a leaf from a Book of Hours. British Museum, London, Addit.
MS 18855, f. 108v. Early sixteenth century.

He is, at the same time, minutely sensitive to the special qualities of this mortal and dangerous beauty, which lies before him, personified in the goddess Venus, and subject to diurnal change:

> 'And on a bed of gold she lay to reste,
> Tyl that the hote sunne gan to weste.
> Hyre gilte heris with a goldene threde
> Ibounden were, untressed as sche lay,
> And nakyd from the brest up to the hede
> Men myghte hyre sen . . .'
>
> (265–70)

In fact, the guise of such beauty is determined by those very temporal laws and conditions which were said to have no power over the rest of the garden. The midday heat, the awaited dusk, the man-made temple with its protective darkness are all necessary to this incomparable vision of glimmering and languid nakedness. The contrast between Venus in her temple, and Nature in hers—the one secret, the other open, the one an artefact, the other natural—has, of course, an obvious moral significance. But the poem as a whole is rather more interested in lengthening and contracting its perspectives upon love and loveliness of various kinds than in landscaping the perilous rose garden out of paradise. And who can say that its freedom of movement is not, artistically, most satisfying? The still and sultry afternoon pleasures of the temple of Venus, the fresh, crystal-clear exhilarations of the park of Nature, 'so sote and grene', are offered to us with full imaginative confidence. It is probably unfair either to find fault with the adjustment of attitudes to content, or to find false reconciliations. As Chaucer presents his paradisal garden, it is full of promises and revelations, not all of which seem to be properly fulfilled or understood in terms of theological or philosophical truth. The garden symbolism is rich, but handled with some arbitrariness. At the very end, we are not quite clear why the garden of Nature, 'vicaire' of God, should have been introduced in the limited, though delicious terminology of *amour courtois*, nor why, with such an announcement, we should not have found Venus, rather than Nature, in sole command. The garden wall encloses but does not resolve all of its varieties and contraries. Like the dreamer, we note, but without perfect comprehension, that one part of the garden has a different climate and time scheme from the rest. The subjects of Venus, who live 'in an old chaos of the sun / Or old dependancy of day and night',[47] are distinguished from the subjects of Nature, whose destinies are planned in a context of paradisal stability:

> 'ay cler day, to any manes syghte.' (210)

97

Even then, the distinction is blurred, whether by design or accident: as the moment of departure from the garden draws near, the poet-dreamer sees the setting sun:

> 'dounward drow the sonne wonder faste.'
>
> (490)

Urgent, time-dominated creatures temporarily disturb the timeless noon of the garden.

We are bound to suspect that here, as in the *Roman de la Rose*, gardens of various origin and significance are being pressed into new and unfamiliar services; their inhabitants are sometimes not those we might have expected. We recognize the landscape, but are surprised at the figures—the disciples of Genius in the *parc* of the Good Shepherd, the talkative representatives of domestic bliss and the aspirants to *amour courtois* in the garden of eternal life. And it may be, indeed, that outside strictly religious and narrowly secular fields the old divisions were becoming blurred. Certainly it seems in works such as the *Roman* (as completed by de Meun) and the *Parlement* that the separate identities of gardens and garden dwellers are vaguely rather than distinctly realized, with de Meun's goddess of love threatening the exclusive rose garden with violent entry by all:

> 'Tuit iront a procession,
> Senz faire i point excepcion,
> Par les rosiers e par les roses,
> Quant j'avrai les lices descloses.'
>
> (20743–6)

('All, without any exception, shall march in among the rose-bushes and roses, when I have broken down the barriers.')

and Chaucer's goddess admitted uneasily to a small but beautiful portion of a garden whose nature is part temporal, part eternal.

It may be very important that Chaucer never again turned to an enclosed garden setting as a defining structure for a whole poem. Perhaps he recognized that these formal designs, invaluable for isolating areas of experience, for concentrating and deepening vision, whether secular or religious, were incapable of conveying the diversity of his interests and the flexibility of his attitudes. The ambiguities and silences which we notice in the *Parlement* probably represent a very real dilemma in the poet, who was attracted as an artist to the rich texture of feeling and decor in the European literature of *amour courtois*, but was aware, as artist and thinker, of the narrowness of its range and vision of life. Gardens figure in several of Chaucer's later poems, but they are not particularly vital to the conduct of the narrative. The 'litel herber' of the *Legend of Good Women* and the 'yerd' of book II of *Troilus and Criseyde* are of this kind. Both have a rather technical interest for their precise references to fashionable garden design—the arbour, the enclosure within an enclosed garden, which in the *Legend* is already the 'garden room' favoured by so many fifteenth-century poets and painters, and the sanded alley walks, the turfed benches, which would remain parts of formal garden repertoire for five centuries. But where gardens are used significantly, it is for Chaucer's special and limited purposes.

In the *Franklin's Tale*, for instance, the lady Dorigen is taken to a garden by sympathetic friends in order to provide her with consolation and distraction in the absence of her husband. The garden looks innocent enough in its careful adjustment of nature and artifice, 'so ful it was of beautee with plesaunce' (917). It is at the fine point of man-ordered loveliness, calling up comparison, in its sensuous and restorative qualities, with the earthly paradise alone:

> 'Nevere was ther gardyn of swich prys,
> But if it were the verray paradys.'
>
> (911–12)

But this May garden, which should have helped to restore Dorigen to happiness, is, in fact, very far from paradisal in its implications, though it may be Eden-like. It is here that she is importuned by the love-sick squire, Aurelius, and led into making a bargain which is far more sinister than she thinks:

> 'I seye, whan ye han maad the coost so clene
> Of rokkes that ther nys no stoon ysene,
> Thanne wol I love yow best of any man.'
>
> (995–7)

In this garden, her trial and temptation take place, and it is interesting that she has retreated here, away from the wild sea shore, which so much reminds her of the perils her husband may be undergoing. The unwisdom of her passionate questioning of God, as she gazes out from the cliffs at the 'grisly rokkes blake':

> 'Why han ye wroght this werk unresonable?'
>
> (872)

is logically and subtly demonstrated, since she finds more unreason and danger in the 'fair creacion' of the garden than in the 'foul confusion' untutored nature. And it is to that same garden that she is commanded by her husband, in order that she may pay the price for her foolishness. As she takes her way

> 'Unto the gardyn, as myn housbonde bad,
> My trouthe for to holde, allas! allas!'
>
> (1512–13)

there is no mention of garden pleasures. May has passed; it is now 'the colde frosty seson of December', with its pale wintry sunlight marking out the anatomy of truth.

But if Chaucer intended, in the *Franklin's Tale*, to hint that a false sense of security could be induced by gardens resembling paradise, he made quite sure of that point in the *Merchant's Tale*. Here, with an almost destructive delight, he presents us with a garden whose beauty would tax the descriptive powers of Guillaume de Lorris:

> 'That he that wroot the Romance of the Rose
> Ne koude of it the beautee wel devyse'
>
> (2032–3)

but which is designed as a place for sensual sport. It could be said that so also is the garden of Guillaume de Lorris: the grass is soft as velvet

> 'On which men might his lemman leye
> As on a fetherbed, to pleye.'
>
> (1421–2)

The handling of this fact by the French poet is, however, extremely delicate. There is a joyful, celebrative, faintly wistful air about the descriptions of love-making, both in the French original and in the Chaucerian translation:

> 'The daunces thanne eended were,
> For many of them that daunced there
> Were with her loves went awey
> Undir the trees to have her pley.
> A! lord, they lyved lustyly!'
>
> (1315–19)

Whatever we are to learn later of the garden and its inhabitants, we are asked to share, temporarily at least, in the poet-dreamer's admiration of these courtly and passionate rituals. By comparison, Chaucer is harsh, almost crude, in his phrasing, as he insists that we understand what the walled garden is for:

> 'And thynges whiche that were nat doon abedde,
> He in the gardyn parfourned hem and spedde.'
>
> (2051–2)

And since the old man January, owner of the garden, has created it as a hiding place for his legitimized (or married) lust, it is only appropriate that it should become the setting for his wife's adventure in a pear tree. The garden encloses beauty and the beast, as we are very forcibly reminded when January invites his young wife, May, to join with him for 'pleye' in the garden, and uses the language of the *Song of Songs*:

> 'Com forth, now, with thyne eyen columbyn!
> How fairer been thy brestes than is wyn!
> The gardyn is enclosed al aboute;
> Com forth, my white spouse! out of doute
> Thou hast me wounded in myn herte, o wyf!
> No spot of thee ne knew I al my lyf.
> Com forth, and lat us taken our disport.'
>
> (2141–7)

The ironies are multiple. The old man's febrile desires are only barely masked by courtly and biblical expressions; particularly telling is his transference of the 'garden enclosed' image from the beloved herself, 'hortus conclusus soror mea sponsa', to that 'gardyn, walled al with stoon' (2029), made not so much in honour as in contempt of real love—'whan he wolde paye his wyf hir dette / In somer seson'.

In these two poems, Chaucer found an effective formula for the garden. It is quite in keeping with this that his great collection of people and stories, the *Canterbury Tales*, should have been set, not, as Boccaccio's, in a garden or series of gardens, but along a busy medieval highway. By this time he has come to terms with the special quality of his own creative energies, and with the special potential of the garden motif.

The limitations, rather than the potential, of this motif were increasingly apparent, over the medieval period, in secular verse. Few later secular poets use garden imagery as dramatically as Chaucer in the *Franklin's Tale* and the

Merchant's Tale. The clear exception to this is the Scottish poet, William Dunbar, whose savage and brilliant exposé of sensual married life, in *The Twa Mariit Wemen and the Wedo*, is overheard from the thick hedge surrounding a 'gudlie grein garth'. The three 'gay ladeis' who tell such tales of misery, cruelty and lust are seated in 'ane grene arbeir / All grathit in to garlandis of fresche gudlie flouris'. The garden, in its shining and profuse beauty, all light and dew and birdsong, is mocked by the repulsiveness of its inhabitants. Apart from this, most gardens in secular poetry of the fifteenth century are purely decorative surroundings for complaints and debates,[48] comparable to the charming *trompe l'oeil* borders of late Flemish manuscripts, though less concerned than those marginalia with fidelity to the shape and texture of garden detail—flowers, fruit, butterflies and insects.

But this is not to imply that all religious artists, on the other hand, made an equally rich use of the garden. The finest of them make it yield rare and abundant fruit: others are satisfied with more modest returns. The anonymous author of *Pearl*, writing at the same time as Chaucer, and with a theme not unfamiliar to the man responsible for the *Book of the Duchess*—human loss and reconciliation—begins and ends his poem in a garden:

> 'Blomes blayke and blwe and rede   *yellow*
> Ther shynes ful schyr agayn the sunne.'   *bright*
>
> (27–8)

There is a strong suggestion of enclosure—no walled garden, but an 'erber grene' into which the poet has to enter:

> 'To that spot that I in speche expoun
> I entred in that erber grene.'
>
> (37–38)

He has retreated even more decisively into grief by such an entry, for the 'erber' encloses him, solacing his loneliness with all kinds of sensuous beauty:

> 'Yif hit was semly on to sene,
> A fayr reflayr yet fro hit flot'.   *fragrance*
>
> (45–6)

only to torment his imagination with reminders of physical decay:

> 'Such ryches to rot is runne.'
>
> (26)

That the *Pearl* poet must, and will, seek to extend rather than to contain his vision is indicated by small touches. The 'erber grene' does not exist in isolation. Beyond the garden there is a landscape, briefly but memorably referred to:

> 'In Augoste in a hygh sesoun,
> Quen corne is corven wyth crokes kene.'
>
> (39–40)

Garden and fields may owe as much to literary and pictorial conventions as to personal reminiscence, but whether these lines record some calendar picture for August or August in the north-western counties of England, the fact remains that this garden has a setting, and one felt to be significant. The poet's private mourning in his 'erber' is in one sense a retreat from the occupied landscape of crops and men. We are meant to contrast the intense, and even unnatural luxuriance of the garden—its Maytime peonies scenting the August air, its flowers and spice plants as thickly spread as in a tapestry—with the vigour and fruitfulness of the agricultural scene. The very sound of the alliterative language, sharp and incisive for dry stalk and keen blade, soft and dense for crowded flower bed reinforces this contrast:

> 'Gilofre, gyngure and gromyloun,
> And pyonys powdered ay bytwene.'
>
> (43–4)

And it is significant that the garden serves only to frame and define the poet's problem: his fierce rebellion against bereavement, and his stubborn despair. Such a place—part secret trysting ground, part garden of remembrance—can isolate, and concentrate emotions. But more is needed than description of the symptoms of loss. This garden, at once intoxicating and claustrophobic, can only help the poet to embroider the fabric of grief; it can suggest little in the way of solution. It already contains what is sought, the lost pearl, imprisoned and inaccessible. Its replacement, in dream vision, by a more varied and open countryside is, therefore, a vital step in the thematic progress of the poem. Not that the garden is totally rejected: in this as in other matters it is characteristic of the poet that he works by change, by transformation. The visionary landscape is different, in substance as in layout: there are cliffs, woods, vales and waters, and they are of a clear Paradisal nature, glittering with a light which prepares the dreaming poet for 'aventure ther mervayles meven', 'experience of wondrous things'. The transmutation of natural and passing beauty into a durable form which mirrors or is analogous to 'the artifice of eternity' is a necessary and powerful prelude to the transmutation of human sorrow into spiritual acceptance. Only by removing the ground of action from a world which celebrates 'whatever is begotten, born and dies', to one in which the revolution of seasons is stilled, and the accident of death precluded, can the poet win for his dreaming self a measure of calm. The contrast is dramatic, as he exchanges his little mundane 'paradise garden', with its flowers shining in sunlight, for a land which proclaims itself, in every detail, a heightened and perfected vision of what the senses are accustomed to register. Here the pearly gravel, the silver leaves have a lustre which shames the rays of the sun:

> 'The sunnebemes bot blo and blynde   *dark*
> In respecte of that adubbement.'
>
> (83–4)

The banks of the river are like thread of gold; the river bed is fiery with precious stones, emerald, sapphire and other rare jewels (118); the rocks are of crystal. Such signals of proximity to the Earthly Paradise[49] are not lost upon the dreamer. Across the river, he is certain, that 'mote', that 'walled city' lies:

> 'Forthy I thoght that Paradyse
> Was ther over gayn tho bonkes brade.'
>
> (137–8)

He has exchanged a garden for a vision of the Earthly Paradise as a city or castle in a landscape—a familiar medieval variation upon the walled garden of Genesis, particularly in the literature of the Alexander legends. In some versions, Alexander faces Paradise, after his journeying up the river Phison, as a 'city of marvellous height and expanse', with moss-grown walls rising steeply out of the water:

> 'The passage throw the quilk the flude come doun
> Was like a postrum of a wallit toun.'[50]

But the distinction between the first garden and 'Paradys erde' (248), 'the land of Paradise', is not harshly or narrowly made. It is important that the Pearl maiden, when she first speaks to the dreamer from across the water, refers to the Paradisal 'garden' in which she is standing:

> 'As in this gardyn gracios gaye,
> Hereinne to lenge for ever and play,
> Ther mys ne mornyng com never nere.'
>
> (260–2)

Less consistently than Dante,[51] the poet nevertheless suggests the spiritual resolution of ordinary garden imagery. The August garden may be left behind, but it has served to conduct the dreamer to his dream of immortality —in a primitive way, it indicates how life springs eternally out of death, 'uch gresse mot growe of graynes dede' (31)—and by the power of its hot scents it has worked a mysterious sleep upon him:

> 'I felle upon that floury flaght,   *lawn*
> Suche odour to my hernes schot;   *mind*
> I slode upon a slepyng-slaghte.'
>
> (57–9)

Then, too, phenomena in the dream countryside are sometimes analogical to those in the garden. In both there is a strong perfume—of flowers and herbs in the garden, of fruit trees in the dream world:

> 'So frech flavores of frytes were,
> As fode hit con me fayre refete.'   *refresh*
>
> (87–8)

Light suffuses the 'erber grene', emanates from the hill slopes, woods and waters of the new landscape. If the dreamer recognizes that in the one case it is of natural, in the other of divine origin, he is still reminded of starry winter nights on earth as he gazes into the miraculous depths of the jewelled river:

> 'In the founce ther stonden stones stepe,
> As glente thurgh glas that glowed and glyght,
> As stremande sternes, quen strothe-men slepe.'
>
> (113–15)

In fact, the relationship between garden and Earthly Paradise is a web of reference and change. The original idea of a garden of consolation is revealed as inadequate for the poem's purposes, but it is not destroyed, rather expanded and transformed. An essentially figural mode of thought—the revelation of the fullest possible meaning of a person, object or event in terms of another, equally 'real'[52]—is at work here. The meaning of earthly beauty is displayed to the dreamer not as he first understood it, a poignant tale of flowering and decay, but as an intimation of God's first and ultimate gift of beauty to man in Paradise. Consequently the crystallizing of the world of August into the dazzling world of the dream is no mere literary conceit in honour of a poet's heightened perception that:

> 'River and rill are endowed
> With robes whose embroideries hold
> Drops of silver and filigree gold.'[53]

Nor is it a cold allegory of the warring of body and soul. Rather, it allows that there is a correspondence between the 'movements of the soul and the sense organs of the body'.[54] So, while the corporeal senses are captured in the first garden, the second 'garden' captures the spiritual faculties, proceeding not by denial of delight, but by transmutation of the ground and the quality of delight. The joy that rises in the dreamer as he explores the 'floty vales', 'stream-watered valleys', of his dream is an exhilaration, not an exhaustion of the senses; it is a substantial passion, based upon an apprehension of eternal beauty as it is reflected in 'the dubbement dere of doun and dales' (121), 'the dazzling splendour of hill and dales'. And this 'strength of joy' (128), first stabilized in the dreamer by the radiant landscape, is to be further strengthened by the appearance and words of the Pearl maiden, who demonstrates to him that the everlasting 'ground of bliss' is set beyond any earthly garden, even beyond the Earthly Paradise, in the Paradise of Christ, the New Jerusalem, 'that clene cloystor'.

The final vision of the poem is of a city, not of a garden or garden landscape, a change of symbolism not quite unexpected either in terms of typological doctrine or in terms of the poem itself. The ultimate 'fulfilment' of the garden of the Earthly Paradise by the city of the New Jerusalem was an accepted alternative to its fulfilment by a Heavenly Paradise: the two gardens, the two cities, the two concepts, were interchangeable 'figures'.[55] But, more specifically, the dreamer has already thought of the Earthly Paradise as a 'mote', situated somewhere beyond the river and crystal cliffs which so invite and refuse his exploration: he has imagined his transfigured Pearl living 'in castel-walle' (917). Moreover, he has been told of the relationship between the two cities of Jerusalem—the one 'there the olde gulte was don to slake' (942), 'where (man's) ancient sin was redeemed', the other 'that lyght of Godes sonde' (943), 'which descended through grace of God' into the vision of St John the Divine. His view of the Earthly Paradise as part garden or park landscape and part city in that landscape prepares us for the transition to a vision of the Heavenly Paradise as St John's splendid four-square city of 'brende gold bryght', based for ever upon solid foundations of those very 'noble jewels' (118) which had earlier been glimpsed in the sparkling waters of the river. Yet even here, the sight of the City of God, with its images of light, purity and everlastingness focused upon the river issuing from the heavenly throne, does not quite obscure the dreamer's memory of another life. True, these waters are lit with a mystery:

> 'Sunne ne mone schon never so swete
> As that foysoun flode out of that flet;'   *copious, ground*
> (1057–8)

but for all the 'glymme pure' that ravishes his being, it is an earthly phenomenon that the dreamer instinctively chooses to convey the drama of that moment when he first becomes aware of the procession of maidens, led by the Lamb, moving through the 'golden gates that glent as glasse' (1106), 'through the golden streets, crystalline-bright'. We are returned to the sublunary world of overlapping seasons and times of day to recall the precarious beauty of dusk when 'the moon rises in all its splendour, and the daylight has not yet completely faded':

> 'Ryght as the maynful mone con rys
> Er thenne the day-glem dryve al doun,
> So sodanly on a wonder wyse
> I was war of a processyoun.'
> (1093–6)

So precise and moving is the evocation of that particular, subtle moment on the borderland of day and night, that the ending of the poem, with the dreamer back in his rich summer garden, cannot really surprise us. Unlike Dante, this poet-dreamer is admitted to a vision and an understanding of God's mysteries which are substantial but limited always by the imperfect working of his will in God's. His rash attempt to join the heavenly procession shows him to be far removed from the state of grace in which Dante declares his will to be turned, like sun and stars, in the orbit of love.[56] Out of the 'aventure ther mervayles meven', his life is to be led nearer to the flowery ground of humility:

> 'Then wakned I in that erber wlonk;   *lovely*
> My hede upon that hylle was layde
> Ther as my perle to grounde strayd.'
> (1171–3)

In a work such as this, the function of the garden is intimately related to the development of the main theme: described, transmuted, and returned to, the garden is an image of the dreamer's progress from an absorbed and selfish preoccupation with his own feelings to a larger understanding of his potential and of the way in which God intends that potential to be drawn upon for the management of his life. The Earthly Paradise and the Celestial City provide a wider and deeper perspective for the little 'erber' than the August cornfields the dreamer first describes, but arbour and meadow are still his ordained world, from whose impermanent beauty he can look out to the 'kythes that lastes aye' (1198), 'the regions of eternity'.

Pearl has its special felicities as a poem which exploits the significance of the garden in a religious setting, but all medieval religious artists had an advantage over secular in the latent symbolic value of the decorative material with which they were able to surround and fill their gardens. The growing enthusiasm, as the fourteenth passes into the fifteenth century, for painting the Virgin Mary in an enclosed garden setting, lavishly provided with plants, fruits and flowers, is in some ways comparable to the enthusiasm for painting lovers and courtiers in gardens (Plate 31). The calendar illustrations for April and May, occurring in religious manuscripts, but often entirely secular in concept,[57] are increasingly attracted to this motif, and so are the illustrations for romances. But however static and elaborate the religious gardens become, they are bound to be partially allusive, appealing not only to the eye, but to the understanding; they ask to be deciphered, as well as viewed. Not every Madonna of Humility, seated on flower-starred grass, is accompanied by a complex symbolism of flowers, but every Madonna in a garden enclosed by wall, palisade or rose hedge is enclosed in a symbol of her own nature and power—'hortus conclusus soror mea sponsa'.

Within this enclosure, all manifestations of natural beauty can be themselves, and more than themselves; the harmony of sensuous and spiritual worlds is, temporarily, complete. In the finest of the later medieval paintings of this kind—Stefano da Zevio's *Madonna in the Rose Garden* (Plate 32a), from Verona, and the anonymous Frankfurt *Garden of Paradise* (Plate 21)— observational realism is sensitively adjusted to spiritual meaning. The enclosure with its fountain or pool, its flowers and birds, speaks of known conventions and realities of secular society; it also speaks, eloquently, of the pattern of suffering and love into which Mary and Christ are eternally set. The fountain repeats the theme of enclosure: Mary is the 'fons signatus', the fountain sealed against all but God. Zevio's trellised hedge of roses, red and white, is a tribute to the rare and exclusive beauty of the Madonna, in her star-encrusted crown, but it is also a reference to love and purity, to the passion of Christ and the compassion of Mary, to blood and milk—a study in images of transformation less bizarre but not less effective than Richard Crashaw's epigram *Upon the Infant Martyrs*:

'To see both blended in one flood,
The mother's milk, the children's blood,
Makes me doubt if heaven will gather
Roses hence, or lilies rather.'

The twin subjects, love and pain, are reintroduced in the figure of St
Catharine, who is seated nearby with a wreath of gold laurel. The roses
of martyrdom surround her symbols, sword and wheel; the roses of purity
link her, mystically, to the Christ-child. Peacocks in this garden, poised above
rose spray, are birds natural to all paradisal states, imaging an earthly loveliness both exotic and familiar, and confirming, as religious symbols,
resurrected and eternal life. So birds and flowers are more than charming arabesques to the garden dwellers. Their commentary is graceful but significant.
In the same way, the detail of the Frankfurt *Garden of Paradise* attends to both
botanical and spiritual truth, fusing them in a decorative scheme which
appeals powerfully to the senses and, from there, to the mind. The meditative
Virgin, turning the pages of a book, warns us that this garden can be 'read';
iris and lily are twin symbols of purity—the iris streaked with sorrow, as the
Virgin was disfigured with grief at the Crucifixion:

'Nou goth sonne under wod:
Me reweth, Marie, thi faire rode.'[58]
('Now sinks the sun beneath the wood:
I pity, Mary, thy fair face.')

The lily of the valley, growing near the Christ-child, recalls both the language
of the Canticles—'Ego flos campi, et lilium convallium' (2:1)—and a traditional association with the return of spring and the Advent of Christ. Daisies
and violets, on the thickly-spread turf, allude to the innocence and humility
of Christ Incarnate who, in vulnerable form, plays among them. Strawberry
plants, bearing fruit and flower, and symbolic of perfect righteousness, fill
the space between Christ and a group of his saints, Michael, George and
Sebastian. St Dorothy picks cherries, the virtuous fruits of paradise, from a
brightly clustered tree. St Martha draws water from a flowing well, as grace
and truth is 'drawn' from the Virgin, the 'fountain of living waters' (Cant.
4:15). The whole garden is alive with goldfinches: over beauty hover
reminders of the passion of Christ. Beyond the garden wall, the intense blue
of the sky alludes not simply to perfect weather, but to perfection; the
garden is held in a paradisal equilibrium which may show itself in cloudless-
ness, but which is as much a spiritual as a climatic condition. This rich and

fluent statement, although phrased celebratively rather than analytically, served to exercise as well as to stimulate devotion.

But not all 'Mary' gardens of the later medieval period harmonize pictorial and symbolic content in so persuasive a way. The danger was that mystery would yield to delight, or that, in the effort to save mystery, the delights of the garden would become mere catalogues, patterns of religious metaphor. Some fifteenth-century Madonnas in Gardens differ very little from their secular counterparts—the ladies in spring and early summer calendar pictures, the ladies in illustrations to certain of Boccaccio's stories from the *Decameron*. The trellised roses, the turfed bench, the flower-spread grass belong to both. Often both are pictured against elaborate arbours which have so far lost their original purpose of sheltering and enclosing that they now often serve simply to project the main figure into bright relief. The splendid tabernacle, given as a new year's gift to Charles VI of France in 1404, already expresses this less private concept of worship in its garden arbour, which backs, and does not pretend to enclose, Virgin, Child and angels with an arched trellis of gold, and clusters of jewelled and enamelled fruit.[59] The world of secular magnificence has been admitted to this garden: the king and one companion kneel before the holy group, and another attendant holds the king's white horse, at the base of a double flight of steps. In da Zevio's rendering of the garden theme, the relationship of Madonna to flower-hedged enclosure is still very clear. The severe, shining, crenellated wall of the Frankfurt *Paradise* presents its message unambiguously. But in Stephan Lochner's *Madonna in the Rose Arbour* (Plate 32b), the Virgin is seen against a raised arbour which is more beautiful and intricate than immediately significant. So too in Schongauer's *Madonna in the Rose Garden* the concept of enclosure has weakened: the rose hedge is now only a decorative panel behind the Virgin.[60] These representations of secluded garden retreats have almost as much to say to us of medieval gardening practice as of devout symbolism. We know that illustrations to Boccaccio's *Decameron* were actually used for gardening treatises, so exact and particular were some of their versions of the gardens in which ladies meditated or received their lovers.[61] But many religious paintings could have served equally well. Two treatments of the *Madonna of Humility* associated with the Master of Flémalle place the Virgin against a structure resembling less a wall than the brick-sided bench, topped with herbs and flowers, which became a marked feature of later medieval gardens and garden art.[62] The Flemish illuminator of the Harleian *Roman de la Rose* manuscript uses such a bench inside the high wall, doubly enclosing the whole of the rose garden; so does Jan van Eyck in his *Madonna at the Fountain*. But for van Eyck, as for the Master of Flémalle, the bench is only a gesture towards enclosure. The close photographic precision with which brickwork and vegetation are rendered, and the care taken, in one case, to establish a clear relationship between garden and surrounding landscape, indicate other preoccupations.[63]

These strong interests in horticultural and topographical realism tend sometimes to dominate. Although all of these pictures contain clear and delicate reminders of traditional religious meaning—fountain, lily pot, dove, oriole, rayed emanation—they are quite distinct in feeling and appeal from da Zevio's view of Paradise as a garden of fluttering wings and flowers suspended mysteriously in space. And they are similarly remote from the Frankfurt *Paradise*, in which botanical realism is ringed and limited not only by a wall, but by the pure, deep, limitless blue of the *aether* beyond the wall. It is in fact quite difficult to decide, in many fifteenth-century religious paintings, whether the enclosure motif has any more than a purely decorative function—an encircling device, for defining and limiting the subject. The required response may be aesthetic rather than devotional. Such doubts are not dispelled by what can be observed in the field of secular painting. The trellised or wattled enclosure is increasingly used by artists illustrating the rituals of the courtly life: lovers converse, make music, courtiers feast and play chess in this setting. The Book of Hours made in France for John, Duke of Bedford, about 1423, frames a wide variety of marginal subjects, sober and fantastic, with a neat circle of wattle: a green-clad figure, symbolic of autumn plenty, standing in an orchard, and two naked men fighting beneath a fruit tree, a shield slung in its branches.[64] Animals are trapped within identical structures. They are featured many times in the illustrations to that practical book of hunting—the *Livre de la Chasse*, written for Gaston, comte de Foix, in the later fourteenth century. The most famous of the *Chasse* manuscripts[65] pictures the capture of the wild boar, the wolf and the hare within these enclosures. In some cases, the text upholds the artist's rendering of the scene: the wild boar is enticed into a fenced *vergier*, or orchard, by his greed for apples; the wolf is taken within a double row of fencing, the two concentric circles operating as a simple version of a maze.[66] But the 'enclosed garden' format is clearly chosen whenever possible: if the text speaks of 'un clos ou de champs ou de vignes ou de vergier' for hare hunting, it is the flower-strewn garden with its pretty palisade which is selected for illustration.[67]

The combination of hunting and enclosed garden motifs in fifteenth-century tapestry and painting is not unusual (Plate 33). Larger animals of the chase, peacefully contained among garden shrubs by these circular wattled devices, suggest that art rather than life has dictated presentation.[68] Even if we should regard their setting as the game park rather than the garden—the gardens of Boccaccio's *Decameron* admitted wild creatures as well as formal arbours—it is still possible that realism is here tempered with fantasy. The delicate fence could be a feature of design, just as it could be a mark of the artist's right to sever himself from fidelity to ordinary visual experience. Animals, trees and flowers are chosen and held, as in a bouquet, for our inspection and pleasure. The point is made, most dramatically, by the picturing of the hunting episode, during which the conversion of St Hubert took place, in a fenced garden, rather than, according to tradition, 'in a clearing of a wood'.[69] Two later fifteenth-century illustrations show the animal at bay, crucifix between its horns, in a crowded enclosure of grass, flowers and leaping dogs.[70]

And, over that century, there are few religious subjects which will not acquire their elegant ringed setting. An exquisite manuscript painting of *God presenting Eve to Adam*, made about 1415 in the French workshop of the Boucicaut Master (Colour Plate II), employs a fragile circle of wattle to mark out its main groups of figures.[71] But this is in no real sense an excluding paradisal wall. Animals wander through a gap in the fence to the glowing landscape beyond, which is fed by the water of life, and graced by trees, birds and angels. Most earlier and, indeed, contemporary pictures of Adam and Eve in Eden seek to isolate them within a walled surround, choosing either to ignore what lies beyond, and filling vacant space with rich decorative patterns,[72] or to make the merest gesture of recognition towards non-paradisal regions. The Boucicaut miniature celebrates perfect created beauty both inside and outside the wattled fence. The concept of enclosure, with its strong religious significance, has been adapted as an artistic device. It marks out a central area, intensifying its appeal to us, without in any way suggesting a thematic separation from the rest of the landscape. A contemporary miniature, from the same workshop, relates the *Expulsion of Adam and Eve* from a high-walled garden into a world of labour where vegetation and light are still paradisal; the severe octagon of the garden wall, like the pure round of the wattled fence, acts as a focus for the eye, not as a key to meaning.[73]

It need not therefore surprise us to find, in a Flemish manuscript of about 1500, the rough stable of the *Adoration of the Shepherds* ringed by that same precise wattled fence, which now encloses not only the Nativity group, but sportive rabbits (Plate 34a). The setting is reminiscent of the secular gardens of love, with their 'varii bestiuoli' ('bestis smale of gentil kynde').[74] And it is suggestive that, later in the book, an identical scene—enclosure, rabbits at play, and beyond the enclosure, a pastoral landscape of great charm—is used to surround a section of plain script.[75] In such a context, we might well hesitate before pronouncing upon the relationship of Virgin and Child to a fenced garden which seems to be part of a larger descriptive stereotype, and

VII *St John the Baptist in the Wilderness,* by Geertgen tot Sint Jans. Gemälde-galerie, Staatliche Museen, Berlin. Late fifteenth century.

to have only slight thematic value. Another Flemish manuscript painting, of the same date, deals in an even more complex way with ideas of inclusion and exclusion. The *Virgin and Child, with St Anne* enthroned (Plate 34b), rest on the flowered grass inside a low brick enclosure. But that enclosure is precisely located outside the far higher walls of a manor house garden. Despite the sharpness of the visual terminology, the religious meaning of the picture is ambiguous. The final development, from complexity into contradiction, may well be seen in a south German miniature which places the Virgin outside her own *hortus conclusus*: seated on its low wall, she turns her back upon its significance.[76]

But, of course, this disruption of religious coherence by interests which appear to be partly, at least, aesthetic, was not sudden or universal. The coexistence of old and new could not be better pointed than by comparing the Boucicaut miniature with that view of Eden taken by the Limbourg brothers in their famous *Fall and Expulsion* (Plate 23a) from the *Très Riches Heures*, illuminated for Jean, duc de Berri, before 1416.[77] The paintings are contemporary: they could hardly differ more in their modes of interpretation. The fragile grace of the Limbourg figures is enhanced by the protective wall which clasps them in their flowery paradise; it is also rendered pitiable, as they step with delicate fearfulness from garden to narrow strip of undefined desert and mountain beyond. The structure of the painting impresses twin ideas of enclosure and expulsion, and despite the rich sources of some of its detail,[78] it presents a strictly defined religious message. In the Boucicaut *Eden*, an uncertain religious message is amply compensated by freedom of artistic invention: the differences, however, are important.

For the desire to preserve and to enforce the symbolic meaning of the enclosed garden was not exhausted by the fifteenth century. It is now, for instance, that garden and hunt are perfectly reconciled in the allegorical narrative of the Lady and the Unicorn. Martin Schongauer's great altar painting, made between 1471 and 1478 for the Dominican church at Colmar,[79] describes, in two panels, the miraculous capture of the Unicorn, emblem of Christ, in the closed garden of the Virgin. Here, Gabriel, huntsman of the Annunciation, has been admitted to the walled enclosure of rose and lily, tower and sealed fountain. But in a miniature from Bruges, after 1500 (Colour Plate III), the symbolism is more exact: Gabriel, with dogs and hunting horn, stands just outside the garden gate, and watches the leaping entry of the Unicorn. The presentation of orthodox religious allegory in what approaches a lively secular mode, the setting of the garden into a hazy landscape, under a luminous sky, the envisaging of the whole picture as an essay in overlapping harmonies of blue and green, admit us momentarily, if not to a real world, to a version of reality. The lineaments are familiar, the substances are rare. But the final symbolic meaning is unmistakable. Not simply the inclusion but the dominant position of so many Marian emblems in that small garden space—the burning bush, the tower of David, the gateway of Ezekiel—require us to penetrate the 'gentle mysterie',[80] and persuade us, further, that the deep border to the scene, strewn with flowers and butterflies, may have more than a decorative part to play. For these are the flowers that might so easily have grown in the *hortus conclusus*, reflecting the beauty and power of the Virgin: the rose and carnation of love, the violet of humility, all touched by the wings of resurrection.

Further reconciliations are made in those *Unicorn Tapestries* which commemorate the marriage of Anne of Brittany and Louis XII of France in 1499. The world of aristocratic ritual and secular realism, the world of hunt and courtship, death and marriage, is replaced, finally, by the image of the wounded but revived Unicorn, resting in a fenced plot, and secured to a tree of pomegranates.[81] Particular historical references are absorbed by the larger symbolism of Christ mystically united with his Beloved, the Church, in an enclosed 'paradise of pomegranates'.

And, perhaps in militant response to the growing fascination which the natural world was exercising, fifteenth-century religious art can show itself as rigorous and formal in its approach to garden themes as that of the twelfth century.

Diagrammatic portrayal remained, sometimes centred about the figure of the Virgin, sometimes replacing her with the composite symbols of her nature: fountain, well, closed gate, tower, olive and cedar, rose and lily. These simple commemorative patterns, through which treatises such as the *Speculum Humanae Salvationis*[82] conveyed the lessons of biblical history (Plate 35a) to a wide, semi-learned public, have their literary equivalents: poems of praise to the Virgin which are little more than devout catalogues of images. John Lydgate's *Balade in Commendation of Our Lady* significantly draws upon twelfth-century Latin verse for its precisely mapped Mary garden:

> 'O closid gardeyn, al void of weedis wicke,
> Cristallyn welle, of clennesse cler consigned,
> Fructif olyve, of foilys faire and thicke,
> And redolent cedyr . . .
> Paradys of plesaunce, gladsom to all good,
> Benygne braunchelet of the pigment-tre . . .
> Rede rose, flouryng withowtyn spyne,
> Fonteyn of fulnesse, as beryl corrent clere.'[83]

These anatomies of gardens had a continuous life in devotional books of the fifteenth and sixteenth centuries. Both as art and literature in honour of the Virgin, the 'garden shut up from the beginning',[84] they served celebrative and meditative purposes—sometimes providing only the bare minimum of natural features to stimulate acts of worship, sometimes allowing sensuous perception into the choice and arrangement of detail.

Their power is well represented in the early sixteenth-century Grimani Breviary:[85] significantly, a 'Mary garden' concludes the book (Plate 35b), following upon a very different kind of painting—Virgin and Child in a flowering field which leads back into an idyllic countryside of trees, shepherds and grazing sheep. The free naturalism of that painting is succeeded by the much more complex mode of the Mary garden. Distant prospects of rocks and architecture direct the eye towards heaven, where the crowned Virgin is blessed by Christ and angels; she is surrounded by words and symbols of adoration, the sun, moon and stars—'Tota pulchra es, amica mea, et macula non est in te' (Cant. 4:7), 'Pulchra ut luna, electa ut sol' (Cant. 6:9), 'Stella maris'. In the foreground lies a garden, complete with gateway, well, tower, olive, cedar, lily, and rose bush in enclosed plot, all clearly labelled with their traditional biblical appellations: 'turris David', 'cedrus exultata', 'oliva speciosa', 'fons hortorum', 'plantacio rosae', 'puteus aquarum viventium'.[86] The Virgin is absent, but the garden is redolent with her presence: an angel holds a mirror to reflect the 'well of living waters', and the mirror is rimmed with the words that image her, 'speculum sine macula' (Sapientia 7:26). So Mary, mirror without flaw, reflected the divine, In such a picture the distinction between perceptual truth and symbolism is denied. The turreted gateway which, from a rocky slope, commands a view not only of the garden but also of a city, is a landscape feature in the grand manner, but it is also a literal reference to Mary as the 'porta celi', opening upon the City of God. The very deliberate written commentary upon the meaning of the garden and landscape components may be seen as a literary intrusion. But it does compel us to recognize the artist's intent—not simply the checking of our emotional responses to a lavish and detailed portrayal of natural forms, but the rigorous co-ordination of thought and sensibility. The interdependence of biblical text and visual image is at its most explicit here: the book of the senses receives its *imprimatur*.

The *hortus* miniature of the Grimani Breviary brings us closer than before to the emblem books of the sixteenth and seventeenth centuries, which both formalize and exploit this open relationship of art and literature, of picture and text.[87] The full statement of the theory of emblematic art may be new, but the materials are medieval. For many medieval artists, paintings were silent poems, to be 'read' by the eye; for many poets, verses were eloquent pictures, appealing to the mind's eye as well as to the eye of the senses:

> 'Pulchra ut luna, thu bere the lambe,
> As soone that shyneth moste clere.
> Veni in ortum meum, thowghty damme,
> To smelle my spyces and erbes in fere.
> My place ys pyghte for the plenere,
> Full of bryghte braunches and blomes of blysse.'[88]

Henry Hawkins's *Partheneia Sacra* (1633) takes that same enclosed garden as a central device for an elaborate set of devotional exercises. Its old power is undiminished:

> 'Being so mysterious and delicious an Object, [it] requires not to be rashly lookt upon, or perfunctoriously to be slighted over, but, as the manner is of such as enter into a Garden, to glance at first thereon with a light regard, then to reflect upon it with a better heed, to find some gentle mysterie or conceipt upon it, to some use or other; and then liking it better, to review the same again.'[89]

In this particular form, its mysteries and its delights codified and enlarged upon, the survival of the *hortus conclusus* was assured. But it is significant that Hawkins was a Jesuit, working in a specific and ultimately medieval religious context. The frontispiece to his book, a walled garden containing all the known symbols of the Virgin, is directly, even severely, in line with medieval diagrammatic versions of that subject. Only in the accompanying text does he allow some delighted observation its place: looking into the lily, perfect type of the Virgin's purity, he sees that 'the seed remains in these hammers of gold'.[90] The scrupulous attention which he pays to the spiritual application of detail allows a small margin for the recording of pure pleasure—'even to behold them were a great delight'. It is, nevertheless, as in medieval antecedents, a strictly limited area. Accuracy is always less important than forcefulness of description, a situation as familiar from the Frankfurt *Garden of Paradise* as from the Grimani *hortus*. In one, botanical truth is powerful, but the intensification of reality more so; in the other, the disposal of natural landscape features is convincing, but the strength of the picture lies in the cumulative effect of its display of images.

This is a fitting sequel to what the fifteenth century can show us. The preservation of the enclosed garden in the safe and narrow specialized setting of religious exercises highlights both its potential and its limitations—its ability to define and concentrate, its inability to expand and comprehend.

It is significant that emblem literature showed itself interested in a strict version of that most strict of medieval walled gardens, 'the garden shut up from the beginning', the Virgin herself. As Henry Hawkins points out, other forms of Paradise were not so secure:

'For that the Garden of Eden, or Terrestrial Paradise, was not so exempt from Sinne, but the place where Sinne began; and was not so free from the Serpent, but that he could get—in and work the mischief.'[91]

The concept of enclosure was felt by many later medieval artists to be inhibiting, but it was, nevertheless, in this very 'inhibition' that its original spiritual power lay. For many, the walled garden remained incomparable:

'I speake not heer of the Covent-Garden, the garden of the Temple, nor that of the Charter-house, or of Grayes-Inne walkes, to be had and enjoyed at home; nor of the Garden of Padua, or of Montpelier, so illustrious for Simples. I speake not of the Garden of Hesperides, where grew the golden Apples, nor yet of Tempe, or the Elizian fields. I speake not of Eden, the Earthlie Paradice, nor of the Garden of Gethsemany, watred with Bloud flowing from our Saviour's precious bodie; But I speake of Thee, that Garden so knowne by the name of Hortus Conclusus, wherein are al things mysteriously and spiritually to be found.'[92]

The freeing of the Virgin from the charmed circle of her wall or wattled fence, the placing of her in a varied landscape, offered rich rewards to the senses. But, like the opening of the rose garden of secular love to the voices and gestures of common sense, this is a diffusion of essential strength. Inevitably, the walled garden was called upon to serve purposes and masters unsuited to it. The lesson to be learnt from the *Roman de la Rose*, from Chaucer's poetry and from the experiments of fifteenth-century artists is that these gardens cannot really be adapted or changed without being destroyed. Only where change was not desired, where, indeed, reaffirmation of medieval forms and ideas was felt to be positively advantageous, could the old magic still work. The more private philosophies of love and worship still had need of the garden, whether for its gift of 'delicious solitude' to the meditating poet,

'Here at the Fountain's sliding foot,
Or at some Fruit-trees mossy root,
Casting the Bodies Veste aside,
My Soul into the boughs does glide.'[93]

or for its precise iconography of delight:

'Put off thy shooe, tis holy ground,
For here the flaming Bush is found,
The mystic Rose, the Iv'ry Tower,
The morning Star and David's bower . . .
The Garden shut, the living Spring,
The Tabernacle of the King . . .
The untouched Lilly, full of dew,
A Mother, yet a Virgin true.'[94]

'See where my love sits in the beds of spices,
Beset all round with camphor, myrrh and roses,
And interlaced with curious devices
Which her from all the world apart incloses.
There doth she tune her lute for her delight,
And with sweet music makes the ground to move,
While I, poor I, do sit in heavy plight . . .
Not daring rush into so rare a place
That gives to her, and she to it, a grace.'[95]

Chapter Five

THE LANDSCAPE OF THE SEASONS

Nothing perishes except with a view to salvation; and all things return to that beauty for which they are destined at our creation, had we not sinned in Paradise.[1]

Nothing except his personal narrative of birth and death more urgently signalled to medieval man of mutability than the changing aspects of landscape and weather. Watching the country year turning 'in yisterdayes mony', his need was various—to endure, to record, even to celebrate, and, first and last, to accept that beyond the apparent wilfulness of nature lay a divine and beneficent will. For this, whether he was artist, poet or philosopher, he had much to draw upon besides his own painful or delighted observation. He had inherited from the ancient world, if at one or two removes and in partial versions, theories, forms and materials relevant to his search for ways of dealing with the vanishing and recurring phenomena of the earth. In the poetry of Lucretius and Virgil were arguments for the orderly operation of Nature in the movement of planets and the linked progress of seasons. Man could 'read' the heavens and use their information to guide his daily actions:

'Si vero solem ad rapidum lunasque sequentis
ordine respicies, numquam te crastina fallet
hora, neque insidiis noctis capiere serenae.'[2]
('But if you pay heed to the swift sun and the moons, as they follow in order, never will tomorrow's hour cheat you, nor will you be ensnared by a cloudlesss night.')

The passing of the seasons, from flowery spring to winter, 'its teeth chattering with cold',[3] had been presented as mythology, a crowded procession of deities, a tableau in the Palace of the Sun:

'Verque novum stabat cinctum florente corona,
stabat nuda Aestas et spicea serta gerebat,
stabat et Autumnus calcatis sordidus uvis
et glacialis Hiems canos hirsuta capillos.'[4]

('Young Spring was there, wreathed with a floral crown; Summer, all unclad with garland of ripe grain; Autumn was there, stained with the trodden grape, and icy Winter with white and bristly locks.')

and as actuality—the labours of rural life most closely bound to a seasonal and ultimately, to a cosmic cycle:

> 'redit agricolis labor actus in orbem,
> atque in se sua per vestigia volvitur annus.'[5]

('The farmer's toil returns, moving in a circle, as the year rolls back upon itself over its own footsteps.')

Both modes would reappear in medieval poetry, both rich and formal personification and also the more informal chronicling of country toil— the preparation of the land, the pruning of vines, pressing of grapes, the feeding of swine in autumn woods, followed by winter feasting, when 'merry winter calls and looses care'.[6]

In the arts, a fairly elaborate notation for seasons and months already lay to hand. The stone Calendars of Roman times, with their tabulations of month, deity, feast, date of nones and agricultural routine, had been given a more sophisticated setting by Hellenistic frieze and mosaic, Roman manuscript and wall painting. Here, in pictorial and plastic form, the frame of reference was widened to take in specific religious rituals, signs of the zodiac and personifications of natural features—June with the torch of summer heat, Winter warmly clad for the cold.[7]

But this mixed legacy—philosophical, semi-scientific, mythological, practical and descriptive—was partly accepted and partly transformed to meet new and pressing medieval demands. It was inevitable that seasonal change would work with special potency upon Christian thought and feeling. The pleasure with which earlier Latin poets contemplated the ripening of a summer landscape was frequently crossed by a melancholy awareness of the imminent death of such beauty:

> 'mirabar celerem fugitiva aetate rapinam
> et, dum nascentur, consenuisse rosas.'[8]

('I marvel at the swift thefts of age in flight, and the roses falling, even as they come to bloom.')

and of the sudden destructiveness of nature:

> 'Vidi ego odorati victura rosaria Paesti
> sub matutino cocta iacere Noto.'[9]

('I have seen the rose gardens of sweet Paestum, that should have lived on, lie blasted by the south wind of the morning.')

This is quite different, however, from the poignancy and even the violence of the medieval response. In one limited context, the brief life of the rose could always extend an invitation to act, rather than to contemplate: the moral drawn by Propertius and confirmed by the pseudo-Ausonius would become familiar in the scholar's lyrics of the twelfth century—'utere, ne quid cras libet ab ore dies!' But not all of the consolations open to those earlier poets were either available or appropriate to their medieval successors. Had they been able to read more than a little of Lucretius, they would have found something of a sympathetic nature in his candid comments upon a world 'so full of imperfections', or in his questioning of natural disaster, 'Why do the changing seasons bring pestilence in their train?'[10] But it is not certain that they could have found common ground in his rational tolerance of complex causes—'non simplex his rebus reddita causa'[11]—and in his reliance upon the power of the mind to sustain, even when solutions are out of the question:

'sed mage pacata posse omnia mente tueri.'[12]
('[True piety lies] rather in the power to contemplate the universe with a quiet mind.')

A philosophic framework such as that of the *Georgics* could more easily have been adapted. With its stress on a close-knit relationship between divine intent, nature and man's industry, it reduced confusion, and gave a picture of responsibility and recompense not quite unlike that of Christianity:

'pater ipse colendi
haud facilem esse viam voluit, primusque per artem
movit agros, curis acuens mortalia corda . . .
. . . labor omnia vicit
improbus et duris urgens in rebus egestas.'[13]
('The Great Father himself has willed that the path of husbandry should not be smooth, and he first made art awake the fields, sharpening men's wits by care . . . Toil conquered the world, unrelenting toil, and want that pinches when life is hard.')

But if these similarities are interesting, it is the differences that are really significant. What can only be described as the tension of the Christian attitude to man and nature compared with the resolved though still compassionate Virgilian view stems ultimately from the high and personalized drama of the Christian myth of the Fall and Expulsion from Eden. For Virgil, the substitution of the Age of Jove for the Golden Age of Saturn, and the imposition of the need to work for the fruits of the earth, prompted regret and reconciliation: for the Christian apologist, the contrast between Eden and the outside world was an integral part of an eschatology, a matter of physical life and spiritual death.[14] The passage of the year through the landscapes and activities of the months was a trenchant commentary upon man's loss of that original garden of everlasting life and spring. However the theologians argued over the precise significance of the Vulgate statement,

'Maledicta terra in opere tuo'
('Cursed is the earth in your labour')[15]

the general potency of God's curse was inescapable: the extent of the change in Nature after the Fall may have been open to debate, but no one could doubt that seasonal suffering and seasonal toil were causally related, first and last, to the sins of mankind. No classical poet could ever feel the rigours of winter with such passionate concern for what they symbolized. Ovid, in in bleak Pontus, 'a country gripped by stiffening cold' ('adstricto terra perusta gelu'),[16] was exiled only from Rome and civilization; but medieval man, in winter moods, felt himself to be exiled from grace:

'And þas stanhleaþu   stormas cnyssað;
hrið hreosende   hrusan bindeð,
wintres woma,   þonne wonn cymeð,
nipeð nihtscua,   norþan onsendeð
hreo hæglfare   hæleþum on andan.
Eall is earfoðlic   eorþan rice,
onwendeð wyrda gesceaft   weoruld under heofonum.'[17]
    ('And storms beat upon these granite cliffs,
    A driving tempest lashes the earth,
    The clash of winter, when darkness falls,
    Night-shadows thicken, and send from the north
    Fierce showers of hail, in hatred of man.
    All is hardship in the earthly kingdom:
    Fate decrees change in this sublunary world.')

For many medieval poets, the image of exile in winter, on an ice-cold sea,[18] potently conveys both the quality of northern European landscape and the inner desolation of the spirit. Even the return of summer cannot always dispel a restless sense of exclusion from warmth and joy:

'Swylce geac monað geomran reorde,
singeð sumeres weard, sorge beodeð
bittre in breosthord.'[19]
('So, too, the cuckoo warns, with sad note,
Guardian of summer, it sings, and strikes the heart
With keenest sorrow.')

For summer itself was subject to change, an unwilling traveller:

'Estas in exilium
iam peregrinatur,
leto nemus avium
cantu viduatur.
pallet viror frondium,
campus defloratur . . .
et ethera silentio turbavit,
exilio dum aves relegavit.'[20]
('Summer to a strange land
Is into exile gone,
The forest trees are bare
Of their gay song.
The forest boughs are wan,
Deflowered the field . . .
And silence grieves the air,
For all the birds are into exile gone.')

And when the image of exile is exchanged for that of ordered procession, the truce between permanence and impermanence, solace and sorrow, is often uneasily observed. The progress of the year, from the 'colde frosty sesoun of Decembre' to August 'quen corne is corven wyth crokes kene', represented, at best, a divine stabilizing of the sad inevitable flux of matter in a post-lapsarian world: God's comfort, made necessary by God's discipline of man in his fallen state. Artists painting or sculpting, poets versifying, peasants experiencing at first hand the activities and labours of the months were all bearing witness to a system of punishment and reward acknowledged first by Adam and Eve, when they stepped through the gates of Eden, relinquishing perfect beauty for the beauty of imperfection:

'The world was all before them, where to choose
Their place of rest, and Providence their guide.'

Henceforward, the unpredictable but often dazzling pageants of the earth would torment and delight. On the one hand, there would always be panic, as the aggressive, intemperate world of wind, frost and heat demanded its victories:

> 'Hu sculon wit nu libban   oððe on þys lande wesan
> gif her wind cymð, westan oððe eastan,
> suðan oððe norþan?   Gesweorc up færeð,
> Cymð hægles scur . . .
> Hwilum of heofnum   hate scineð
> blicð þeos beorhte sunne,   and wit her baru standað.'[21]
> ('How shall you and I now live or endure on this earth
> If the wind constantly blows, from west and east,
> From south and north?   The skies darken,
> Hail-showers fall . . .
> Sometimes the fiery sun beats down from the heavens,
> Scorching us, naked as we stand.')

On the other hand, there would always be relief, as providence asserted itself above disaster:

> 'No hwæðre ælmihtig   ealra wolde
> Adame and Euan   arna ofteon,
> fæder æt frymðe,   þeah þe hie him from swice,
> ac he him to frofre let   hwæðere forð wesan
> hyrstedne hrof   halgum tunglum
> and him grundwelan   ginne sealde;
> het þam sinhiwum   sæs and eorðan
> tuddorteondra   teohha gehwilcre
> to woruldnytte   wæstmas fedan.'[22]

('But the almighty father would not withdraw all of his favours from Adam and Eve, though they had deceived him. The sky he gave them as consolation, set with holy stars, store of earth's riches, ordered each lusty species, on land, in sea, to breed abundantly, and fill man's need.')

If man was destined to strive against uncertainty, in landscape and weather, God had indicated to him both the certainty which lay beyond, and the possibility of minimizing, even controlling, uncertainty. The regular movement of stars in the heavens, the regular pattern of growth in plants and men said something to him of 'the variance now, the eventual unity'. If he was always to be subject to the chance of ruined vineyards and frost-charred crops, he could still legitimately believe in a norm of labour and fruitfulness— the reconciliation of God and his creation in the harvesting of the resistant earth. Christian philosophy very early on began its task of composing a picture of man and the natural world which would make peace between faith and experience. In the sixth-century *De Consolatione Philosophiae*, Boethius persuasively argued for that same Lucretian 'power to contemplate the universe with a quiet mind',[23] but it was a power won by the suppression rather than by the acceptance of awkward features. The design of the picture is admirable, as so many succeeding poets and thinkers acknowledged:

'Omnium generatio rerum cunctusque mutabilium naturarum progressus et quidquid aliquo mouetur modo, causas, ordinem, formas ex diuinae mentis stabilitate sortitur.'[24]

('The engendrynge of alle thynges and alle the progressiouns of muable nature, and al that moeveth in any manere, taketh his causes, his ordre, and his formes, of the stablenesse of the devyne thought.')

And so is the accommodation of sensuous detail to the bordering truths of change and death:

> 'Isdem causis vere tepenti
> Spirat florifer annus odores,
> Aestas Cererem fervida siccat,
> Remeat pomis gravis autumnus,
> Hiemem defluus inrigat imber.
> Haec temperies alit ac profert
> Quidquid vitam spirat in orbe.
> Eadem rapiens condit et aufert
> Obitu mergens orta supremo.'[25]

('By thise same causes the floury yer yeldeth swote smelles in the first somer sesoun warmynge; and the hote somer dryeth the cornes; and autumpne comith ayein hevy of apples; and the fletyng reyn bydeweth the wynter. This atempraunce norysscheth and bryngeth forth alle thynges that brethith lif in this world; and thilke same attempraunce, ravysschynge, hideth and bynymeth, and drencheth under the laste deth, alle thinges iborn.')

This copy book account of cosmic and seasonal equilibrium served the Middle Ages well, and was translated into numerous European vernacular languages. But even here, in the tranquil settlement of problems, the sensitive quality of those problems is only too clear. Order and disorder could be observed in natural phenomena: if the stars preserved 'their ancient peace', the same could not be said for the winds of heaven, whose sudden actions were so frequent and destructive:

> 'Cum nemus flatu Zephyri tepentis
>   Vernis inrubuit rosis,
> Spiret insanum nebulosus Auster:
>   Iam spinis abeat decus.'[26]

('Whan the wode waxeth rody of rosene floures in the fyrst somer sesoun thurw the breeth of the wynd Zephirus that waxeth warm, yif the cloudy wynd Auster blowe felliche, than goth awey the fairnesse of thornes.')

The paradox of a universe which illustrates not only regular patterns of change but also disruption of that regularity is not so much resolved by Boethius as dissolved in the philosophic concept of a divine intelligence whose operation can never be more than partially comprehended by man. So, too, is the paradox of a world which puts forth natural beauty as matter for both admiration and suspicion: Lady Philosophy underlines the human dilemma when she passes from sympathy to censure in her dealings with the 'beauty of the countryside':

'Est enim pulcherrimi operis pulchra portio. Sic quondam sereni maris facie gaudemus; sic caelum sidera lunam solemque miramur.'[27]
('Why schulde it nat deliten us, syn that it is a ryght fayr porcioun of the ryght faire werk? And right so ben we gladde somtyme of the face of the see whan it es cleer; and also merveylen we on the hevene, and on the sterres, and on the sonne, and on the moone.')

But when natural beauty stirs delight, it invites attachment to things which can never be possessed by man but which may, disastrously, possess him. Delight enslaves in that it leads beyond the satisfaction of need to the indulgence of sensation:

'An vernis floribus ipse distingueris aut tua in aestivos fructus intumescit ubertas?... Terrarum quidem fructus animantium procul dubio debentur alimentis. Sed si, quod naturae satis est, replere indigentiam velis, nihil est quod fortunae affluentiam petas.'[28]
('Artow distyngwed and embelysed by the spyrngynge floures of the firste somer sesoun, or swelleth thi plente in fruites of somer?... Soth is that, withouten doute, the fruites of the erthe owen to be to the noryssynge of beestis; and yif thow wilt fulfille thyn nede after that it suffiseth to nature, thanne is it no nede that thow seke aftir the superfluyte of fortune.')

Only, perhaps, within the sheltered confines of a religio-philosophic treatise could all of the delicate balances be adjusted, and man achieve a properly harmonious relationship with a universe whose moving rituals of earth and sky taught so many apparently contradictory lessons. In the *De Consolatione*, a work which arbitrated between ancient and Christian worlds in a way which was as satisfying to King Alfred in the ninth century as it was to Chaucer in the fourteenth, little is made—in specifically Christian terms—of the theme of exile and expulsion. The language is occasionally suggestive of something more than the historical facts of Boethius banished from Rome and imprisoned in Pavia:

'Ac si te pulsum existimari mavis, te potius ipse pepulisti.'[29]
('And yif thou hast levere for to wene that thow be put out of thy cuntre, thanne hastow put out thyselve rather than ony other wyght hath.')

It goes no further towards making the agonizing point that man first created his own confusion, and took upon himself the responsibility for living in a world so perilous and so seductive. But that point would be made, time and time again, by Christian theologians; it is not surprising that, in practice, ways of regarding and describing the substance of the vast regions to which man had been unwillingly, but justly, relegated, were not always self-evident, or easily arrived at. Imagining and giving artistic or material form to the garden paradise were, if not evasions, certainly simplifications of the problem. With spiritual analogues never far away, life in the garden had definable moral reference, whether favourable or unfavourable. Outside the garden lay endless tracts of a more difficult nature—obdurate, dangerous, rich and sometimes perturbingly beautiful. Part divine gift and part human penance, the landscape of field and forest, hill and lake provoked a whole range of responses, many conflicting.

In a situation where nothing was really clear, it would be surprising to find medieval writers and artists single-minded or even consistent in their procedures. Philosophic detachment and spiritual doctrines of rejection or transformation offered ways out which were, indeed, acceptable and powerful. A world so Janus-faced could be turned into moral allegory. The earth's potential for good or ill could be 'interpreted' as man's inner struggle to direct his activities towards the fruitful life of the spirit, not towards the barren life of the material universe:

'Nec terra in se maledicta est; sed *Maledicta*, inquit, *in operibus tuis*, quod ad Adam dictum est. Tunc terra maledicta est, si habeas opera terrena, id est opera saecularia.'[30]
('The world is not accursed in itself, but accursed, as God said to Adam, "because of your actions". So the world is accursed when we engage in worldly, that is, non-spiritual activities.')

The difficulties could be surmounted, or perhaps by-passed, by stressing the transmutations worked by God. For the twelfth-century mystic,

Hildegard of Bingen, if instability in the seasons and in human beings demanded notice:

'Et sicut terra in frigore et in calore fructus suos non aequaliter profert, sic etiam ipsa (anima) male et bene operando inaequalia opera habet.'[31]

('And as the earth, in cold and heat, yields its fruits unequally, so the soul, through good and evil, is unequal in its works.')

man still reigned, god-like, upon his throne of earth, sustained by the divine law of love:

'Dominus etenim in coelo in potentia sua potenter regnat, et sidera quae per ipsum accenduntur et reliquam creaturam inspicit. Sic et homo super sedem, quae terra est, sedet, et reliquae creaturae dominatur, quia signis omnipotentiae Dei insignitus est.'[32]

('So God reigns in all his power in heaven, and looks upon the stars that, through him, fire the skies and on every created thing. And so man, set on his throne of earth, rules over all other creatures, holding power next in token through God's omnipotence.')

But visionary and allegorical solutions could not totally satisfy. The old biblical words were inescapably real for a good part of humanity:

'Maledicta terra in opere tuo; in laboribus comedes ex ea cunctis diebus vitae tuae. Spinas et tribulos germinabit tibi, et comedes herbam terrae.'[33]

('Cursed is the earth in your labour: in toil shall you win sustenance from it all the days of your life: thorns and hardships shall it bring forth for you, and you shall eat the grasses of the earth.')

Convenient, and, if possible, interesting formulas were needed in order that man's close physical and emotional involvement with nature could be given a religious context which would frame but not inhibit the need for expression too severely. The resetting of classical motifs for the picturing of seasons and months into a specifically Christian scheme provided one such formula. What lay within the reach and the sight of man, as he laboured or engaged in the different rituals of management of the earth, was a reasonable area for the attention of the medieval writer or artist. It offered material for practical informative purposes, and for more extensive statements about the universe, for the simplest accounts of man, soil and weather:

'By thys fyre I warm my handys;
And with my spade I delfe my landys.
Here I sette my thynge to sprynge;

VIII *Gethsemane, the Agony in the Garden*, by Giovanni Bellini (d. 1516).
National Gallery, London.

And here I here the foulis synge.
I am as lyght as byrde in bowe;
And I wede my corne well I-now . . .
At Martynesmasse I kylle my swyne;
And at Cristesmasse I drynke redde wyne.'[34]

and for the great sculpted programmes of Romanesque and early Gothic cathedrals, which group the same simple occupations around Christ Panto-crator, giver of wheat and wine.[35] So, in the Christian dispensation, the world outside Paradise was most safely recomposed about the work of man, and, especially, about his patient husbandry of earth and animals, as this was dictated by processes of growth, by planetary cycles, and by human need, divinely implanted. And if, in the interests of faith and unity, a selective use of material was required, if the order rather than the hazard of seasonal involvement was to be emphasized, there was still some room for observation of variety within the pattern.

Unpromising as it may seem, this limitation of landscape to prescribed areas of human activity had virtues which were not to remain narrowly religious. Admittedly, strict control of subject matter was prompted by the need to make some sense of 'all-devouring mutability',[36] to relieve the pain of a situation which could never, in this life, be altered, but which might, by simplification, be partially understood. And admittedly, the shaping of a man-centred attitude to the natural world was significantly Christian in its acceptance of the biblical hierarchies of creation. To be concentrating upon man's non-paradisal realm had its disadvantages: where there were no absolute certainties of approach, free composition was difficult, and the temptation to adopt stylized schemes and motifs was strong. No one can study the Calendar pictures of the Middle Ages without seeing evidence of an instability of viewpoint. The status of landscape is frequently in doubt, as also its mode of portrayal. Innovation alternates with convention: advances are as often denied as accepted. Similarly, to be so absorbed with the round of man's labour was, if not a deterrent, at least a check to the rapid development of a full 'landscape art'. Even at the close of the fifteenth century it was easier for poets and painters to turn their attention to the woods and fields than to lift their eyes to the hills and, beyond, to the remote mountain ranges.

But given an imposed formality of structure and an imposed conformity of attitude, they managed, gradually, to find potential in their theme of man and the changing seasons. Those very conditions which restricted some aspects of their work were able to encourage others. For problematic as it was to deal with the world outside the paradise garden, this was the only

129

world in which those problems could be overcome, the only ground upon which the victories could eventually be won. A vision of landscape which was both harmonious and comprehensive had to be achieved in the restless context of seasonal growth, not in the happy finality of an eternal spring, whatever the moral implications. Some of the excitement as well as the pain of this situation is expressed by an anonymous English poet of the fourteenth century, as he imagines God's words to Noah, after the Flood:

> 'Sesounes schal yow never sese of sede ne of hervest,
> Ne hete, ne no harde forst, umbre ne drouthe,   *storm*
> Ne the swetnesse of somer, ne the sadde wynter,
> Ne the nyght, ne the day, ne the newe yeres,
> Bot ever renne restles; regnes ye therinne.'[37]

And although the range of material offered to the eye by the diurnal world could be and often was regarded as an embarrassment, that range was both needed and exploited—tentatively by the creative artists of the Middle Ages, and most completely by those who inherited from them. Medieval artists may frequently have sought retreat from the perplexing variety of natural landscape into formulaic versions of it or into disciplined gardens of sensuous and spiritual delight; they did, however, lay claim to an area of experiment which only their heirs would fully occupy, but which would meanwhile attract them to journeys of exploration and discovery. Even their dominant interest in humanity at work had its positive contribution to make: without the impetus of the 'labours of the months', which recorded the year-long and unbroken relationship of man, beast and earth, it is doubtful whether the sombre seasons of the year would have received more than cursory attention. Out of a purely human concern for the importance of the months of November and December, when swine were fattened on acorns and killed for winter sustenance, grew subtle muted paintings of autumn woodlands. Bruegel's *The Return of the Herd* (Plate 36), with its balanced attention to the harsh life of herd and herdsman and to the economical beauty of bare tree and rock, completes a long line of November studies from the preceding century. And it could be argued that out of the medieval conviction that winter is a state of siege, when man is best occupied at home, by the fire, holding the line against dissolution, grew the desire to picture the snow-bound landscape that so threatened him. In this sense, Bruegel's *The Hunters in the Snow* (Plate 37) fulfils, rather than escapes from, the earlier February Calendar scenes which look outside hesitantly, or turn away from winter's violence.

It is, therefore, the choice of a landscape of action to express seasonal movement that provides us with the most rewarding, though not necessarily the most straightforward evidence about medieval man, nature and art. That choice was not, of course, universally respected: the well-loved classical mode of personification was never totally relinquished, and it is to a kind of symbolic figure, indicative of the significance of a month or season, that Chaucer refers in his comment on the Squire—'He was as fresh as is the month of May'. It is this mode which is still employed by countless manuscript painters of the fourteenth and even fifteenth centuries for times of the year as various as January, April and May—the double or triple-faced god Janus, with winter viands, or youthful creatures with branch and flower, celebrating endurance and new life. In Chaucer's poetry, as in that of Boccaccio, May can still appear as goddess in a formally coloured tableau of seasons, months and planets:

> 'In May, that moder is of monthes glade,
> That fresshe floures, blew and white and rede,
> Ben quike agayn, that wynter dede made,
> And ful of bawme is fletyng every mede;
> Whan Phebus doth his bryghte bemes sprede. . .'[38]

Painters of fifteenth-century Ferrara were to revive more than one classical motif in frescoes of the 'triumph of the months'—the barque of Venus, April deity of love and beauty, drawn by swans to a shore thronged with aspirant courtiers.

But the real 'triumphs' lay elsewhere, in the concept of the months as landscapes of activity, whether practical or courtly: in May, for instance, as a summer parkland, just beyond castle or town walls, visited and enjoyed by the leisured classes; in April as a chequer board of grove, garden and field, each dedicated to its proper seasonal ceremony—ploughing, sowing, flower gathering, courtly conversation and hare hunting. Such scenes decorated one room in the palace of the bishop of Trento (Plate 39), not long after Chaucer's lifetime.[39] Even more decisive are those great hall frescoes commissioned by the dukes of Ferrara, the D'Este family, for the Palazzo Schifanoia (Plates 38a and b). These distinguish clearly between a stylized setting, full of iconographic sense, for their mythological themes, and real northern Italian countryside, full of the signs and occupations of the rural year, for those areas which depict the life of Ferrarese nobility and citizens.[40]

Some of this potential is already hinted in art of the eleventh century. Man's business with the outdoor world through all twelve months was recorded in glancing strokes by two English manuscript painters[41]—shepherds at work with their flocks, peasants bending to the corn with sickles, loading their waggons, and feeding the swine under September trees. Nothing could better illustrate both the uncertainties and the strengthening impulses of earlier medieval artists, faced with this subject: the two sets of Calendar pictures are rich with reminiscences of the past, tentative explorations into the future. On the whole, landscape is rather summarily alluded to; the selection of detail is still controlled by practical needs—woods for September, corn fields for June.[42] And the portrayal of such natural features is stylized, with trees, for instance, in formal design, indebted to Nordic interlace and classical acanthus, and corn a solid auburn swathe. By comparison, the patterns of men, animals and implements are tense and energetic—heavy oxen, followed by lightly poised figures of ploughmen, a graceful frieze of arms and scythes, raised in summer hay fields, the vehement attitudes of February and March, when trees are pruned, and the soil opened for sowing. But in two cases, a May pastoral and an October hunt (Plates 40a, b), the eye is engaged more closely with pictures which suggest contour and variety—the hillsides of shepherds and huntsmen, the pools of water fowl and hawk. No one could pretend that this is landscape painting of a high order. It is nevertheless a statement of some importance about man, his use and enjoyment of the natural world. While the artists do not feel free to range widely in their observation, they have made some modest claims. Their landscapes are inhabited, and inhabited by different sorts of men, with different interests in pool, hill and animal. The shepherds are watched by others, more elaborately dressed, who stand at some distance from their labours, landowners perhaps, but spectators certainly. So, already, some place has been made for appreciation of a scene which originally recorded only participation. Even more strikingly, the hunt of October is dedicated to the pleasure of the huntsman's experience: the variousness of nature is celebrated through man at leisure, not through man at work, combating the hostility of earth and weather.

No other manuscripts of the same century, illustrating seasonal themes, are led to such experiment. The eleventh-century artist who provided simple paintings to accompany the sections *De Temporibus* and *De Vicissitudinibus Temporum* for a manuscript of the encyclopaedic treatise *De Universo*, by Rabanus Maurus,[43] neglects landscape entirely—only the actions of men interest him, and even then, action often gives way to stylized gesture. If winter demands more vigorous treatment for its ploughing and wood chopping, and autumn for its grape harvesting, spring still is satisfied with a symbolic figure carrying green branches, Chaucer's 'green and lusty May'.[44] The verbal context of these paintings gives them the richness they so deliberately reject as works of art. Seasons and months are seen as part of a universal pattern, with correspondences in the times of the church year, events in the Old Testament, states of spirituality. The direction is allegorical: summer foretells heavenly bliss, winter foreshadows the end of life:

'Aestas autem venturae jucunditatis praefiguratio est ... Aestas futura beatitudo ... Hiems vero tribulationem significat vel terminum mortalis vitae.'[45]

This Christian preoccupation with further meaning is permanent. At any time from the ninth to the fourteenth century, the warm dry season of summer can serve to remind man only of a spiritual state of ease. The summer hillsides from which William Langland passes to his visions of heaven, earth and hell, are hardly glimpsed again; sun and birdsong are most evocatively used for that 'futura beatitudo' promised to the patient poor:

'Now lorde, sende hem somer, and some manere ioye,
Hevene after her hennes-goynge, that here han suche defaute!'[46]

The background of concern is powerful. So, too, winter, though more frequently presented to the eye, and with some asperity—the seeds locked into midwinter soil, the mean shelter of stripped woodland[47]—essentially signifies suffering, 'vero tribulationem significat'. Langland's real theme is 'wo in wynter-tyme', the cold. night vigils by the cradle, the peasant in the rain-soaked lane:

'And yit is wynter for hem worse, for wete-shodde thei gange,
A-fyrst sore and afyngred ...'[48]

Only momentarily can his eye afford to be caught by icicles melting in December sunlight:

'as men may se in wyntre
Ysekeles in eveses, thorw hete of the sonne,
Melteth in a mynut-while to myst and to watre.'[49]

And for the most part, seasonal change is an image of mutability which should delay man no longer than it takes to contemplate death: fear lingers in the summer orchards:

'Lo, lo, lordes, lo! and ladyes, taketh hede,
Hit lasteth nat longe that is lycour swete,
As pees-coddes and pere-Ionettes, plomes and chiries.

133

That lyghtliche launceth up litel while dureth
And that that rathest rypeth roteth most saunest.'[50]

It is not surprising, therefore, that the advances made in the two early
English Calendar series are not sustained by most works of the twelfth and
thirteenth centuries, which are, on the whole, content to re-embody seasonal
material in schemes of cosmic significance. But it is still right to stress the
importance of the continual use of seasons and months motifs, even when
little is being done to extend their range. From the medieval point of view,
however terse and commonplace their mode of statement, these records of
man's year were invested with a seriousness which blended semi-scientific
interest with philosophic and religious belief. They bore witness to systems
greater than themselves. From the longer historical point of view, they
usefully preserved channels of communication for later artists and poets. If
they showed a strong tendency to establish themselves as stereotypes and to
remain unchanged over considerable periods of time, they were at least
accepted, familiar and available. They were the moulds into which new
materials, drawn from new areas of observation, could be poured. And they
provided, for the changing conditions of the later Middle Ages, a structure
and a sanction.

Both the nature of and the attitude to stereotyped seasonal portrayal in the
thirteenth century are clearly set out in the encyclopaedic *De Proprietatibus
Rerum*, compiled about 1240 by Bartholomaeus Anglicus, or Bartholomaeus
de Glanville, a Franciscan friar teaching in Paris. Book IX, which deals with
years and months and the Feasts of the Church, is part of a vast demonstration
of the theological basis of the heavenly hierarchies and the natural world. Its
context is the same as that of seasonal labour in the great sculpted designs of
cathedral doorways from thirteenth-century Amiens or Chartres.[51] And its
content is similarly composed—single figures, playing their traditional rôles,
by fireside, in field, vineyard and forest. The fourteenth-century English
translator of Bartholomew's work, John of Trevisa, follows his Latin source
closely to give us these little pictures in which action is stilled to gesture,
'frozen by distance'. Typically, January and February are indoor scenes of
feasting and warming—January has the double-faced god of the year 'with
two frontis . . . etinge and drynkynge of a coppe', February 'an olde man
sittinge by the fire hetynge and warmynge his feet and hondis'.[52] One
glance outside is sufficient; the distant sun cannot pierce the cold that envelops
the earth—'that tyme is moste stronge colde for the sonne is fer'. March 'is
ypeynt as it were a gardiner', pruning in 'ful chaungeable and unstedfast'

weather. April and May look less to practicalities than to pleasure: April is painted 'beringe a floure', May is summed up as a courtly hunting scene, 'a yonglynge ridinge and beringe a fowle on his honde', an 'aventure' in a countryside of green woods and luxuriant pastures, where 'alle thingis that beth alyve beth ymened to ioye and to love'. The months of high summer and autumn centre on peasant existence: June 'is ypeynte makynge hay, for that tyme hey is ripe in meedis', July, with its 'gret passinge hete', reaps with sickle, August threshes in a barn. September, 'ende of somyr', works 'in a vineyerd as a gardeyner gadringe grapis in a basket'. October sows seeds in the cold, dry soil. November is the swineherd among falling leaves, 'a cherle, betynge okes and fedynge his swyne with mast and ackornes'. December kills the domestic animals. With the exception, perhaps, of the month of May, details are chosen for their functional virtue: landscapes can be deduced from what Bartholomaeus writes about the year—they are hardly mirrored in his words. There is a strong sense of the need to control and simplify a world whose weather only rarely ceases to be 'chaungeable and unstedfast', the need to combat the difficult nature of soil and extremes of temperature. Like Langland, Bartholomaeus sees how winter torments wild creatures ('greveth and pricketh') and tests mankind. The conformity of his seasonal 'portraits' is a mark of unwillingness to be disturbed by that variety of seasonal life which would later 'disturb', but in a more creative way, poets such as the author of *Sir Gawain and the Green Knight*, Gavin Douglas, and painters such as Bruegel.

Similar attitudes are taken up in thirteenth-century poetry. One anonymous *January Song* from northern France speaks only of chimney corner and feasting:

> 'A la cheminée
> el froit mois de genvier,
> voil la char salee,   salted meat
> les chapons gras mangier;
> bon vin a remuer,
> cler feu sans fumée.'[53]

The jongleur Colin Muset gives us a mere glimpse of what lay beyond those comfortable occupations—the muddy roads of northern Europe, travelled by princes and their struggling retinues:

> 'Quant je voi yver retorner,
> lors me voudrois sejorner,
> se je pooie oste trover
> large, qui ne vousist conter . . .

> ne seroie pas envious
> de chevauchier toz boous
> apres mauvais prince angoissoux.'[54]

(When I feel winter coming on, I like to stay indoors, if I can find a generous host who will not count the cost . . . I am not anxious to ride mud-spattered behind a bad-tempered, arrogant prince.)

It was not until the next century that any northern European poet took his readers into the midst of real winter landscapes, asking them to register, with painful precision, just what rigours of climate and countryside drove men to fire, food, and shelter—to the closed door and the mind closed against the fragile and economical beauty of winter:

> 'the paragon of art,
> That kills all forms of life and feeling
> Save what is pure and will survive.'[55]

But at least these thirteenth-century poets are not bound by the strict and very ancient pictorial tradition for January. It is not the two-headed god of the dividing year who feasts the month away, but man himself. While some artists, quite early on, begin to displace Janus by a human figure, male or female, their dominant January image, well into the fourteenth century, was symbolic.[56] Poets seem to have been freer to choose, to re-interpret, to coalesce. February warming, January feasting are merged into one scene of conviviality and presented not objectively, as narrative, but from the very centre of the writer's experience. For other months of the year, too, the verse of this century stirs towards new ground, new action. The English author of *Kyng Alisaunder* takes a varied view of spring, summer and harvest, with more than one part of medieval society engaged, characteristically, in a landscape, and more than one part of nature illustrating the basic theme of growth, fruition and conservation. Certainly no Calendar picure of comparable date has such a variety of descriptive detail within a single frame, and it is ironic that the closest artistic parallel might be found in the eleventh century, which can show us an October hunting scene roughly similar to the harvest hunt of *Alisaunder*:

> 'Whan corne ripeth in hervest-tyde,
> Mery it is in felde and hyde . . .
> Knighttes willeth on huntyng ride—
> The dere galpeth by wode-syde.'[57]

If we look at an English Calendar series of roughly the same period, that of the so-called Peterborough Psalter,[58] the adventurous spirit of the English 'Alisaunder poet' seems more remarkable. This elegant and graceful manuscript, illuminated by some of the finest East Anglian craftsmen, pictures the months and their occupations in simple medallions of bright gold (Plates 41a–e). Its statement about man and nature is concise, controlled—one symbolic figure labours beneath an unchanging burnished sky. This Adam, isolated in the glare of eternity, has no right to see more than the earth he sows, the sheaf he binds; the variety of the world, man's shifting relationship, in his different rôles, to field and forest, are of no interest. What matters above all is the ineluctable succession of God's year, represented not only in an agricultural but also in an astral region. This is made visually clear by the strict parallelism of medallions, containing earthly labours and heavenly zodiac signs. The 'oolde pees' of the sky affirms the hard-won peace of man's dealings with his chosen world. Hints of a flickering desire to say more than this come rarely: the appearance of a girl with flowers for the month of May, instead of the more traditional youth on horseback, eloquently though briefly speaks of the elaboration of this scene in terms of a spring love idyll, an elaboration already begun in poetry, as *Kyng Alisaunder* proves. But it will not be long before painters will untie the girl's clasped bunches of flowers, and scatter them over the meadows to form an embroidered ground for courtship or betrothal.

While most of these thirteenth- or early fourteenth-century Calendar pictures confirm established patterns, their innovations are sometimes significant for what future artists may make of them. So, for instance, the bread baking motif for the month of December, which now occasionally replaces the familiar pig killing scene,[59] has nothing of its own to contribute to the development of seasonal landscape painting. But it helps to focus attention upon one kind of domestic activity in that winter world, an activity not simply concerned with life indoors, but with the bare woods of December, from which wood must be carried to light the oven-fires. And even in their rôle as perpetuators of tradition, the Calendar series did more than conserve. Though we may properly admire the efforts of the *Alisaunder* poet to extend the range of actors and material in his vignettes of the months, it is not his April passage, enlarged out of courtly literature, which is most impressive:

> 'Averylle is mery, and langeth the daye:
> Levedys dauncen and thai playe.
> Swaynes justneth, knighttes tournay,
> Syngeth the nighttyngale, gradeth the jay.'[60]   *chatters*

137

Rather, it is his description of Autumn, which puts together details from a group of labours of the months, and sees the rural work of August, September and October as one broad panorama: vineyards, cornfields, orchards, with pasturing animals just beyond the border of vision, but indicated by the presence of the watchful hayward:

> 'In tyme of hervest mery hit is ynough—
> Peres and apples hongeth on bough,
> The hayward bloweth mery his horne,
> In everyche felde ripe is corne,
> The grapes hongen on the vyne.
> Swete is trewe love . . .'[61]

Some of these details may have come from observation of the English countryside in late summer, but the sequence of loaded vines and pear trees makes observation of Calendar conventions just as likely a source—the continental grape harvest of September and October familiar in English cycles of the twelfth and thirteenth centuries. And though the hayward sounds a particularly convincing note, he has his counterpart in earlier manuscript paintings: eleventh-century English Calendar artists can show us a horn blower in a June cornfield, as well as a huntsman with horn in a September wood.[62] The poet's originality lies in his skilful adaptation of the classical motif of narrative 'punctuation',[63] in his combination of elements from diverse sources, in his evident enjoyment of rich associations, and not necessarily in his authentic version of a real English harvest. The Calendar themes stimulate others to action and experiment, while themselves exploring, tentatively, new approaches, new patterning.

The quality of that tentative exploration can be sampled in the Calendar from one of the most famous of all fourteenth-century English manuscripts, Queen Mary's Psalter.[64] Lavish and expansive, compared with the almost contemporary Peterborough Psalter, in its treatment of the months, it still imposes strict limits upon itself (Plates 42a–f). In deep winter, life is spent indoors: the fire that warms the February bedroom escapes as smoke through the chimney and the picture frame into the empty space of the manuscript page (f. 72v), not into the cold air of East Anglia, where it was painted. Little attention is paid to evocative colour, except from a purely aesthetic point of view: the corn of August (f. 78v) is greyish, against a red diapered background; the oak trees of November (f. 81v) are still green against a sky of tooled gold-leaf. Men, plants and animals are formalized into a design for action: grass and corn cutting (ff. 76v, 78v) are elegant as ballet movements. But if landscape is never allowed to speak for itself, at least the artist increases the number of occasions on which it might do so. The accompanying zodiac signs are presented informally, translated into human and outdoor experience, their symbolic and mythological context obscured. In this way, December, confined in its Calendar picture to the 'labour' of pig killing and butchering, only vaguely suggested as taking place on brown wintry soil, acquires a rustic goatherd scene for its sign of Capricorn (f. 83r). Similarly, March (f. 73v) is represented by both tree pruners and shepherds, April (f. 74r) by courtly flower pickers and peasant herdsmen—the additional episodes constructed wittily and thoughtfully about the signs of Aries and Taurus. The same diapered or tooled backdrops serve for labour and for sign. What is significant is the artist's desire to expand his illustration of the months in the direction of naturalism, and in the interests of variety.

The earlier decades of the fourteenth century are points of departure for landscape in art, as older motifs and attitudes harden or are perceptibly changed by the discoveries of new materials and of new tastes. The occupations of the months are everywhere—sculpted high into capitals, they can momentarily lose their human figures, and appear as a tangle of leaf and animal. So, in the stone of Southwell Minster, household pigs search hungrily among gigantic oak leaves for the acorns of November. Although naturalism is not complete, there is an unfamiliar sense of the eye's excitement by luxuriance and disorder in nature. So, too, in the margins and *bas-de-pages* of manuscripts, the activities of the year crowd against the severe lines of the Latin text, as if to invade the area of understanding with the living world of the senses—in the mid-century Luttrell Psalter (Plate 43a), for instance, which has something of Langland's passion for the hard facts of that country sequence from winter sowing to autumn harvesting, and attempts valiantly to record the effort of bringing 'harvest home' over the hill, or up the border of the page.[65] Even the artist of Queen Mary's Psalter interprets autumn threshing more freely and vigorously when he works in the informal space left vacant by the script: his peasant figures are more substantial, their movements stronger (Plate 43b).

In a great deal of this Calendar art, however, landscape is only fragmentarily present. The 'realism' of the Luttrell Psalter is still directed towards human beings and their immediate practical context in field or highway. There is the same impression of a countryside waiting to be admitted to our vision as there is in the words of Langland's plowman, Piers; both painting and poetry admit no more than plough, soil and grain sack, animals, plants and men:

'Ac ich have porett-plontes, perselye and scalones,
Chiboles and chirvylles and chiries sam-rede,
And a cow with a calf, and a cart-mare,
To drawe a-feld my donge the whyle drouth lasteth.
By this lyflode we mote lyve tyl Lammasse tyme;
And by that, ich hope to have hervest in my crofte.'[66]

Some medieval artists never needed to question this situation: others found it less satisfying. Not that there is any very clear division between those two groups at such an early date. Certainly, the first Calendar pictures to contain landscape only and the first vernacular poems to contain descriptions of the seasons unconcerned with agricultural labours come from the first half of the fourteenth century. But this is an area of experiment in which restlessness is more noticeable than decisive action, and it would be difficult to isolate any one movement as most important, either for the present or the future of seasonal landscape in art. If we are interested in the tendency of much fifteenth-century Calendar painting to focus upon courtly activities in country settings—a tendency particularly marked for the spring and early summer months of April, May and June, with their flower gathering, be-trothal and maying ceremonies, their motifs of 'aventure', and of hunting—then the sonnets of the fourteenth-century Italian poet Folgore da San Gemignano may seem significant for what is yet to come.[67] His pictures of the months are selective in their own special way: the landscape is extensive but adjusted to the nature of the 'signorili e cavallereschi' who inhabit it. Castles in the high Alps, cities on the plains are mentioned:

'D'agosto si vi do trenta castella
in una valle d'alpe montanina,
che non vi possa vento di marina . . .'[68]
    (For August I give you thirty castles in a valley of the mountainous Alps where no sea wind blows . . .)

But this Alpine August is a time for horse riding, not for looking at scenery. The streams in the mountain valley run 'gently and evenly, day and night', 'che vada notte e di traente e rasa'. Not for Folgore that later taste for 'a castle, precipice-encurled / In a gash of the wind-grieved Apennine'.[69] Good health and fine living come first. It is as a resort in the hot Italian summer that the Alps appeal—'where you shall be as healthy and bright as a star', 'per istar sani e chiari come stella'. What Folgore likes best in all the world is to be found in the June sonnet: a countryside of gently rolling slopes, flowered meadows, gardens and orchards, watered by sparkling streams and fountains. This is not substantially different from the landscape of the walled gardens of love—fresh, aromatic and pleasurable:

> 'Ch'abbia nel mezzo una sua fontanetta
> E faccia mille rami e fiumicelli,
> Firendo per giardini e praticelli
> E rinfrescando la minuta erbetta.
> Aranci, cedri, dattili e lumie
> E tutte l'altre frutte savorose
> Empergolate siano per le vie.'[70]

('And, in its midst, a little fountain with a thousand branches and rivulets, cutting through gardens and little lawns to refresh the little grasses. Oranges, citrons, dates and sweet lemons, and all savoury fruits shall be trained into long pergolas for the walks.')

And the occupations of the months are suitably similar—singing, dancing, the crowning of a prince of revels.[71] These graceful scenes, which never allude to the more basic labours of the land, or the men who are engaged in them, are forward-looking in that they assume the right to consider the seasonal world from a purely secular point of view. Palaces, thronged with courtiers, decorate the month of March, but;

> 'chiesia non v'abia, mai né monastero;
> lassate predicar i preti pazi.'[72]

('Let it have no church nor convent. Leave the silly priests to their gabble.')

For such purposes, which are as courtly as they are secular, the traditional labours of the months, with their moral, philosophical and practical implications, could not be attractive. Folgore allows them, occasionally, a brief entry into his descriptions, but in a changed form. January feasting, 'banquets with fires of burning rushes', 'corte con fochi di salette accese',[73] is one thread in a fabric of winter existence which weaves each episode of the patrician day into a sequence of festivity. Fortified with 'sweetmeats, comfits and sharp mixed wine', 'tregèa, confetti e mescere arazaio', protected by 'cloth of Douai and of Russia', 'vestiti di doasio e di rascese', the Sienese can venture briefly into the cold for snowballing with young ladies. The passing reference, in the December sonnet,[74] to the 'porci morti' which appear at table, evades rather than calls up the familiar pig killing 'labour' for that month.

But it could be argued that this Tuscan poetry was both enriched and impoverished by the exclusion of work from its world of beauty and pleasure. Folgore's 'alert interest in landscape'[75] is alert only to a particular kind of natural setting. Although he searches wide areas,

> 'Di guigno dovi una montagnetta
> Coverta di bellissimi arboscelli,
> Con trenta ville e dodici castelli,
> Che siano entorno ad una cittadetta.'[76]

('For June I give you a little mountain covered with the loveliest little trees, with thirty villas and twelve towers, not far from a little town.')

he looks for homogeneous rather than various material. The walls of the garden are down, the view is unimpeded, but the eye only registers, on a slightly larger scale, what the garden has conditioned it to expect and to desire:

> 'Fontane d'aqua che non vi rincresca,
> Donne e donzelle per vostra compagna.'[77]

('Fountains of water that shall never weary you, ladies and maidens for your company.')

If, indeed, this poetry does 'foreshadow' the Calendar painting of 1400, it does so in a very partial sense: it cannot prepare us for the best of early fifteenth-century work. The April, May and June landscapes of the *Très Riches Heures*, made before 1416 by the Limbourg brothers for Jean, duc de Berri, both confirm and resist the selective principles operating in Folgore's verse.[78] May, for instance, is given over entirely to the aristocratic festival of maying in the woods surrounding the castle and town of Riom; it is a countryside quite dedicated to the recreation of a particular social class, who responded, as we know from poetry, to the occasion of May as much as to its appearance:

> 'Du moys de may me vint la souvenance
> Dont maintes gens ont la coustume en France
> En ce doulz temps d'aler le may cueillir.'[79]

April brings a betrothal to the forefront of the picture, making the 'occupational' flower-picking a mere arabesque to that ceremony. Castles and castle garden again point to the control of landscape by courtly vision, as by courtly ownership. Outside the castle walls are parks with well-regulated tree lines, and the type of *arboscelli* which Folgore liked to imagine on his hill slopes. Even so, there is a greater variety here: the formal castle garden and the castle park are backed by a river, with slightly rougher land on the further bank. Two fishermen ply their nets, oblivious of their mannered overlords among the trees. June returns to the life of the peasant, and the labour of hay making on the edge of the Seine: it may be true that there is more of Queen Mary's Psalter than of Bruegel's *Hayfield* in its delicate arrangement of figures and implements, but at least it accepts the importance of the agricultural event, and widens out from this to observe the subtle gradations of colour in the grass and foliage of June. The peasant's occupation is still at the centre of the June world. In fact, whatever new pressures are exerted, whatever new models and materials come the way of fourteenth-century artists and poets, few of the really interesting advances in seasonal landscape portrayal are made quite outside the 'labours of the months' tradition.

And here, French Calendar painting for the first half of the century is much more important than Italian courtly verse. The experiments conducted by French artists such as Jean Pucelle are probably already influential in the more varied Calendar programme of Queen Mary's Psalter,[80] and they were to remain a vital source for themes and treatment well into the fifteenth century.[81] Pucelle and his associates, who illuminated books for a series of royal and aristocratic patrons from Jeanne d'Evreux, queen of Charles le Bel, to Jean, duc de Berri, made innovations in ways which increased the potential of the landscape element in Calendar pictures without dissociating it completely from its occupational character. Whereas Folgore in his sonnets cut himself off from whole areas of landscape experience by his preoccupation with the exclusive tastes of Sienese nobility, Jean Pucelle and his atelier, working in no less demanding circumstances, managed to get the best of more than one world. So, while some manuscripts stay close to tradition, and picture the months in occupations only, some are more adventurous. The first volume of the Belleville Breviary, illuminated about 1325, has a Calendar series which, even in its present fragmentary state, can be judged to be both experimental and influential. Close copies of this series in other manuscripts allow us to see, for the first time, beneath the arc of the travelling sun, the seasonable months reveal themselves in bare trees, heavy rain, budding branches, corn fields and acorn woods.[82] Not only have they been released from medallion and picture frame and set beneath the inverted bowl of heaven: they have been freed of human activity. With the exception of December (Plate 44a), which keeps a peasant to cut essential firewood, these landscapes stand alone—simple, and still restricted to a few components, but independent (Plate 44b). And in one manuscript of the group, the Prayer Book of Bonne of Luxembourg, painted before 1349, a further resolution is made (Plate 44c); the rainy skies of February, from which so many medieval Calendar figures had escaped to the cheerful fireside, become part of an outdoor scene which accommodates the zodiac symbol. Pisces, the sign of the Fish, suggests, as in Queen Mary's Psalter, a fishing episode; what is unique to the Prayer Book of Bonne of Luxembourg is the entirely appropriate fusion of seasonal detail and human activity. The artist has turned from the traditional indoor occupation for February, and has found a way of seeing man in a landscape, occupying himself usefully and naturally during the bleak days of 'February fill-dyke'.[83] This is a far more interesting 'blueprint' for landscape composition than the comprehensive but casual descriptive formulas of Folgore da San Gemignano. And it has been achieved in association with a traditional set of assumptions about man, nature and weather. Even in those landscape vignettes from the Belleville Breviary and its copies which reject a figure element, the choice of terrain and vegetation is still dictated by the old cycle of man's labours on earth: oak trees in November, pared branches in March, corn in August are still connected with the necessity of winter provisioning, tree pruning, harvesting (Plates 45d, a, b). Man the labourer is only just out of the picture; his hand is awaited. It may be significant, too, that where appropriate the zodiacal sign is often partly integrated into the landscape. So, as if to compensate for the loss of man-at-work, Virgo enters the August cornfield, Sagittarius hunts in November woods, and Libra gazes upon the loaded vines of September, as a courtly woman, with her symbolic scales only half in view (Plates 45b, d, c). It was a composite type of picture, landscape and labour, which formed the basis for the finest Calendar series ever commissioned by Jean de Berri—the *Très Riches Heures* (Plates 50a and 51a). For here, while the traditional occupation for the month may be transformed, or re-set into a more varied context, it is never totally disregarded. And while landscape appears in ravishing protean shapes as the year demands, it never dominates: courtiers or peasants, often both, are its constant inhabitants, utilizing it according to the customs of their appointed lives.

The passage from the Pucelle Calendar vignettes to the full miniatures of the Limbourg brothers is not a simple history of the copying, or even the compilation of various earlier Calendar motifs. And certainly, the development of landscape painting from 1325 to 1416 cannot be covered by that history, simple or complex. It was part of a 'process in which every form of imagination was involved, and which concerned the entire attitude of man towards his physical environment'.[84] To understand how the brief landscape notation of a Pucelle-type February—a few trees in the rain, or a single fisherman on the banks of a stream—could become the full statement of the Limbourg version, much more than French Calendar art has to be taken into account. Between 1320 and 1400 French painters were learning, from

Italian models, the elaborate art of perspective. From Italian scientific books, herbals, and *Tables of Health*, or *Tacuina*, they were studying illustrations of the physical world remarkable for fidelity to observable truth, and often, too, for a capacity to go beyond their prescribed duty of clarifying the text, as didactic purpose is overtaken by creative delight.[85] Sometimes the plant or condition of nature prompts the artist to imagine a landscape setting for his subject—a river scene for the fishing of pieces of aloe wood from the water, or a harvest scene for the gathering of cereals.[86] The debt of French, and, later, Franco-Flemish illuminators to Italian inventiveness in detailed 'nature studies' of all kinds is easily proved. The transmutation of the December miniature (Plate 51a) in the *Très Riches Heures*—the brutal and practical killing of the domestic pig replaced by the aristocratic ritual of the boar hunt—was worked with the help of a sketch from an Italian zoological picture book.[87]

Yet it remains true that Calendar art, and in particular that of northern Europe, was a strong cohesive force, acting upon rich but dispersed materials. The Pucelle manuscripts and their copies made modest beginnings, compared with the bold and free work of the Limbourgs in their most mature phase. All, however, confirm that the Calendar offered a natural means of expression for man's changing responses to his environment. It is significant that the Italian illustrator of 'Ordium', 'cereal', in one of the best-known of the *Tacuinum* manuscripts, reproduces a July or August harvesting scene of Calendar type when he wants to enlarge the scope of his composition: the mould was already prepared.[88] Similarly, when Jacquemart de Hesdin, before 1388, painted for the *Petites Heures* of Jean de Berri a Nativity (Plate 46a) which was to stress the newly-realized pathos of this winter event— 'Goddes sone whan he wolde be born / . . . he ches that tyme that was moost noyous and harde / as the colde wynter / nameliche to a / yong childe'—[89] he turned to a Calendar motif, picturing Joseph hunched in his chair, as many earlier artists had pictured February-by-the-fire (Plate 46b).[90] The 'moste stronge colde' of that time of year, always recognized but only ever partially substantiated in visual terms, is here given a fresh and powerful form: beyond the thin supports and worn thatched roof of the shed rise slate-green hillsides, shafted with white light, as if with powdered snow. Whether some devotional text persuaded Jacquemart to fulfil the implied conditions of February in the Calendars, we cannot know. But whatever his motives— pressure of a special religious context, awakening interest in wintry country-side—his action was to adopt a ready-made artistic convention for indicating man's suffering in hard weather. The old Calendar scene has been extended, not destroyed. It may not be without relevance to the developing Calendar landscape that in a slightly later work, the Brussels Hours,[91] also made for

145

Jean de Berri, Jacquemart provides events in the cycle of Christ's life with appropriate seasonal setting (Plates 47a and b): the leafy trees of the *Visitation* miniature give way to bare trees and icy hillsides in the *Annunciation to the Shepherds* and the *Flight into Egypt*. Those bare trees, at least, had already been chosen to characterize December and January in the Calendar vignettes of the Pucelle manuscripts.

There were, of course, some major artists of these years in northern Europe whose interest in landscape was strong, but not specifically directed towards its seasonal aspect. The part played by the phenomena of the outside world in the painting of the unidentified Boucicaut Master is very great indeed,[92] yet his versions of those same episodes from the life of the Virgin and Christ (Plates 48a and b)—Visitation, Annunciation to the Shepherds, Nativity, and Flight into Egypt—repeat, like a *Gloria*, a single flowering landscape of shrubs and trees, lakes and hills, in which farmhouses and swans speak of peaceful domesticity, and a sky exploding with rayed sun and stars speaks of divinity now incarnate.[93] The world of the Boucicaut Master is really concerned, in spite of its array of familiar detail, with 'bright shoots of everlastingness': shining tree trunks, gold-tipped bushes recall the transmutations worked upon nature by God. The fiery trellis of the sun proclaims, temporarily, a truce with wasting Time. When Calendar art provides this painter with episodes for border decoration, they are chosen from a strictly limited range—April flower picking, for instance, harmonizes with the atmosphere of golden afternoon which so often settles, like a luminous haze, over the central pictures.[94] It is not surprising that in a manuscript illuminated under his direction, the French translation of the *De Proprietatibus Rerum*, no attempt was made to interpret the Calendar descriptions of book IX.[95] The many landscapes accompanying the text (Colour plates II and IV) are charged with the light and colour of an endless summer day, whose perfect sky brings to mind the *aether* of Paradise as much as the 'gret passynge hete' of July. Variability is a theme of the Boucicaut Master only in so far as it can be treated in terms of light—the shifting tones of dusk, when sun, stars and darkness are in easy commerce. The English *Pearl* poet recollected that moment of equilibrium as he gazed into the Holy City—the moon rising through a sky still faintly sunlit.[96] The French painter saw it in the city of Paris (Plate 49), chequered with glinting rooftops and deep shade, the sky barred by sun and pierced by stars.

Nearly contemporary, *Pearl* and the art of the Boucicaut Master, especially as it appears in the Boucicaut Hours of 1405,[97] complement each other: both poet and painter describe a world of radiant forms in which colours, already rich, are burnished, glazed, and rinsed with gold and silver. The verbal glitter of the dream land, in *Pearl*, is exactly matched by the visual splendour of Boucicaut techniques: they alone could have given substance to its jewelled waters and luminous forests. In this particular English work, with its theme of immutable life and beauty,[98] the anonymous poet uses seasonal material only in a limited, even polemical, way. August 'quen corne is corven wyth crokes kene' has a very precise Calendar reference, but it also symbolizes a state of mind from which the poet-dreamer has to be won. The fruitfulness of the season is both comfort and torment: the grounds of his final consolation must be sought elsewhere. But that sensitivity to the sights and sounds of high summer, and to their special Calendar formulation, is real enough, even when briefly indicated. In another of his poems, *Sir Gawain and the Green Knight*, it has fuller play. That Calendar motifs should have some life in this romance, is not surprising: the action is intimately related to the cycle of the seasons and their festivals—beginning with a January feast, and ending in January snow. At least three of the winter indoor scenes are reminiscent of Calendar patterns for January and February. The celebration of the New Year at Camelot, which opens the poem, could be regarded in the same light as the Limbourgs' January picture from the *Très Riches Heures;*[99] in the one, a legendary king, in the other, a mortal prince, is complimented. The old occupation of the feasting winter deity is transformed, as indeed it had already been transformed by Folgore da San Gemignano, into a brilliant tribute to pleasure and magnificence:

> 'For ther the fest was ilyche ful fiften dayes,
> With alle the mete and the mirthe that men couthe avyse:
> Such glaum ande gle glorious to here,   *noise and revelry*
> Dere dyn upon day, daunsyng on nyghtes . . .
> For al was this fayre folk in her first age,
>   On sille.'[100]   *hall*

Gawain's arrival, on Christmas Eve, at the castle in the forest is a sophisticated version of February-by-the-fire:

> 'A cheyer byfore the chemné, ther charcole brenned,
> Was graythed for Sir Gawain graythely with clothes . . .   *prepared*
> And he sete in that settel semlych ryche
> And achaufed hym chefly, and thenne his cher mended.'
>
>   (875–6, 882–3)

As in many of the later Calendar pictures for January and February, warmth and food are combined:

> 'Sone was telded up a tabil on trestes ful fayre,   *set up*
> Clad wyth a clene clothe that cler whyt schewed . . .
> Segges hym served semly innoghe   *men*
> Wyth sere sewes and sete, sesounde of the best.' *various fine stews*
>   (884–5, 888–9)

Even the knight's awakening on a cold January morning and his preparation for that last stage of the journey to the Green Chapel reads curiously as if the poet were remembering some February vignette of the type found in Queen Mary's Psalter—the dressing of a nobleman, in a bedroom warmed against the 'wylde wederes of the worlde':

> 'Deliverly he dressed up er the day sprenged,   *quickly*
> For there was lyght of a laumpe that lemed in his chambre.
> He called to his chamberlayn, that cofly him swared . . . *promptly*
> Fyrst he clad him in his clothes, the colde for to were . . .'
>   (2009–11, 2015)

There are no literary precedents for this intimate, strongly imagined scene: the visual arts can, at least, provide a sketch for it. Yet the visual arts can provide only the barest suggestions for the poet's vivid and specific treatment of those 'wylde wederes' prudently avoided by Calendar figures. Even the glacial rocky slopes of Jacquemart de Hesdin, the rainy river banks of Jean Pucelle are tentative approaches to winter's meaning compared with this full encounter. The links with Calendar art are still clear—the poet's attitudes are man-centred, outraged as he is by the suffering of his hero in a winter landscape[101] which would be best viewed through a castle window, its cold light reflected upon the walls of a comfortable bedroom. Gawain will eventually have that pleasure—

> 'And Gawayn the god mon in gay bed lyges,
> Lurkkes whyl the daylyght lemed on the wowes.' *walls*
>   (1179–80)

But before then he must travel unseasonably, and realize, with Langland's peasants, that 'winter was worse' (726). What sets this poet apart from both Langland and the Calendars is his desire to substantiate the quality of winter in a series of startling and evocative natural images—nights of sleet, among crags and frozen waterfalls, days of frost, in tangled forest and swamp:

'For werre wrathed hym not so much that wynter nas wors,   *troubled*
When the colde cler water from the cloudes schadde
And fres er hit falle myght to the fale erthe.   *brown*
Ner slayn wyth the slete he sleped in his yrnes,
Mo nyghtes then innoghe, in naked rokkes
Theras claterande fro the crest the colde borne rennes   *stream*
And henged heghe over his hede in hard iisseikkles . . .   *icicles*
Bi a mounte on the morne meryly he rydes
Into a forest ful dep, that ferly was wylde,   *exceedingly*
Highe hilles on uche a halve and holtwodes under   *on each side*
Of hore okes ful hoge, a hundreth togeder.   *grey, huge*
The hasel and the hawthorne were harled al samen,   *entwined together*
With roghe raged mosse rayled aywhere.'   *spread everywhere*

(726–32, 740–45)

The choice of detail strikes an unusually personal note—who, before this, had noticed the thick rough moss growing in virgin forest, or the twisted thickets of hazel and hawthorn? Langland had made mention of the plight of birds and beasts in winter time, subdued by misery:

'thorw wynter thow hem grevest,
And makest hem wel ney meek and mylde for defaute.'[102]

but the context prevents any sharp realization of the scene. The real subject of the passage is patient poverty, and the natural world provides an analogy, no more, for man's condition. Where Langland notices resignation, the *Gawain* poet notices, and records, pain:

'With mony bryddes unblythe upon bare twyges,
That pitosly ther piped for pyne of the colde.'   *pain*
(746–7)

So, too, with Gawain's ominous dawn: December becomes January in a night of blizzard unimagined by any painter until long after the medieval period. The Calendar pictures can prepare us for the February snowscape of the Limbourgs, for the village snowshower in which Bruegel sets his most moving *Epiphany*,[103] but these are domestic winter-pieces by comparison. Here, beyond the shivering animals and peasants, beyond Gawain, uneasily sheltered—'Thagh he lowkes his liddes ful lyttel he slepes' (2007)—lie mountainous snow-filled valleys; the castle is beleaguered, swept by storm:

'Bot wylde wederes of the worlde wakned theroute;
Clowdes kesten kenly the colde to the erthe,

Wyth nye innoghe of the northe the naked to tene.   *pain, torment*
The snawe snitered ful snart, that snayped the wylde;   *stung the wild animals*
The werbelande wynde wapped fro the hyghe   *whistling, swooped*
And drof uche dale ful of dryftes ful grete.'

(2000–2005)

It is not difficult to find the traditional elements in this description, followed as it is by a version of February 'dressing-by-the-fire'; man and beast are still very much part of the landscape. But both the range and the particularity of vision are new. The driving snow and the shrill wind evoke a desolate and entirely credible terrain, far from farmyard and village street, a countryside familiar, no doubt, to fourteenth-century travellers, though rejected by fourteenth-century poets and artists as material for their art.

Nothing could better stand for that norm of medieval attitude and practice, here so strikingly questioned, than Chaucer's December verses in the *Franklin's Tale*. Calendar vignettes are not starting-points for him: rather they are admired models. His conflation of January feasting and February-by-the-fire motifs to serve as one picture is interesting, and will become more common in fifteenth-century Calendars. On the whole, however, it is a careful, even conservative version of Calendar winter that Chaucer decides to give us. In his exemplars,[104] Janus has not been displaced, the landscape takes in nothing but agricultural detail, the implications of the months are social and religious:

> 'And this was, as thise bookes me remembre,
> The colde, frosty seson of Decembre.
> Phebus wax old, and hewed lyk laton,   *copper*
> That in his hoote declynacion
> Shoon as the burned gold with stremes brighte . . .
> The bittre frostes, with the sleet and reyn,
> Destroyed hath the grene in every yerd.
> Janus sit by the fyr, with double berd,
> And drynketh of his bugle-horn the wyn;
> Biforn him stant brawen of the tusked swyn,
> And 'Nowel' crieth every lusty man.'[105]

By themselves, these lines are little more than pleasantly submissive to tradition: their context makes that submission intelligible. The narratives of both *Sir Gawain* and the *Franklin's Tale* are involved with seasonal change; in one case, the involvement is dramatic, in the other, purely conceptual. Gawain's ordeal is heightened by the delay of a year before he can set out on his quest. The ineluctable movement of the seasons and their festivals is, in this tense situation, unnerving. Seasonal stability contrasts with the instability of human affairs:

'A yere yernes ful yerne and yeldes never lyke.'   *passes quickly*
(498)

The cycle of the year is described in terms of weather and plant growth, whose natural struggles for dominion or survival end in tranquillity:

'Wrothe wynde of the welkyn wrasteles with the sunne,
The leves laucen fro the lynde and lyghten on the grounde,   *fall*
And al grayes the gres that grene was ere;
Thenne al rypes and rotes that ros upon fyrst,
And thus yirnes the yere in yisterdayes mony   *passes*
And wynter wyndes ayayn, as the worlde askes.'   *returns*
(525–30)

Only man is stabbed by fear of an unknown future as the autumn moon rises:

'Til Meghelmas mone
Was cumen wyth wynter wage.   *foretaste*
Then thenkkes Gawan ful sone
Of his anious vyage.'   *difficult journey*
(532–5)

In the *Franklin's Tale*, the passage from May to December charts, almost symbolically, the passage of unthinking confidence into stern reparation; what is promised carelessly in May is demanded in December. The seasons decorate and even underscore the theme, but their function is never that of capturing the imagination. May is an artful garden in sunlight, December a warm room in time of frost: the replacement of one by the other marks a changed temper and atmosphere rather than a real change of landscape or climate. It is as if, by choosing extremely formal models and materials for his May and December, Chaucer warns us that the poem's locus of action is only superficially in Brittany and in Orleans. Dorigen, walking to her winter garden moves into reality, out of delusion:

'My trouthe for to holde, allas! allas!'[106]

Seasonal landscape in *Sir Gawain and the Green Knight*, backed as it may be by Calendar and rhetorical tradition, reaches artistic maturity in some very special ways. Whether we are following Gawain on his journey or reviewing the whole sequence of yearly change, there is an imaginative freedom about the composition which is not easily paralleled in the visual arts. The deep summer perspectives of the Boucicaut Master, the chilly steep-rising hillsides of Jacquemart de Hesdin may come to mind, but they do not convey in paint what the *Gawain* poet conveys in words—the vision and the sense of a natural world which makes many different demands and bestows many different gifts upon man. It is this variousness of material and attitude which distinguishes his work in the romance. Winter is, by turns, horrifying and beautiful: it repels and engages. The eye takes in the strangeness of the cloud-topped hills, the glittering of the mountain becks, the whiteness of the snow:

'Mist muged on the mor, malt on the mountes; *hung about, was breaking up*
Uch hille hade a hatte, a myst-hakel huge. *mist cape*
Brokes byled and breke bi bonkkes aboute, *bubbled, splashed*
Schyre schaterande on schores, ther thay doun *dashing white on the banks*
 schowved . . .

Thay were on a hille ful hyghe;
The whyte snaw lay bisyde.'
     (2080–83, 2087–88)

The landscape, subjected to close scrutiny or powerfully and suggestively distanced, is, by turns, local, identifiable, and more generally symbolic of states of mind, of emotions. The forms which the year's phases take may derive, ultimately, from medieval treatise and Calendar; illustrations to herbals, rhetorical set-pieces on the character of the seasons, Pucelle miniatures of tree and plant life may all contribute:

'Wela wynne is the wort that waxes theroute, *Very lovely*
When the donkande dewe dropes of the leves, *moistening*
To bide a blysful blusch of the bryght sunne.'
     (518–20)

But the excitement they generate is not derivative:

'Wrothe wynde of the welkyn wrasteles with the sunne.'
     (525)

No other writer or painter of these years gives the impression of being capable of even holding in reserve such a wealth of responses to the outside world.

And this must set the English poem apart, even from the most lavish and sophisticated series of Calendar pictures to be produced within the following decades—the last work commissioned from the Limbourg brothers by Jean de Berri. The Calendar of the *Très Riches Heures* is as remarkable an advance upon all earlier miniatures—even upon the earlier Calendars of the Limbourg atelier—as the descriptive poetry of *Sir Gawain and the Green Knight* is upon earlier comparable writing. But it is still a little more readily explicable in a medieval context than the romance. Here, too, variousness is a distinguishing feature, demonstrated in themes and modes already partly approved by medieval taste. Innovation, for this Limbourg Calendar, consists less of moving into entirely new areas of attention and sensibility than of extending old. It is a triumph of compilation, in which diverse materials and impulses are brought to exquisite harmony. And, further, it is a triumph of equilibrium—a quality not only of style but of attitude: by comparison, the seasonal poetry of *Sir Gawain and the Green Knight* is extravagant, exploratory. For there are limits to the Limbourgs' naturalism. Nothing could be more remote from Gawain's travels through 'mony misy and myre' (749) than the slow quiet journey of man and beast up the smooth, snow-covered inclines of the February miniature (Plate 50a). Nothing could be more remote from those wild autumn skies filled with wind and sun (525ff) than the Limbourg October, with its peasants at work under a clear blue firmament, only hinting of winter transparency. The mountains of the poem, ringed strangely with mist, are arresting, both physically and imaginatively. The mountains of the Calendar are accommodated to pleasure: soft cones of summer lightness, they are no more than a dream of distance.[107]

But if, for the Limbourgs, it is still true that 'the world is a garden, beautiful and secure',[108] the garden now admits more than ever before. And if the Calendar is a magnificent compilation, it is also intricate and inventive. Characteristically medieval in their willingness to work with motifs announced by others, the Limbourgs were unusual for the variety of their sources, for their unerring sense of how to bring widely differing elements into pictorial unity, and for their tact in adjusting fresh interpretation to old themes. So, while they return us, in many of their miniatures, to the occupations of the months, those occupations are allowed to prompt a landscape more detailed and extensive than any hitherto. Hints in earlier painting and poetry are developed to the point of originality: the art of composition assumes a major creative rôle. The February picture, building upon ideas and exemplars only partially recoverable, combines December wood chopping[109] and its own motif of warming with a snowscape which, for the first time in painting, is not only unmistakable but aesthetically bold and pleasing. Folgore da San Gemignano had written of snowballing in January,[110] and January snow, faintly dusting the hillsides of earlier nativity scenes,[111] had already fallen more thickly in one fresco (Plate 50b), from Trento, in northern

Italy.[112] The month of 'banquets with fires of burning rushes, rooms and beds with beautiful embroideries'[113] had been given its outdoor character at last, more fully than in the Pucelle manner, with its few bare trees. For here, as in Folgore's verses, courtiers play at snowballing. But what persuaded the Limbourgs to set February in deep snow—a month which the Pucelle artists had begun to elaborate as a rainy season—we can only guess. Both manuscript and fresco painting lie behind their work; among the books in Jean de Berri's library they must have known the *Petites Heures* (Plate 46a), which linked February warming and icy countryside,[114] and on their travels in Italy[115] they might have heard of, or seen, some January fresco similar to that of the Torre dell' Aquila. Drawing, no doubt, upon a number of sources, and encouraged by the ambitions and expert tastes of their patron, they designed a version of February which is as wealthy in its reminiscences of the past as it is in its forecasts of the future. Two winter occupations come from the religious Calendar tradition. Their setting, with depth suggested by carefully placed spires, rooftops and peasant driving a laden donkey into the middle distance, has a more complicated line of descent. Represented in simpler form, by earlier Limbourg miniatures,[116] it may have come to the notice of the brothers from other manuscripts associated with the court of Jean de Berri. In a Crucifixion picture, from a Book of Hours thought to have been painted in 1405 under the direction of Jacquemart de Hesdin, we find the same moulded hilly landscape, stretching away, with the same distancing devices of buildings and driven beast.[117] And if the source of this landscape setting can ultimately be found in a Sienese fresco of the preceding century (Plate 55),[118] the finished Limbourg picture of farm, farmyard, copse and 'a bread-white hill over the cupped farm' owes something also to garden formalism, to border detail. The farm is neatly enclosed in its wattle fence; the trees, slim and close-set, are familiar; pecking birds, bee hives, farm implements are not, in themselves, strange to the decorative borders of manuscripts.[119] But here, all is presented in natural logical relationship: the reasonable beauty of the scene, in which the activities of man and animals are closely integrated with the weather, is satisfying in its thoroughness. Here we can believe in the vital connection between leaden brooding sky and midwinter snow, between peasants, drowsing by a cheerful fire, and the swing of the woodcutter's axe, between huddled sheep and labourers swathed against the cold. The potential of the old Calendar themes is released, and an adequate language found for describing afresh the old 'landscape of action'. But more than that—in a domestic and agricultural context quite alien to the *Gawain* poet the Limbourgs have conveyed something of that same feeling for the sensuous power of winter, its appeal to the interested eye as well as the numbed body:

'... The smell of hay in the snow and the far owl
Warning among the folds, and the frozen wold
Flocked with the sheep-white smoke of the farm-house cowl ...
The puffed birds hopping and hunting ...
And all the woken farm at its white trades.'[120]

Other miniatures in the cycle pay more attention to courtly life, and to courtly compliment. The great castles of Jean de Berri, rising against gold-flecked, lapis-lazuli skies of oriental brilliance, acknowledge the ties of patron and artists, as they also acknowledge, in pictorial terms, those other terrestrial hierarchies—peasant and overlord, field, forest and seigneurial park. But except for the months of April, May and August, courtly pursuits remain accessories to the Limbourg vision of the world; spring pageants of love and summer hunting expeditions test their expertise rather than their originality. Once again, it is the month and its labours which engage them most rewardingly—the austere prelude to spring, in March ploughing and sowing, the peaceful outcome of harvest and sheep shearing in July, the return to harsh earth and thin sunlight in October. Appropriately, for January and December, the beginning and end of the year's turning, the established labour is not so much replaced as transformed by courtly demand. Behind the ceremony of the Duke's New Year Feast, Janus presides, while the death of the wild boar in the forest of Vincennes commemorates, in its bright ritual of violence, the more casual and practical slaughter of the domestic pig in meagre farmyards. This December painting (Plate 51a) says almost as much as that of February about the meticulous balance of old and new in Limbourg art. The pattern of activity is traditional—a mid-season death. The setting is borrowed from tradition with its thick wood, such as romance or dream poem might have prescribed, curved, like a garden wall, about a tableau. But the form of that tableau is taken from a Lombard pattern book, not from a northern European Calendar,[121] and the mood of the scene is complex, at once mysterious and explicit, melancholy and energetic. Here, on a short December day, the piled woods, rich with the colours of dissolution, enclose man and dying beast; beyond them, the chalk-white towers of the château de Vincennes are stark as branch and twig already stripped for winter. The leaping dogs, the watchful huntsmen, the trees thrusting from a cloud of autumn leaves surrounded the torn animal on the dark earth with emblems of continued life.

In the *Très Riches Heures*, seasonal landscape achieves that status which earlier Calendar painters had tentatively proposed for it. Not quite independent, it respects old contexts, old affiliations. The twelve phases of the year rest beneath the arc of the zodiac and are dominated by the golden chariot of the sun; the deep blue of the sky of France merges into the deeper tones of the unchanging heaven of the constellations; man, beast and nature observe and conform. But, given this restatement of an ancient pattern, the Calendar of the *Très Riches Heures* quietly confirms that the pattern allows for a wider range of interpretative skills than had been suspected. It neglects nothing that tradition could supply, but it claims the right to adjust, expand and add according to personal taste and individual observation. Most important, it confirms not only the seriousness of Calendar themes, but their virtually untried artistic potential. If the April and May miniatures are still influenced by garden imagery, if winter, in February, is still a shade prettier than experience registers, the last contribution of the Limbourgs, the October miniature, moves in a direction which can only lead to Bruegel. Thoughtful, robust, confidently and minutely observed, this version of autumn and its appointed labours marks the arrival of the Calendar on the threshold of high art. While the truth of the biblical text is undiminished— 'maledicta terra in opere tuo, in laboribus comedes ex ea cunctis diebus vitae tuae'—its power to limit vision and dictate approach is passing.

Similar to the *Roman de la Rose* for the way in which it gathered up and re-expressed all preceding descriptive material—secular or religious, courtly or philosophical, northern European or Italian—the Calendar of the *Très Riches Heures* had no such immediate effect as that poem. Not until the end of the fifteenth century did artists begin to assimilate and re-produce, in their own way, what the Limbourgs had brought into life. In the Calendars of the intervening years, some progress is made, but on a small scale, and with reference to modes and styles from which the Limbourgs had departed. The Calendar of the Bedford Hours,[122] for instance, painted about 1423 for John, Duke of Bedford, Regent of France, preserves an older format. Winter is predominantly an indoor existence, and landscape slips easily from naturalism to decorative artificiality. Seasonal change is indicated by occupation only—the trees of November are as fresh as those of April, and the skies, star-studded, scrolled and diapered, are varied for beauty, not for time of year. Artists working for the Angevin court, at about 1418, used an earlier Limbourg Calendar as their model—that of the *Belles Heures*, made between 1402 and 1413 for Jean de Berri (Plate 52a). Although it is clear, from miniatures outside the Calendar series, that they knew of the *Très Riches Heures*, yet their most famous book, the *Grandes Heures de Rohan*,[123] is patterned upon the older, single-figured plan which the Limbourgs eventually rejected (Plate 52b). The modest quatrefoils of the *Belles Heures* are enlarged to full-page representations, but the months are evoked as flamboyant ceremonies, with activity and zodiac symbol woven into a thick even tapestry of tree and sky.

The world of the seasons, however, often closely associated with country labours, begins to assert itself in painting outside the strict Calendar tradition, just as it does in poetry, as we shall see in the next chapter.[124] The enthusiasm of fifteenth-century artists for looking beyond the confines of wall or wattle fence, beyond the fixed spring or summer of the paradise garden to the mutable landscape of cornfield and forest,[125] is symptomatic. The backgrounds to fifteenth-century religious pictures increasingly register not only devotion but time of year: Sassetta's *Journey of the Magi*[126] has the frosty earth and leafless trees of January, its pale skies scored by a line of snow geese. The Dijon *Nativity* of the Master of Flémalle is backed by a taut precise winterland, trees delicately traced in still air. Bellini's *Madonna of the Meadows* unites season, labour and religious theme in a particularly moving way: Virgin and child are presented against an early spring 'landscape of action', the pure cold tones of countryside, the intent, obedient attitudes of man and beast harmonizing with the mood of the pensive woman seated on the grass.

For all this, there are an equal number of paintings which ignore such matters. The growing delight of Flemish artists in landscape work, either as broad hinterland to religious subject or as a detailed vista, glimpsed through open door and window, did not always guarantee a special interest in the changing shades and aspects of the terrestrial year. The tendency to codify and stabilize was always strong: a formula, once proved successful, would be adopted, time after time. And so the rose garden was often exchanged for a domestic landscape of equally formal components—swan, farmhouse, meadow and orchard sleeping in a June haze as unvarying as the reflected light of Paradise.[127] The flowers of summer may accompany an autumn *Visitation*, while the foliage and colours of spring may serve for the whole sequence of events from Visitation to Crucifixion.[128]

Not surprisingly, it was the Calendar, with its strong attachment to the concept of change, which decisively established the natural world as material both serious and sufficient for artists. The completion of the Calendar of the *Très Riches Heures*, by Jean Colombe, working about 1480 for its new owner, Charles, duc de Savoie, begins to make this clear. Freed from the necessity of particular courtly compliment such as the Limbourgs willingly recognized, Colombe provided a November acorn gathering, equally preoccupied with Savoyard landscape and with seasonal labour. Castle, like village, is scaled down to allow rock and tree and distant river to invite the eye. In the immediate foreground, peasants and their hungry

animals on the edge of a dark wood, stress, even more than the labourers of
the Limbourg October, the sombre urgency of the autumnal day.

What Colombe lacks in grace and precision of style, he makes up in
vigour and expansiveness. The slight sense of aesthetic distancing which
makes itself felt in some parts of the Limbourg miniatures has disappeared,
and we are more closely involved with both labour and countryside. And
those Flemish manuscript painters of the late fifteenth and early sixteenth
centuries who eventually turned to the whole cycle as model often interpreted
it more in the spirit of Colombe than in the spirit of the Limbourgs. His
appreciative rendering of stocky peasants, intent upon their work, and of
landscape almost uncomfortably present to the senses was attractive to them.
Hence, in the most extreme examples, the crowding of picture space with
every kind of realistic detail—a foreground busy with human activity, a
background filled with natural and man-made features of town and
country.[129] The vitality of the old occupation motifs is undiminished;
against the misty screen of trees in December, pig-killing and bread-baking
are still as frequent as aristocratic boar-hunting, and no February snow scene
lacks its humble fireside and woodyard.[130] Even the splendid Calendar of
the Grimani Breviary,[131] based directly upon the Calendar of the *Très Riches
Heures*, increases its social realism at the same time as it opens up landscape
vistas unexplored by the Limbourgs. The February miniature is more explicit
than its original in every way, from icicles hanging from cottage eaves,
and small boy urinating in the snow, to windmill and windblown trees on
the horizon. The December miniature (Plate 51b) reduces the mystery
of the Limbourg scene, thinning the dense forest to sparse woodland, letting
in the cool light of winter, and rationalizing, as the Limbourgs never
attempted to do, the spatial relationship of castle and hunt by a careful
tracing of path and horsemen in the middle distance. The assertive and
zestful realism of the Grimani Calendar is accompanied by a waning
interest in zodiacal detail. The golden chariot of the Limbourg sun has faded
to a spectral paleness—it is an apparition, not a controlling force, moving
through a heaven bereft of the old constellations, above a world no longer
conscious of their power. Around the main picture and Calendar area, small
marginal vignettes, set into arches and columns, illustrate religious subjects
and further seasonal episodes. The 'pageant of the months' takes on a new
meaning, as many activities, many aspects are put on record—the June hayfield enriched by heron catching and eel fishing, the July harvest and sheep
shearing by goose-boy on a river bank, the December boar-hunt by domestic
pig-killing and by the baking of bread (Plate 52c). This view of the year, its
landscapes and occupations, is comprehensive enough to bring Bruegel to
mind. It is still, however, a disparate view, which awaits harmonization into a

single vision. Significantly, it is the Grimani rendering of Jean Colombe's November which goes furthest towards reaching that harmony. Here a number of country pursuits—swine-tending, hare-hunting, preparation of the earth—are pictured in muted autumn scenery, gently receding over misty fields from oak wood to distant church spire. In this instance, the balance of human figures and the landscape they inhabit is perfectly maintained. In other places, and noticeably where no very clear lead was given by the original, that balance is more uncertain. Courtly retinues, celebrating the seasons in April, May and August, sweep through the countryside, practically obscuring it. Once again, it is agricultural labour and animal husbandry rather than the outdoor pastimes of the nobility which encourage the artist to look intently and creatively at his surroundings.

In the Grimani Calendar we sometimes have to accept the sacrifice of compositional grace to dramatic liveliness, of elegance to bold coverage, but this is not true of one other Calendar painted in Flanders in the early sixteenth century, by Simon Benninck, of Bruges.[132] Knowing that Bruegel was familiar with Calendar landscape in Flemish manuscripts, and used it as a ground base for his fine commissioned studies of the seasonal year,[133] we might still hesitate before allowing more than the Grimani November to be a positive anticipation of what was to come. Parts of individual pictures look clearly towards Bruegel: the thick mass of ripe corn in the Grimani July miniature, half-reaped, and the single tree, shelter from summer heat, are to be central features of Bruegel's *Corn Harvest*. But Benninck's work, on at least two occasions, tells us that the transformation of Calendar art was already complete when Bruegel began his series. The March and December miniatures (Colour plates v and vi) concern themselves with the labours of the months, one with the horticulture and forestry of early spring, the other with the winter 'labour' of the boar hunt, as the Limbourgs had interpreted it, a century earlier. The ease with which these subjects are accommodated in a landscape they have helped to suggest, the skilful proportioning of human interest and natural beauty, the precision of design and the subtle range of colouring all speak of lessons learnt from the past, and redirected towards the future. Appropriately, the March miniature both records, and dismisses, the enclosed garden. In the foreground, ladies visit a formal plot where a peasant digs over a patch of earth—part of the fence is down, and the whole area exposed to the sounds and sights of wood cutting, of life in farm and castle, and in the open countryside beyond moat and barn. The equilibrium, so characteristic of Limbourg painting, is here too, but it has to operate in a field of observation wider and more varied than that of the Limbourgs. For these reasons, Benninck's version of their December boar hunt is instructive: closer, in many respects, to the Limbourg format, even to the Limbourg spirit, than the Grimani main *December* miniature, the picture emerges as one of the most original of these seasonal descriptions which lie between medieval and Renaissance periods. Where the Grimani artist increases the number of huntsmen present or arriving at the scene of the kill, Benninck reduces it; he keeps the vivid impression of an event in the still depths of a forest—the place is protected and secluded. The castle background has disappeared, and in its place, woods heaped upon woods stretch to a range of rocks and a bright horizon. Paintings such as this, of tangled undergrowth and sharply etched trees, of shaded skies and obdurate winter crags, must have prepared the way for Bruegel's dark and powerful essay on man, beast and season, *The Return of the Herd* (Plate 36).

Chapter Six

LATE MEDIEVAL

The Art of seeing Nature is a thing almost as much to be acquired as the art of reading the Egyptian hieroglyphics.[1]

This chapter will be mostly concerned with the development of landscape realism, of the 'landscape of fact',[2] outside Calendar pictures, in the fourteenth and fifteenth centuries: the emphasis is on elements of structure, perspective and form, on the concept of *scene*, though the seasonal themes delineated in the previous chapter will be touched on where relevant. The story of this development begins with the stylized relics of high medieval and the *locus amoenus*, and ends with the triumph of landscape as an independent art form in the *Aeneid* Prologues of Gavin Douglas, and in the paintings of Giovanni Bellini and of Bruegel. There is consciousness of change, especially in Italy, but no steady development; separate traditions overlap, are submerged, re-appear, so that at any one time there can be a century of difference between Milan and Venice, Paris and Bruges, London and Edinburgh. But the general direction of change is clear: from an observation of nature which always and systematically subdues natural phenomena to larger philosophical and spiritual meanings, which is essentially symbolic, to an observation of nature which finds the beauty of appearances philosophically explicable and aesthetically satisfying, and which can rest therefore on its actual forms. The reasons for this change, which amounts to no less than a change in the nature of perception, are no doubt deep and various, but the contribution of particular individuals, of particular poets and painters with perceptions bolder than most, and the technical skills to translate them, should not be underestimated: Petrarch, perhaps Petrarch above all, the Limbourgs, Van Eyck, Piero della Francesca. The renewal of classical influence played its part, and so did changes in the natural environment, for it can hardly escape notice that the two great centres for the growth of landscape painting, Flanders and northern Italy, were also the two most advanced industrial and urbanized areas in Europe. Cities produced the taste, for, as we have seen, all landscape is urban pastoral; they also provided the fashionable demand, and the technology (as in the development of oil painting) to satisfy it.

It is possible that 1500 is too early a date to declare the emergence of landscape as an independent art form, though it suits our tastes to do so. The

161

artists of the Grimani Breviary[3] had an ostensible 'subject' for all their minatures, to which landscape was still accessory, and Giovanni Bellini's foregrounds are still dominated by religious figures. Even Giorgione's *Tempesta* presumably has a subject, whatever it may be. Perhaps we have to wait till the seventeenth century, till Vermeer, for the truly objective landscape of fact. It is certainly possible, at the other extreme, to look too early for burgeoning realism in medieval landscape art. Accuracy of natural form is one of the signatures of early Gothic, but it has little to do with taste for, or even the apprehension of, landscape. Much has been made, for instance, of the leaves of Southwell Minster, where the delicate carving, in exact imitation of nature, of leaves of oak, maple, vine, hawthorn, rose, hop, ivy, and other trees, in the chapterhouse and its vestibule, seems to mark a new naturalism around the end of the thirteenth century.[4] Pevsner associates this with a decline in the monastic spirit of *contemptus mundi*, and a growing delight in nature's beauty as evidence of God's creative love, first expressed by St Francis and then philosophically systematized in Aquinas.[5] He associates it further with the detailed and accurate descriptions of animals and plants in the *De Animalibus* and *De Vegetabilibus* of the roughly contemporary Albertus Magnus. Albertus, in contrast to other encyclopaedists such as Vincent of Beauvais, who concentrate on the medical use and symbolic purport of plants, actually describes what he has seen in the oak and the maple, commenting:

'It is not sufficient to know in terms of universals; we must seek to know every individual thing according to its own nature.'[6]

But the case can be pressed too hard. The leaves of Southwell evince no more than a limited and *ad hoc* naturalism, and are not evidence of a radical change in the mode of perception. It is a sporadic realism, no more than had been long familiar to the Middle Ages from the illustrations to works on natural history, such as the *Herbarium* of Sextus Apuleius Barbarus (MS Bodley 130), illustrated at Bury St Edmund's, or to treatises on hunting, such as the *De arte venandi cum avibus*, done about 1250 for Frederick of Sicily.[7] There is no sense of scale in the Southwell leaves, of relations in space; no attempt, as Pevsner says, 'to place individual objects into relation with each other or nature as a whole'.[8] Without this sense of space, such realism as there is can be only local and fragmentary, truth to nature always being subordinated to the integrity of the pattern. The same may be said of similar carvings, done about the same time, in the chapterhouse at York minster, and of the wonderfully accurate carvings of rose bushes, strawberry plants, vines, watercress, ferns, acorns and maple leaves which begin to appear, from about 1250, on the façade of Notre-Dame at Paris. As for Albertus, his commitment to the world of individual and actual forms is equally sporadic, for he mixes with it a dependence on classical, biblical and encyclopaedic material as fanciful as that in Alexander Neckam's *De Naturis Rerum*, nearly a century earlier. The occasional startling accuracy of his descriptions, or of similar descriptions in practical treatises, such as that of the behaviour of ducks in the *De arte venandi cum avibus*,[9] or of particular pictures and carvings, seems to have been absorbed without impact into a symbolic programme of equally startling inaccuracy. Though it is important that this ability to record objectively should never have been entirely lost, and though the observations of naturalists and their illustrators were to play a specific part in the later development of landscape art, it is still true that in these earlier centuries the medieval mind seems to have had an extraordinary capacity for ignoring or assimilating without notice what was doctrinally irrelevant. It sought in nature 'not knowledge but edification, not enlightenment but the exemplification of preconceived ideas'.[10] Nor was the *contemptus mundi* in decline; in fact, it might be said that what Europe took from the Franciscan movement was more than anything a renewed sense of the spirit of apostolic self-denial.

The realism of early Gothic book illumination, whatever may be said of the importance of Calendars in preserving traditions of the labours and therefore of potential opportunities for seasonal landscapes,[11] is equally limited. The tree in the picture of *Abraham entertaining the Angels* in the St Louis Psalter (1256) is recognizably an oak, but leaves and acorns are disposed according to a purely decorative pattern, and the foliage as a whole is rigid and solidly outlined as if by the lead moulding of a stained-glass panel.[12] Landscape motifs are being used to categorize rather than to represent; their conventional shorthand indicates a garden, a forest, water, outdoors, but does not attempt to remind us of it visually. There is some sense of dimension, if only that of foreground and background, but the background is impenetrable with *rinceaux*, diapers, tessellations or architectural features, a surface rather than a view, and the foreground has the figures distributed decoratively in a line across it. This is the character of book illustration well into the fourteenth century, and in England for still longer. The *Gloria* picture in the De Lisle Psalter (*c.* 1330), with its sheep climbing up the borders, shows how the sense of scene is still totally controlled by the frame and page surface.[13] Whatever movement towards realism there is takes place in the borders, where the artist has greater freedom to experiment and is less dominated by the stylized ritual of miniature and initial. Hence the borders full of naturalistic birds, animals, leaves and flowers in the East Anglian psalters of 1300–50, particularly the Ormesby, Gorleston and St Omer Psalters, and in French manuscripts of the same period.

Occasionally, this peremptory naturalism will invade the picture, as in the *Apocalypse* scene of MS Royal 19.B.xv, where the sketchy but freely drawn and just recognizable trees repeat the experiments of the same artist in the *bas-de-page* of the Magi in Queen Mary's Psalter.[14] But on the whole, in East Anglian manuscripts at least, this border ornamentation means little in the development of landscape; the attention to detail is quite unmatched by a sense of its placing, and the minute realism has in the end no more reality than the fantasy of the grotesques. Perhaps an exception should be made in the case of some of the *bas-de-pages*, the vignettes of everyday life and noble recreation, influenced by Calendar material, such as the falconry scene in the page of *Jesus in the Temple* in Queen Mary's Psalter,[15] where an extraordinary visual realism is combined with a power of organizing a scene which adumbrates, if it does not state, the principles of landscape composition.

In French book illustration, as in English, it was in the margins and *bas-de-pages*, as well as in the specialized context of the Calendar pictures, that the movement towards realism first asserted itself, especially in the work of Jean Pucelle, in the birds, monkeys, dragonflies and butterflies of the Belleville Breviary. There is nothing in English quite like the *trompe l'oeil* butterfly of f. 24.[16] Pucelle also made a break with tradition in showing the months, in the Calendar pictures, by a changing landscape rather than by human figures, thus preparing the way for the Boucicaut Master and the Limbourg brothers.[17] But Pucelle himself makes little of this: his miniatures remain surface adornments of the written page, with the fragile and decorative elegance which is characteristic of this Gothic style. Without the intervention of the Flemish painters, it is likely that his influence would have petered out in a fashionable and pretty mannerism, as it does in the miniatures of Jean Bondol, 'le maitre des boquetaux', with their scalariform terrain and characteristic stylized little clumps of trees, or *boquetaux*. It is this decorative landscape which dominates the other arts, such as tapestry, where 'landscape' is nothing more than the naturalistic marginalia of book illustration transplanted into ornamental compositions without depth or horizon. Something in the physical nature of tapestry would explain this emphasis on surface filling, but the frescoes in the Garde-Robe chamber of the papal palace at Avignon are little different. They illustrate courtly diversions such as fishing and hunting, and show considerable interest, in their forest and garden backgrounds, in natural flora and fauna. There is even a hint of spatial dimension in the fishing picture,[18] in the 'wrong' perspective of the fish tank (Simone Martini's influence has been suggested), but the overall effect, of naturalistic detail disposed according to a primarily decorative scheme, is centrally representative of this Gothic tradition.

It was a very persistent tradition, even in Italy, as in the Lombardy miniatures of the late fourteenth century. The Book of Hours painted by Giovannino de'Grassi for Gian Galeazzo Visconti (*c.* 1385) is a high-water mark of this aristocratic, refined, decorative art. Another, perhaps the consummation of the Gothic landscape in Europe, is the *Madonna in the Rose Garden* of Stefano da Zevio,[19] packed with symbolic detail, but airless, in a void, dematerialized (Plate 32a). The Frankfurt *Garden of Paradise* reflects the same spirit (Plate 21): the details are very precise, the flowers are all recognizable species, but the composition disdains perspective just as the symbolic significance of everything in the garden disdains the evidence of the eye. Where this tradition of decorative garden landscape does not pertain, there is, except in Flanders and northern France and northern Italy, no tradition of landscape. John Siferwas and Hermann Scheere are the best miniaturists of their period (*c.* 1400) in England, but neither shows any interest in landscape. A *Crucifixion* by Siferwas in the Sherborne Missal[20] has a suggestion of broken terrace in the foreground and some cramped trees in the background which horses seem to be trampling underfoot, but the sky is still a patterned backdrop and most of the foreground action is taking place on what appears to be an actual carpet. The famous *Troilus* frontispiece to Corpus Christi College, Cambridge, MS 61, of Chaucer reading to the assembled court, has perhaps some idea of space, and the castles may be imitated from the châteaux of the Parisian schools, but the bright colours and general liveliness cannot disguise a weird unlikeliness in both detail and perspective.

The persistence of two-dimensional decorative landscape in art is matched by the persistence of stereotyped spring introductions in poetry, particularly in lyric. These have a chiefly formal existence, serving usually to announce a theme of love-longing, which is intensified by the season, as in this poem from the early fourteenth-century collection in Harley MS 2253:

'When the nyhtegale singes, the wodes waxen grene,
Lef and gras and blosme springes in averyl, y wene,
ant love is to myn herte gon with one spere so kene...'[21]

The detail is conventional, and is repeated from poem to poem, functioning like a kind of shorthand when reduced to the minimum:

'Nou sprinkes the sprai,
al for love icche am so seeke
that slepen i ne mai.'[22]

In one poem from Harley 2253, however, the celebration of spring, the *reverdie*, is extended so as almost to swallow the love complaint:

'Lenten ys come with love to toune,
with blosmen and with briddes roune, *song*
that al this blisse bryngeth;
dayes-eyes in this dales,
notes suete of nyhtegales,
uch foul song singeth.
The threstelcoc him threteth oo; *thrush*
away is huere wynter woo,
when woderove springeth. *woodruff*
This foules singeth ferly fele,
ant wlyteth on huere wynne wele *warble*
that al the wode ryngeth.

The rose rayleth hire rode, *puts forth her rosy hue*
The leves on the lyhte wode
waxen al with wille.
The mone mandeth hire bleo, *sends forth*
the lilie is lossom to seo, *lovely*
the fenyl and the fille; *chervil*
wowes this wilde drakes,
Miles murgeth huere makes, *animals make joy of*
ase strem that striketh stille; *flows softly*
Mody meneth, so doh mo, *The passionate (lover) complains*
Ichot ycham on of tho, *I know I am . . .*
for love that likes ille.'[23]

This recalls the embroidery of Latin lyrics on the same theme,[24] but there is independent observation of detail too, of a cataloguing kind, such as seems to be characteristic of Western alliterative poetry, and which we may compare with the naturalistic detail of fourteenth-century marginal illumination. The effect is luxuriously accumulative, occasionally evocative, but not particularly coherent visually as a 'scene'.

Spring openings are also transferred to religious lyric, sometimes simply for the season's impulse to song and celebration:

'Nu this fules singet and maket hure blisse
and that gres up thringet and leved the ris; *springs, the branch is in leaf*
of on ic wille singen that is makeles, *matchless*
The king of alle kinges to moder he hire ches'[25]

but sometimes more subtly, to contrast with the emotions aroused by seasonable meditation on the Passion, as in the poem that Brown calls 'A Springtide Song of the Redemption',[26] or in 'A Spring Song on the Passion':

> 'When y se blosmes springe
> ant here foules song,
> A suete love-longynge
> myn herte thourhout stong.'[27]   *pierced*

In this poem, as Rosemary Woolf says, 'there is an implicit contrast between Christ's former beauty, symbolized by the fairness of spring, and His disfigurement on the Cross'.[28] Other lyrics use winter and autumn openings:

> 'Nou skrinketh rose ant lylie-flour'[29]

to introduce penitential meditations and moralizations on the transience of life. Such seasonal landscapes have no content, it will readily be seen, and are simply 'occasions' for poetry.

Something more is happening in romance, though not in the actual setting of the narrative, where the action is still divided between the charming garden pleasance of temptation or reward[30] and the forest wilderness of the hero's self-exile, as in *Sir Orfeo* and the Lancelot story. Both have an identity as formal as the landscapes of earlier book illustration, the latter, in particular, developing into an indiscriminate catalogue of wild beasts. Chrétien's *Yvain* portrays the knight riding through a forest where wild bulls combat endlessly; the English version, *Ywain and Gawain*, stereotypes the feature automatically:

> 'A faire forest sone I fand.
> Me thoght mi hap thare fel ful hard,
> For thare was mani a wilde lebard,
> Lions, beres, bath bul and bare,
> That rewfully gan rope and rare.'[31]   *cry out and roar*

It is the same wilderness that Gawain rides through:

> 'Sumwhyle wyth wormes he werres and wyth wolves als,
> Sumwhyle wyth wodwos that woned in the knarres,   *monsters, crags*
> Bothe wyth bulles and beres, and bores otherwhyle,
> And etaynes that hym anelede of the heghe felle.'[32]   *giants, pursued*

This wilderness is also adapted for more explicitly symbolic purposes in dream vision and allegory, particularly as a type of *rite de passage* to an earthly paradise, as in Arthur's dream of Fortune in the alliterative *Morte Arthure*.[33]

Outside the forest and the *vergier*, the world of romance remains shadowy. But one group of late thirteenth-century romances, *Kyng Alisaunder* in particular, is exceptional in that it introduces seasons and landscape description as a form of narrative punctuation and transition. The passages are short, usually of about six lines, and are inserted at natural breaks in the narrative. The themes are the seasons, especially spring, and daybreak, with the addition of gnomic comment and little vignettes of everyday life and courtly pastime, as in contemporary pictures of the labours of the months or in the margins of the East Anglian psalters.[34] The seasonal allusions, which are sometimes eliminated and absorbed into the gnomic comment and scenes from life, give a chronological 'feel' to the narrative, but are syntactically independent:

> 'In tyme of Maii the nighttyngale
> In wood maketh mery gale.   *song*
> So don the foules, grete and smale,
> Summe on hylles and summe in dale.
> The day daweth, the kyng awaketh'[35]

and function partly as ornament, partly as a stereotyped means of alerting a listening audience to transitions and new matter. The detail is often conventional enough, as in the typical passage quoted above, but the realism of the genre scenes sometimes carries with it an associated sharpness of observation, as in this dawn scene:

> 'In a morowen-tyde it was,
> That dropes hongen on the gras,
> And maidens loken in the glas,
> Forto atyffen her faas'   *adorn*
> (4101-4)

while this cameo of late summer is explicit in its reminiscence of Calendar themes:

> 'In tyme of hervest mery it is ynough—
> Peres and apples hongeth on bough,
> The hayward bloweth mery his horne....'[36]

There are twenty-seven examples of the device in *Kyng Alisaunder*, nine in

Arthour and Merlin, and one in *Richard Coeur de Lion*: all three romances are usually associated together as the work of a single Kentishman of about 1290. There are isolated examples also in a later romance, *The Sowdone of Babylone*.[37] Those in *Arthour and Merlin* are very similar in form and function to those in *Kyng Alisaunder*, but less elaborate and less subtle:

> 'Mirie it is in time of June,
> When fenel hongeth abrod in toun;
> Violet and rose flour
> Woneth than in maidens bour.
> The sonne is hot, the day is long,
> Foules make miri song.'[38]

A later, more popular redaction of *Arthour* clearly regards the seasons headpieces as extravagances, and abbreviates them sharply, also linking them explicitly to the sequence of the narrative ('So in that tyme . . .').

There are hints for the seasonal headpiece in *chanson de geste* and more elaborate examples in medieval Latin narrative poetry, as Smithers points out,[39] but the origins of the device are in classical epic, where descriptions of dawn and sunset are similarly used as a form of narrative punctuation, often with elaborate development of astronomical periphrasis, and sometimes with allusion to the appropriate activities of the time of day in everyday life.[40] In Homer, a new day begins, and a new episode in the story, when Dawn comes to light the East or brush the sky with rose-tinted hands, to rise from the River of Ocean or the bed of Tithonus and spread her saffron mantle over the world, to deck herself in crimson streamers. There is a similar economy of formulaic repetition in Virgil, but signs too of more elaborate treatment, both in the inclusion of more detailed observation, as when he describes the sea reddening with the rays of dawn,[41] and also in more extended mythological embroidery:

> 'Postera vix summos spargebat lumine montis
> orta dies, cum primum alto se gurgite tollunt
> Solis equi lucemque elatis naribus efflant.'[42]

('Scarce was the morrow's dawn sprinkling the mountain-tops with light, what time the Sun's steeds first rise from the deep flood, and breathe light from uplifted nostrils . . .')

The famous lines, which Virgil himself repeats, in part at least, on three occasions:

'Et iam prima novo spargebat lumine terras
Tithoni croceum linquens Aurora cubile'[43]

('And now early Dawn, leaving the saffron bed of Tithonus, was sprinkling her fresh rays upon the earth.')

became a *locus classicus* amongst rhetoricians (like most lines in Virgil) for illustration of the figure periphrasis. Virgil adds to the dawn transitions a few night scenes, mostly brief, but expanded to a full nocturne to introduce the sleepless anguish of Dido.[44] It is Statius, however, who builds the epic periphrasis into the great set-pieces which were to influence medieval poets so strongly, builds them out beyond the drama of action into an independent rhetorical drama of allusion and conceit. The night scene and land storm which introduce the combat of Tydeus and Polynices are bombastic, hectically coloured, frenziedly allusive:

'Solverat Hesperii devexo margine ponti
flagrantes Sol pronus equos rutilamque lavabat
Oceani sub fonte comam, cui turba profundi
Nereos et rapidis adcurrunt passibus Horae,
frenaque et auratae textum sublime coronae
deripiunt, laxant calidis umentia loris
pectora; pars meritos vertunt ad molle iugales
gramen et erecto currum temone supinant.'[45]

('Far on the sloping margin of the western sea the sinking Sun had unyoked his flaming steeds, and laved their bright manes in the springs of Ocean; to meet him hastens Nereus of the deep and all his company, and the swift-striding Hours, who strip him of his reins and the woven glory of his golden coronet, and relieve his horses' dripping breasts of the hot harness; some turn the well-deserving steeds into the soft pasture, and lean the chariot backward, pole in air.')

Elaborate dawn scenes and sunset scenes, such as this, show how amplification is woven out of mythological allusion, not out of the actuality of dawn and sunset, just as Hellenistic landscape painters went on personifying rivers and mountains in mythological figures long after they were committed to an aesthetic of impressionism. They still draw their mountains with perfect illusionism, and Statius, with a similar bravado, has his *erecto temone*.

Such elaboration has more to do with later medieval poetry, as we shall see, but the importance of the *Kyng Alisaunder* passages should not be underestimated. Smithers speaks of the lyrical headpieces as 'arabesques', serving 'to catch and relieve the eye as it attempts to take in the effect of a large fabric', and comments on 'the abundance, variety and novelty' of individual images within the convention.[46] We might add that their relation to the text is similar to the relation of marginalia to text illustration in the manuscripts of the period; in both, the freedom to experiment releases a new independence of observation which prepares the way for major changes of attitude.[47]

These changes, however, are slow to take effect in England. Chaucer, for instance, takes unexpectedly little interest in landscape, though, as we have seen, he is very much alive to the symbolic and dramatic possibilities of gardens.[48] His extended descriptions of garden scenes in the *Book of the Duchess* and the *Parlement of Foules* are dominated, as descriptions, by models of the *paradis terrestre* from the *Roman de la Rose* and Boccaccio's *Teseida*, which he embroiders with a wealth of affectionate detail but without any radical change of perspective or point of view. Shorter garden scenes in the Prologue to the *Legend of Good Women*, in the *Merchant's Tale* and in the *Knight's Tale* are close to the fashionable mannerism of Machaut, and in the General Prologue to the *Canterbury Tales* Chaucer returns to the older tradition of scientific-philosophic seasons description derived from classical sources and from encyclopaedic treatises such as the *Secreta Secretorum*.[49] There is some seasonal allusion in the *Troilus*, though the lengthiest description[50] again returns to the *Roman de la Rose* and the *Teseida* for its conventional detail; and some elaborate astronomical periphrasis in book V,[51] loftily allusive in the high style, and drawn from epic or quasi-epic sources. The moment of actual observation as Criseyde descends to her garden:

> 'This yerd was large, and rayled alle th'aleyes,
> And shadewed wel with blosmy bowes grene,
> And benched newe, and sonded alle the weyes'[52]

is in sharp contrast. The dawn scene in the *Knight's Tale*:

> 'The bisy larke, messager of day,
> Salueth in hir song the morwe gray,
> And firy Phebus riseth up so bright
> That al the orient laugheth of the light,
> And with his stremes dryeth in the greves
> The silver dropes hangynge on the leves'[53]

has a breathtaking *élan*, but it is literary in spirit, bejewelled and craftily allusive (the fourth line is from Dante). Chaucer's wild places, such as the cave of Morpheus in the *Book of the Duchess*, the forest of Mars in the *Knight's Tale*, or the desert of the *House of Fame*, are all effectively ominous, through evocation of sound as much as anything,[54] but are markedly lacking in the graphic visual quality of their classical models and analogues.[55] On the whole, there is no movement towards landscape realism in Chaucer, the reverse if anything, or at least a declining interest. His spirit, and that of his contemporaries at court, is well reflected in some lines from Sir John Clanvowe's *The Cuckoo and the Nightingale*:

> 'I wente forth alone, boldely,
> And held my way doun by a broke-syde,
> Til I com to a launde of whyte and grene;
> So fair oon had I never inne been;
> The ground was grene, y-poudred with daisye,
> The floures and the gras y-lyke hye,
> Al grene and whyte; was nothing elles sene.'[56]

Here, in quintessence, is the closed and languid serenity of Gothic landscape, decorative, heraldically ordered, horizonless—'was nothing elles sene'.

French poetry provides a fuller record of the working out of the *Roman de la Rose* tradition of idealized garden landscape. The early imitations are perfunctory, and dissolve quickly into allegory and moral commonplace. Baudouin de Condé's *La Voie de Paradis* (c. 1270), for instance, begins with a spring landscape closely imitated from the *Roman*, but it is purely introductory, and fades into a dream in which he joins the pilgrimage to Paradise, where the only landscape is a road with two forks, one broad and the other narrow, as in Deguileville's *Pélerinage de la Vie Humaine*. The forest setting of Nicole de Margival's *La Panthere d'Amors* (c. 1300) remains quite unrealized, and the poet is obviously impatient to explain to us the allegorical significance of its features. The spring morning openings of Jean de Condé's *La Messe des Oisiaus* and Watriquet de Couvin's *Li Dis de la Fontaine d'Amours* are fuller, but it is Guillaume de Machaut (c. 1300–77) who provides perhaps the most extended development of idealized garden landscape. The *vergiers* of his dream visions are anthologies of the traditional 'charms of landscape', with fountains, trees planted to give shade, birds singing so that the woods re-echo with their song, fruits of all kinds, and the ground carpeted with flowers:

> 'Car il n'i avoit lieu ne voie
> Qui ne fust semez de flourettes
> Blanches, jaunes et vermillettes
> Ou d'aucune estrange colour.'[57]

Nothing intrudes on the perfection of these terrestrial paradises: in their brilliance of colour and clarity of outline there are no shadows, no dim and doubtful lines. His appreciation, like that of contemporary painters, is reserved, as Ruskin says,[58] for the 'tender, bright, balanced, enclosed, symmetrical', and there is a habitual smoothing of nature's forms in the interests of a 'love of order, light, intelligibility and symmetry':

'Tout fait par mesure et tout vert.'[59]

Nature must be courtly to be appreciated: these gardens are all settings for the display of the refined sentiment and dialectic of love. Some are explicitly allegorical, such as the enchanted garden of eternal spring, 'L'Epreuve des fines amours', in *Le Dit dou Lyon*;[60] others are ostensibly real, such as the garden of the castle at Durbuy in *Le Jugement dou Roy de Behaingne*,[61] but are constantly invaded by the traditional attributes of the *paradis terrestre*. Enclosure from the 'natural' world is still very important, and the expansion of the garden within its walls generates the need for still further enclosure within the garden, whence the arbour in the Parc de Hesdin in the *Remede de Fortune*, surrounded by its 'haiette d'esglentier'.[62] Such arbours become frequent in late fourteenth- and fifteenth-century garden scenes, and no doubt reflect developments in actual gardens, just as Machaut shows some interest in the latest 'engins' of garden art.[63]

Froissart lacks the vivacity of Machaut. The garden scenes of the *Paradys d'Amour* and *L'Espinette Amoureuse* are thin and faded. A more extended garden landscape in *Le Joli Mois de May* shows clearly the medieval inclination to subdue natural form to human artefact, in its description of a hedge so thick and clean-cut that it seems to be carved:

'Au regarder pris le vregié,
Que tout autour on ot vregié
   De rainselés
Espessement et dur margiet
Et ouniement arrengié;
   Au veoir les
Ce sambloit des arbrisselés
Qu'on les euïst au compas fais
   Et entailliés.'[64]

('The garden was exactly marked out, and bounded by a thick, firm hedge, evenly cut; the shrubs looked as if they had been trimmed to a precise pattern.')

The quality to be praised in gardens is that they are 'bien ordonnez'.[65] Beyond this, Froissart is chiefly interested in nature in so far as it provides topics of praise for his lady. The garden of *Le Joli Mois de May* is designed so that he can compare his lady to it, item by item, and show her superiority to rose, lily, hawthorn, nightingale. The flower poems, such as *Le Dittié de la Flour de la Margherite* and the *Plaidorie de la Rose et la Violette*, are all using nature as a source of allegorical emblems for the virtues of his lady. Landscape cannot exist in itself, but is always an embodiment or reflection of love or the lover's feelings:

> 'Quant je vy là si bel arbril,
> Il me souvint du mois d'avril,
> De ma dame et de sa beaulté,
> De sa noblesce et leaulté . . .'[66]

For the most part, the same is true of Deschamps (1346–1406): the interpretation of nature is always in terms of humane, moral and social values. The garden is the garden of youthful love, contrasted with the desert of age;[67] flower and leaf are used to develop a debate about different kinds of human worth;[68] the praise of May welcomes it as a time of lover's duty and observance,[69] or even for its more general benefits:

> 'Tu faiz aler sanz froidure les nus,
> Les malhetiez de l'iver respassas.'[70]

He develops pastoral themes to some extent, praising the simple life of the country[71]—in contrast to Froissart, whose *pastourelles* are simply frames for pictures of court life, news and *estrifs*—but mostly uses them for conventional anti-court satire. Deschamps writes of the sea, but it is its dangers, its unpredictability, that he stresses, its relation to human life, not the appearance of a seascape;[72] it is generalized into concepts and abstractions of order and disorder, just as the rocky coastline is by Dorigen in the *Franklin's Tale*.

Nevertheless, it is possible to see glimpses of change in Deschamps, not so much in the *Lay Amoureux*, though the spring garden there is extraordinarily rich, as in the *Lay de Franchise*, a poem of park and château scenery in which lovers assemble for the May-fêtes in honour of the god of Love. It is a real event, in a real place, the park of the château of Beauté-sur-Marne, and Deschamps' description of the castle amidst its trees (66–91), though touched with idyll, is unquestionably what he has seen, an idealized transcript of reality rather than a reconstruction of reality. It is impossible not to be reminded of the château and parkland scenery of some of the Calendar pictures in the *Très Riches Heures* of the duc de Berri and in other manuscripts, which we have seen to be most significant evidence of changes in the mode of viewing landscape. Deschamps was in the royal service, first as a military official and then as bailiff of Senlis and 'maître des eaux et forêts' for the duc d'Orléans, and he may well have known the work that was being produced in the de Berri ateliers. It may be fanciful to go on from this to the company's return to the château in the poem:

> 'Sales y sont; par les fenestres perent
> Les beaus moulins, les froumens et li pré' (241–2) *granaries*

and acclaim the first conscious 'view' in poetry since classical times, or to see in Deschamps' elaborate attempts to convey the effect of sunlight on landscape (131–43) a reflection of similar concerns amongst painters such as the Boucicaut Master. Nevertheless, the *Lay de Franchise* is not alone. The praise of château and estate, for which his profession must have given him a connoisseur's eye, is a favourite theme in Deschamps, and we can perhaps recognize in the topics of his praise the source of the new realism. For it is the profitability and usefulness of the well-ordered land that is its primary beauty:

> 'Jardins y a, riviere pour voler,
> Sauvoirs dedens, garanne prouffitable,   *fishponds, warren*
> Vignes entour pour l'ostel gouverner,
> Coulombier, prés et mainte terre arable,   *dovecot*
> Granche, fontaine en .viii. lieux despensable,   *barn*
>   Arbres et noble saussay,   *willow plantation*
> Garanne grant et bonne cave y sçay,   *wine cellar*
> Estuves, baings et le ruissel courant.'[73]   *bath houses*

All these landscapes are in fact allegories of good government, which is perhaps why they can afford a new kind of realism. We can be sure that similar motives operated with painters preparing scenes of the duc de Berri's châteaux and estates, with their rural occupations and courtly pastimes, for Calendar pictures, just as they did with Ambrogio Lorenzetti in Siena. And finally, whilst we can see that Deschamps' vivid pictures of the barren and wintry landscapes of Brie and Flanders are simply exercises in fashionable rhetorical invective, reversing the topics of praise for his favoured Champagne:

> 'Brie froide est, qui n'a grosse riviere,
> Fors boscaiges, nefles sauvaiges, noix'[74]   *medlars, walnuts*

it could still be true that, just as the first true winter scenes are in the de Berri manuscripts, the first objective winter description in poetry, that is, the first in which the tribulations of winter are simply recorded and not used to echo some theme of love or life or death, is in Deschamps, *Balade* 793. Deschamps has no taste for winter, no more than Ovid, exiled in Tomis:

> 'heu quam vicina est ultima terra mihi!'[75]

('Alas! how near to me is the margin of the world.)

or Virgil, who sees nothing picturesque or imaginatively appealing, as the eighteenth century might do, in the metamorphosis of landscape under snow:

> 'sed iacet aggeribus niveis informis et alto
> terra gelu late septemque adsurgit in ulnas.'[76]

('But far and wide earth lies shapeless under mounds of snow and piles of ice, rising seven cubits high.')

but his distaste is for what he sees as real, not for what he interprets as allegorical.

Deschamps' successors show little inclination to pursue his interests in the realistic landscape of good government. For Christine de Pisan, the season of May is still part of the liturgical cycle of love, and her poetry is more concerned with the amorous observances appropriate to the season than with the season itself.[77] An elaborate and brilliant spring morning landscape in the *Dit de Poissy*[78] has an attention to light and colour which has prompted LeFrançois-Pillion to speak of it as the poetic analogue to the new illumination,[79] but it is still a landscape dominated by an *idea*, that of its usefulness to lovers:

> 'C'est zephirus qui boutons novellez
>   Fait espanir   *open out*
> Et ces belles doulcetes fleurs venir
> Et aux amans donne maint souvenir
> De leurs amours'
>
> (155–9)

and still in essence, therefore, no different from Gottfried von Strassburg. Her *Dit de la Pastoure* gives a long idyllic account of the shepherd's life, its cares and diversions, drawn with the thoroughness characteristic of Christine from *Le Vray regime et gouvernement des bergers et bergères* of Jehan le Brie, but it is all in fact no more than a *parabole couverte* for some topical liaison. The isolation of courtly sentiment is still more marked in Charles d'Orléans: the only landscapes he is interested in are the allegorical places of love, 'la forest d'Ennuyeuse Tristesse', 'le boys de Merencolie' or 'la forest de Longue Actente'.[80] The stamp of a thoroughgoing realism in the fifteenth century is an open scorn for pastoral such as is displayed by Villon, for whom the countryside means only flight, exile, hiding.[81]

A totally different kind of landscape realism from that of Deschamps was being developed in England during the late fourteenth century, not in court poetry but in the alliterative schools of the west and north. It is a realism generated as much by the verbal demands of the form as by any altered mode of vision. Its character is in a rich and luxuriant, often indiscriminate accumulation of substantives, an arbitrary concreteness of reference which can break through to a kind of illusory realism, like some early fifteenth-century Italian examples of advanced International Gothic, through sheer weight of sensory allusion, even though there may be no visual coherence or ordering of scene. There is a kind of flaunting bravado about the diction of some alliterative poems in the richer style—the *Morte Arthure*, the *Wars of Alexander* and the *Siege of Jerusalem* particularly—an adventurousness and strutting confidence with words which belongs to a school of poets newly risen. But it is the demands of the medium, of heavy stress, regular alliteration and half-line weighting, which produce the characteristic distributive accumulation in descriptive passages:

> 'Mynsteris and masondewes they malle to the erthe   *churches, strike*
> Chirches and chapelles chalke-whitte blawnchede.
> Stone stepelles fulle styffe in the strete ligges
> Chawmbyrs with chymnes and many cheefe inns
> Paysede and pelid downe playsterede walles.'[82]   *crushed, threw*

Concreteness of effect is produced here more by accident than design, for the technique is essentially one of piling up detail, not of articulation. The density of language, its richness of reference, and its function on many occasions as a thesaurus of synonyms, can often produce visual effects of startling power:

> 'Then come thar-in a litill brid   in-to his arme floghe
> And thar hurkils and hydis   as scho were hand-tame   *cowers*
> Fast scho flekirs about his fete   and fleghtirs aboute   *flutters*
> And thar it nestild in a noke   as it a nest were.'[83]

177

But the arbitrary nature of these effects is perhaps illustrated in *The Parlement of the Thre Ages*, where the poet, out hunting, is stalking a deer:

> 'I waitted wiesly the wynde by waggynge of leves, *watched*
> Stalkede full stilly no stikkes to breke,
> And crepite to a crabtre and coverede me ther-undere.'[84]

There is no reason in the nature of things why it should be a 'crabtre', and no rhetorical advantage, nothing in fact beyond the exigencies of alliteration. This is what I mean by 'illusory' realism.

It is to be expected, therefore, that the natural landscapes of alliterative poetry will have rich surface texture and be packed with sensory detail, like the Pisanello *St Eustace*, but will not necessarily be realistic. The principle of design is accumulation and ornament, not selection and emphasis for the sake of visual organization, and the spring scenes in the *Parlement* and *Winner and Waster* are little different from 'Lenten ys come with love to toune',[85] in their reliance on the catalogue:

> 'Fele floures gan folde ther my fote steppede.
> I layde myn hede one ane hill, ane hawthorne be-syde:
> The throstills full throly they threped to-gedire; *keenly, argued*
> Hipped up heghwalles fro heselis tyll othire; *woodpeckers, hazels*
> Bernacles with thayre billes one barkes thay roungen; *wild geese*
> The jay janglede one heghe, jarmede the foles; *sang, birds*
> The bourne full bremly rane the bankes by-twene; *noisily*
> So ruyde were the roughe stremys, and raughten so heghe,
> That it was neghande nyghte or I nappe myghte.'[86] *approaching*

A more elaborate scene in the *Morte Arthure* has the same basic pattern,[87] though there is another passage in that extraordinary poem which hints at other possibilities:

> 'Now ferkes to the fyrthe thees fresche mene of armes, *goes, wood*
> To the felle so fewe, theis fresclyche byernes, *mountain*
> Thorowe hopes and hymlande, hillys and other, *valleys, border-land*
> Holtes and hare woddes with heslyne schawes, *grey, hazel-groves*
> Thorowe marasse and mosse and montes so heghe; *marsh*
> And in the myste mornynge one a mede falles,
> Mawene and unmade, maynoyrede bott lyttylle, *cultivated*
> In swathes sweppene downe, fulle of swete floures.'[88] *mown*

The opening suggests a certain optimism about the possibilities of a morning's ride—it is again a catalogue of natural features—but the last three lines have a rare and unmistakable impressionism, the very sense of lush meadow land under morning haze. Maybe it is significant that the key detail is agricultural rather than aesthetic.

The poems which depend more closely on Latin sources, such as the *Destruction of Troy*, the *Alexander* poems and the *Siege of Jerusalem*, show little inclination to introduce landscape description. The poet of the *Destruction* pays only brief attention to Guido della Colonna's seasons transitions, though it is interesting to see the characteristic alliterative density of reference emerging, even in this comparatively unadventurous poem, in the description of the isle of Colchos, especially if we compare it with the corresponding passages in the contemporary versions of Guido, one by Lydgate, in the *Troy-Book*, full of bookish and rhetorical allusion, and another in the *Laud Troy-Book*, where Guido's sterile parody of the *locus amoenus* is diffused to the thin fluency of romance.[89] The one freedom the poet of the *Destruction* does allow himself is in the description of storms, especially storms at sea, which are his *tour de force*:

> 'When sodenly the softe aire unsoberly rose;
> The cloudis over cast, claterrit aboute;
> Wyndes full wodely walt up the ythes;   *stirred, waves*
> Wex merke as the mydnighte mystes full thicke;
> Thunret in the thestur throly with all;   *darkness, fiercely*
> With a launchant laite lightonyd the water;   *lightning*
> And a ropand rayne raiked fro the hevyn.
> The storme was full stithe with mony stout windes,   *violent*
> Hit walt up the wilde se uppon wan hilles.'[90]

There is an obvious attempt here to overwhelm the senses in a mass of detail; the confusion of impression, which is as much auditory as visual, is evidently appropriate to the particular circumstances, though it is a cheap enough effect in alliterative poetry. There is a more deliberate realism in another storm description which is less of a set-piece (the one quoted above is headed 'A Storme on the Se' in the MS): it brings vividly to our eyes a sodden landscape which must have been very familiar to the poet if he lived in the north-west of England:

> 'That day was full derke, dymmyt with cloudes,
> With a ropand rayne, rut fro the skewes;   *poured down, clouds*
> A myste and a merkenes in mountains aboute,
> All donkyt the dales wyth the dym showris.'[91]   *soaked*

Whatever reservations we may have about these landscapes and sea scenes in alliterative poetry must be silenced for the poet of *Sir Gawain and the Green Knight*. Here is an eye that can see, and a mind that can organize and select so as to give a strong and coherent visual impression, whether it is of the storm at sea or the whale's interior in *Patience*, the Deluge in *Cleanness*, or the many natural landscapes in *Gawain* itself. The latter are dealt with in more detail elsewhere,[92] but it may be apposite to note here that the most powerful effect of visual realism is to be found not in the great set-pieces of seasons description and winter journey, which have a primarily rhetorical function,[93] but in the almost casual evocation of wild north-country landscape, whether in close focus, as in the boar hunt:

'Then al in a semblé sweyed togeder	*throng*
Bitwene a flosche in that fryth and a foo cragge.	*pool, wood, wicked*
In a knot bi a clyffe at the kerre syde,	*wooded mound, marsh*
Theras the rogh rocher unrydely was fallen,	*in confusion*
Thay ferden to the fyndyng, and frekes hem after.'	*went, men*

(1429–33)

or in broad panorama, as in Gawain's journey to the Green Chapel:

'Thay bowen bi bonkkes ther boghes ar bare;	*go*
Thay clomben bi clyffes ther clenges the colde.	
The heven was uphalt, but ugly therunder.	
Mist muged on the mor, malt on the mountes;	*hung about, was breaking up*
Uch hille hade a hatte, a myst-hakel huge.	*mist-cape*
Brokes byled and breke bi bonkkes aboute,	*bubbled, splashed*
Schyre schaterande on schores, ther thay doun	*dashing, white on the banks*
schowved.'	

(2077–83)

Though one might hesitate to talk about a 'feeling for nature', there is here, without doubt, a communication of its forms both precise and evocative.

For a more self-conscious shift of emphasis in the attitude to landscape we have to move to Italy. Here, as we saw earlier,[94] Giotto and Duccio had created the space necessary for the development of landscape, but had mostly filled it with the remnants of stylized broken terrace structure. However, their declaration of intent was clear enough, in the startling suspended cross of Giotto's *Christmas at Greccio*, leaning away from the viewer and supported by a rope through a pyramidal frame, or in Duccio's *Entry into Jerusalem*, where he portrays a figure leaning out of a window *within* the walls, as if to pull us through the gates towards him.[95] It was clearly enough understood by near-contemporaries such as Boccaccio who, inspired by the famous lines in which Dante contrasts the decline of Cimabue with the rise of Giotto,[96] sees in Giotto the beginnings of a radical new naturalism which will sweep away the ignorant blunders of the Dark Ages:

'Let Nature . . . fashion what she would, he with his style and pen would depict its like on such wise that it shewed not as its like, but rather as the thing itself, insomuch that the visual sense of men did often err in regard thereof, mistaking for real that which was but painted.'[97]

Giotto's example was not immediately followed up. Landscape had to wait until Flemish influence began to penetrate before it could be fully established in Italian painting, and there was even a reaction against Giotto in the middle years of the fourteenth century, a revulsion against his humane realism and towards a more ascetic spirituality which Meiss ascribes to the influence of the Black Death.[98] Such a change of spirit would effectively exclude landscape from frescoes and panel paintings with religious subjects, and there are, of course, very few others. Two of those few are in the Palazzo Pubblico at Siena, and it is noteworthy that both of them, with their political and social 'occasions', show a significant shift towards the landscape of fact. Simone Martini's fresco of *Guidoriccio da Fogliano* in a nightbound landscape is designed to show the Sienese hero riding between the two towns he has conquered. A panoramic view is almost unavoidable, and the dazzling figure of the rider is therefore set against a landscape in which sweeping vistas of bare rock are combined with a minute precision in the portrayal of town and encampment. The contrast between the gorgeous trappings of man and horse and the lunar landscape is too startling for reality, and much else betrays the style of a painter who was to have considerable influence on the formation of International Gothic; but landscape is, in part at least, the 'subject' of the picture. It is the whole subject in the portion of Ambrogio Lorenzetti's allegorical fresco dealing with the *Effects of Good Government in the Country* (Plate 55). Here the theme of the well-ordered land, which we have already seen producing a new kind of realism in Deschamps,[99] allows detail of flowers, trees, cultivated fields, genre scenes of peasant activity and courtly pastime, set in a spacious landscape receding to distant hills. It is admittedly, under its clear and unvaried light, an ideal universalization of the ordered life of nature and countryside, and there is much that is awkward in the perspective, but the observation of reality is extraordinarily direct. These panoramas of Siena and the surrounding countryside are, as Panofsky says, 'the first postclassical vistas essentially derived from visual experience rather than from tradition, memory and imagination'.[100]

Boccaccio himself, in his writing, stands at the junction of traditions, aware of new influences, particularly through his friend Petrarch, and a literary innovator of the first importance, who yet returned in later life to Latin encyclopaedia and moral allegory. The ambiguity of his position is reflected not so much in the traditional pleasure garden of the *Teseida*,[101] used by Chaucer for the *Parlement of Foules*, nor even in the royal gardens of Robert of Sicily in Naples which he describes in the *Amorosa Visione*, but in the garden scenes of the *Decameron*. Here the noble retinue of tale-tellers move on the morning of the third day to the Villa Palmieri on the Fiesolan slopes above Florence, where there is a walled garden, which is elaborately described. It is a paradise,[102] but with some subtle shifts of emphasis which suggest a growing commitment to what is known and seen: a gallery is 'close imbosked with leafage and such flowers *as the season afforded*'; and, of the plants, 'there was abundance of every rarer species *that our climate allows*' (my italics). Paradise gardens, traditionally, are little concerned with such scrupulous qualifications. Towards the close of the sixth day the company find their way to La Valle delle Donne, one of Virgil's natural amphitheatres, with stream, waterfall and miniature lake.[103] The tone of Boccaccio's description is idyllic, and there is paradisal and classical allusion as well as a rich exploitation of the traditional imagery of the medieval garden of love, but it is surely of great importance that he purports to describe a real and identifiable place, stripped of all supernatural elements,[104] offering an idealization of observed reality rather than an iconographic reconstruction of reality.

It is Petrarch, however, who makes the decisive move towards a new vision of landscape. Petrarch has a sense of geography and a grasp of the larger aspects of landscape which we may contrast with what passed for geography in a popular encyclopaedia of the day in England, Higden's *Polychronicon*. He moves easily from country to country, aware of relationship and dimension, able to generalize, like Virgil in *Georgics* II, about the beauties of Italy, travelling for interest and curiosity, not on any moral pilgrimage.[105] His rhapsodic descriptions of his solitary and delightful country home in the Vaucluse, his 'transAlpine Helicon', are touched by pastoral and literary allusion, but they are descriptions of a real place, the farm where he lives, the fountain of Sorgues, his rocky retreats. Above all, there are Petrarch's mountain panoramas. Clark selects one of these, the ascent of Mont Ventoux, to show that Petrarch was medieval at heart, since he compares the difficulty of the climb to the ascent of the hill of Virtue and, when he comes to the top, does no more than open his copy of the *Confessions* of St Augustine, to find this:

' "Men go to admire the high mountains and the great flood of the seas and the wide-rolling rivers and the ring of Ocean and the movements of the stars; and they abandon themselves!" I was stunned, I admit.'[106]

Certainly, Petrarch is not far from Langland here: in *Piers Plowman*, the dreamer is shown a vision of the manifold wonder of creation in 'the myrour of myddel-erde':

'And seih the sonne and the see and the sand after,	saw
Wher that briddes and bestes by here makes yeden,	went
Wilde wormes in wodes and wonderful foules	
With fleckede fetheres and of fele colours ...	many
And siththe ich loked on the see and so forth on the sterres,	
Meny selcouth ich seih aren nouht to seggen nouthe;	marvels, saw, say
Ne what on floures in feldes and of hure faire coloures,	
How out of greot and of gras grewe so meny huwes ...'[107]	earth

But he falls into the trap, looks at the panorama of nature for what it is rather than for what it 'means', and is sharply rebuked by Ymaginatif for his presumption: the wonder of creation is not to sit and look at, but to be *used*, and primarily as a repository of moral examples for man's benefit.[108] It is the orthodox medieval view of nature, and the source of an allegorizing natural history rather than a scientific one. God made all creatures, says Baudouin de Condé,

'Oisiaus par air, biestes par tiere,	
Poisons en mer et en riviere,	
Bois et vregiés et praeries ...	gardens
Mais tout fist Dieus por siervir l'omme.'[109]	

One can see that Petrarch could hardly not have opened his St Augustine on the summit. But the fact remains that he does describe the hard work of climbing with painful accuracy, and he does pay attention to the view when he gets to the top. It would be ridiculous to argue that no one had climbed mountains before, and taken some pleasure in it: what we are discussing, it must be made clear, is a mode of perception expressed in literary terms, what Petrarch chose to write about, not what he chose to do.[110] Within these terms, however, his choice was remarkable: mountains had inspired a universal horror among the Roman poets, except for Lucretius, and for patristic writers they are blemishes in nature, coeval with the Fall, or with the first murder, or with the going down of the Flood.[111] Medieval man approached them with trepidation: John of Salisbury, crossing the Grand St

Bernard, recognizes that he may be nearer to heaven, but concludes, 'Lord, I said, restore me to my brethren, that they come not into this place of torment';[112] and Adam Usk, crossing the St Gotthard in 1402, asks to be blind-folded 'lest I should see the dangers of the pass'.[113] In art, mountains had long had a non-symbolic aesthetic of their own, traceable from the backgrounds of Hellenistic painting, through the framing and patterning devices of Byzantine art, up to Giotto and later.[114] But even here the gloomy symbolism of mountains is not without its potency: they signify the world outside Paradise, the world of sin and malediction, in the *Expulsion from Eden* from the *Très Riches Heures* (Plate 23a), as well as in Dirc Bouts' *St John on Patmos*, where a river separates the heavenly city from a savage mountain landscape, with a winged devil hovering above.

Petrarch's letter, set against this background of traditional belief and response, cannot be dismissed as insignificant. Furthermore, the description of the ascent of Mont Ventoux is not the only evidence of Petrarch's interest in 'views'. In a letter from Capranica, he says:

'All about are numberless hills, not high or hard to climb, and affording broad views'[115]

and in another, from San Colombano:

'To the west we have a wide view over a solitary region, very quiet and pleasant. I don't remember ever seeing from so slight an elevation such a noble spectacle of far-spreading lands. By turning about one can see Pavia, Piacenza, Cremona, and many other famous cities besides. So at least the local people affirm, though it has been too cloudy today to make the test. But for these three cities I have the evidence of my own eyes. To our rear are the Alps separating us from Germany, with their snow-clad peaks, rising into the clouds, into heaven; before us stand the Apennines and innumerable cities . . . The Po itself lies at our feet, separating the fat fields in a giant curve.'[116]

The significance of this taste for 'views' in the development of landscape realism can hardly be over-emphasized, and Petrarch's is the first expression of the taste in post-classical times. There had been panoramas in poetry before, visions in which the world and everything in it shrank to nothingness, as in Dante and, following him, in Boccaccio and Chaucer;[117] or opportunities to see the world as an allegorical battlefield.[118] But Petrarch's is not a vision, but a view, for which he has 'the evidence of his own eyes'. What medieval writer would have regarded such evidence as anything but illusory? Nor does Petrarch wish to *use* the landscape that he sees, neither to subdue it physically, by conquering it, nor subdue it morally, by allegorizing it. All he wants, as he says, is to live and die in it. Dante's places, however accurately described, always have an ulterior significance: in Petrarch they exist for their own sake. 'With Petrarch reappears the cultured enjoyment of Nature.'[119]

To translate this vision into painting or poetry, given the stylistic inertia of any art medium, was a matter of more difficulty. But it happens, and first of all in France. The process has been described in detail, in relation to Calendar pictures, in the previous chapter:[120] the transplantation of the naturalistic flora and fauna of marginal decoration into the miniature itself, as in the *Petites Heures* of Jacquemart de Hesdin; the attempt to free the miniature from the surface of the page by isolating it within painted-in panel borders, as if it were itself a panel painting, as in the Breviary of Renaud IV; and the elimination of gold and decorative backgrounds in favour of blue skies. The Brussels Hours, also attributed to de Hesdin, shows the integration of these features into coherent compositions which Panofsky calls 'the very beginning of naturalism in Northern landscape painting'.[121] The miniature of the *Flight into Egypt* (Plate 47b) has an attention to season in its bare and leafless trees as well as a vista of estuary and mountain landscape which foreshadows much fifteenth-century painting, preoccupied as it is with the same problem of establishing spatial relations in depth. The panel painting of the same subject in the Dijon triptych by Melchior Broederlam looks a good deal less sophisticated by contrast, though it has some sense of space and of the texture of rock and foliage.[122] The most spectacular advances, however, are made by the Boucicaut Master. The scene of the *Visitation* in the Boucicaut Hours (Plate 48a) is still primitive in some ways—the tiny trees at the front are quite out of scale, and the middle ground is still a jolting series of screens or *coulisses*. But in the background a blue lake extends into depth, its ripples reflecting the light of the sun, and the hills around show scenes of human activity; objects thin and pale towards the horizon, their contours growing more indistinct; and the sky, instead of being uniformly blue, fades to a whitish tone on the horizon. The Boucicaut Master has in fact discovered aerial perspective a century before Leonardo enunciated its principles.

It would be a mistake to think that all that these miniaturists had to do was to open their eyes and see what was before them. What we see is what we construct, what our habits of mind teach us to select, and naturalism is to that extent as much a form of interpretation as any other mode of vision. There is no sense, with the Boucicaut Master, that the scales fell from his eyes and that he saw what had hitherto been obscured, but rather that one mode of perception was being excitingly disentangled from another, and a miniature like the *Visitation*, which shows us, in addition to a realistic landscape, the sun shining with individual golden rays, is particularly interesting as a record of the moment of parturition. The work of the Limbourg brothers, in the *Très Riches Heures* of the duc de Berri, represents the further sophistication of the Franco-Flemish school of miniaturists: the sense of space, the detail of natural phenomena and rural occupation, are astonishingly naturalistic, as are many individual features, such as the line of hay ricks receding in careful perspective in the June picture, the snow scene with smoke against the sky in February (Plate 50a), the cast shadows of March. But above all these scenes—and often omitted in reproduction—there is the symbolic representation of the chariot of the sun passing across the sky, with the signs of the zodiac against a deep blue ground sprinkled with gold stars, reminding us that these are Calendar pictures, symbolic of the ordered cycle of the seasons and man's life, and ultimately therefore a reflection of the divine order.

It is necessary to have similar reservations in mind in talking about the extraordinary growth of realism in Flemish landscape art of the fifteenth century. What seems to be simply a statement of the eye's affection may be a subtle visual disguise for some symbolic truth. The crumbling wall with vegetation growing out of it in the *Friedsam Annunciation*, attributed to Hubert van Eyck, is not, or not merely a loving evocation of natural detail, but a symbol of unregenerate nature, the garden of Eden and of man's heart run to rankness, surrounding the combined Judaeo-Christian imagery of the church portal in which the Virgin is framed. Every detail in a picture by Jan van Eyck, landscape included, is part of a visual statement of a conceptual truth: 'No residue remained of either objectivity without significance or significance without disguise'.[123] The exaltation of physical reality in the *Ghent Altarpiece*, the minute precision in its portrayal of flowers, trees, rocks, earth, is a visual aspect of the iconography of the Redemption. The juxtaposition of the human and the divine in *The Madonna and Chancellor Rollin*, the bold faith which can see worldly chancellor in the same plane as Virgin and Child, is reflected in the colonnaded vista of a crowded cityscape beyond (Plate 56). The commitment to reality goes no further than the symbolic programme allows: when he chooses, van Eyck can violate reality deliberately for symbolic effect, as in the *Madonna in a Church*, where the sun shines from the north to show that the 'light of the world' was no earthly light. Or he will close off the background ostentatiously, as he does in the *Madonna at the Fountain*, where two angels hold a cloth of honour behind the Virgin. Nor is the realism that of the copyist; the prospect of Liège in the *Rollin Madonna* is an imaginative reconstruction, with an assembly of detail which includes the tower of Utrecht cathedral. Van Eyck's control over visual statement is almost inhumanly precise, and it is, paradoxically, this precision that makes perfect objectivity possible. Later painters, lacking his subtle sense of the relation of symbolic truth and visual reality, were driven in one of two directions, either towards a more total realism, which might founder in inconsequence, or towards larger and larger statements of symbolic truth, whence the bubbling skies of Bosch and the monstrous decaying vegetation of Grünewald.

For all these reservations, however, the excitement of the eye before these Flemish landscapes of the fifteenth century is in the increasing power and subtlety of their communication of nature's forms. The link with Franco-Flemish miniature is perhaps the Turin-Milan Hours, in which the hand of Jan van Eyck has been identified in seven miniatures. The freedom and boldness of innovation in these scenes already makes the *Très Riches Heures* look mannered and over-refined; the choppy waters of an estuary (*St Julian ferrying Christ*), breakers on an ocean beach (*Prayer on the Shore*—the first true seascape in painting), a night scene for the *Betrayal*, clouds and chiaroscuro effects everywhere. In the *bas-de-pages* there is a contemplative *Baptism* with reflections in quiet waters, and a series of flat landscapes with low horizons, which are perhaps most significant of all, for there can be no single act of choice more telling as evidence of a commitment to realism than to sacrifice half the picture to nothingness: 'A low horizon is always and everywhere a sign of advanced contemplation of nature'.[124] Decorative landscapes always occupy the full frame, and the continuity of this habit can be seen in the more or less contemporary *Grandes Heures de Rohan* (Plate 61) from France, where *The Annunciation to the Shepherds* shows a rocky landscape with trees, grassy slopes and superb genre detail, piled apparently precipitously almost to the upper border.

Van Eyck was not prepared to make this sacrifice in a full-scale painting. In the *Ghent Altarpiece*, where he was presumably committed to an existing design (by his brother Hubert), he contents himself with the bold stroke of making the landscape background continuous across all five panels, painting in rocks, forests and cities in the luminous aerial perspective he has learnt from the Boucicaut Master. In the *Rollin Madonna* he solves the problem in the manner which was to become conventional in landscape painting, obtaining the high horizon which he needs for richness of content and gradations of depth by taking a raised point of view. It is the equivalent in painting of Petrarch's mountain climbing, and shows the imperative demand of landscape realism for the panorama which opens up beyond the enclosing wall or hedge of 'Gothic' landscape. Van Eyck's immediate model is the Master of Flémalle, who introduces the distant prospect as a glimpse seen through a window, giving to the landscape a natural rationale as well as a controlled frame. Van Eyck enlarges the vista, adds colonnades to act as sighting lines, and draws the eye outward into the panorama by the brilliant device of the balcony with men on it who are also looking at the view.

The rest of the century needed only to explore the possibilities opened up by van Eyck. The *St Luke painting the Virgin*, ascribed to Rogier van der Weyden, is a direct imitation of the *Rollin Madonna*, even to the figures on the balcony, and Rogier himself has colonnaded vistas in the *Miraflores Altarpiece* and the *St John Altarpiece*, as well as continuous landscape background across all three panels of the *Vienna Triptych*. His interest in landscape is less intense: there is less sense of space, and construction in depth is often obtained by the comparatively simple device of successive or interlocking 'screens' of hill slope and foliage, which draw the eye outward with something less than inevitability. Rogier seems to have been less sure than his master of the perfect reconciliation of the natural and the divine, and in the Madrid *Descent from the Cross* or the *Calvary Diptych* he shuts out space and place altogether with a blank brick wall, perhaps, says Friedländer, as 'a defence against the threat of secularization'.[125] There is a similar tendency to 'denaturalize' space in Hugo van der Goes, whose Berlin *Nativity* virtually excludes landscape background, and encloses the scene in a frame of curtains held open by prophets. Other painters, with less religious intensity, seem to have been less aware of the threat, whence the perfect but maneristic perspective of Petrus Christus, almost more interested in painterly effects than in communication of a subject. In Dirc Bouts, the significance of the figures is absorbed into the interest in landscape: the deep perspective of the Madrid *Visitation* (Plate 57), unified by the winding path, a device which was also to become conventional; effects of light, both daybreak and full morning, in the side panels of the *Louvain Triptych*; a sunset scene, with light on rippling waters, in the Boutsian *St Christopher* in Munich. He introduces the window prospect even into the half-length *Madonna* in the National Gallery. In the growing autonomy which he allows to landscape he announces, as Panofsky says, 'the possibility of landscape painting as a species *sui generis*'.[126] The elaborate landscapes of Geertgen tot Sint Jans are similarly full of optical refinements, though maybe somewhat repetitive, and his *St John the Baptist in the Wilderness* (colour plate VII) makes a mockery of its title in the luxuriant pastoral landscape, melting back past carefully-sited impressionistic trees and by serene pathways to the distant Jerusalem. St John hardly seems to know what he is doing amid such surroundings. It remained only for Gerard David and Hans Memlinc, at the turn of the century, to make the last refinements on this vision of landscape, and then for Patinir and Bruegel, the great master of sixteenth-century landscape painting, to declare the full independence of the form.

The influence of Flemish landscape realism was widespread in the fifteenth century. In Germany, Conrad Witz took over some of the van Eyckian light effects, and provided in the *Miracle of the Fishes* panel of the St Peter Altarpiece, at about the same time that another German painter was refining on the Paradise garden, 'the first real landscape in the history of European painting (Lassaigne) apart from the miniatures of the Limbourg brothers and the Turin Hours'.[127] The fact that it is a real place that he paints is significant, as it is in Boccaccio, though it must be added that his real place is much less realistic than van Eyck's imaginary ones. In France, miniaturists like Fouquet and Simon Marmion continued the tradition of the Limbourgs, though only one panel painter, the Master of St Giles, bears comparison with Flemish contemporaries.

In Italy, the Flemish influence was decisive and profoundly significant, once it began to make itself felt in the middle of the century. Up to that time, except in Tuscany, the dominant landscape was that of International Gothic, elaborated and embroidered with superb virtuosity by painters like Gentile da Fabriano (d. 1427) and Pisanello (d. 1455). The former's *Adoration of the Magi* in the Uffizi has a foreground crowded with glittering detail, and behind it, without any attempt at transition, an equally crowded background rising to a gold sky. There is some interest in light effects, explored further under the freer conditions of the predella (*The Flight into Egypt*—even here the sun is still a gold disc in relief, and though the morning light laps delicately at the hills, the figures cast no shadows), but the effect of the whole is of the blending of naturalistically observed detail into an overall decorative pattern (Plate 59). This fragmentary naturalism is the quality also of one of the most famous of 'Gothic' landscapes, the Pisanello *St Eustace* (Plate 62) in the National Gallery, where bold lighting, precisely-drawn animals and optical tricks like the stag facing away from the viewer might be thought to stretch the syntax of Gothic to its limit. Yet the shadowy landscape remains totally unreal, without depth or horizon, and any lingering sense of illusion is defied by the coiled scroll in the foreground. All this maybe serves to heighten the sense of 'vision', which is the subject of the picture, and the gains and losses of the next century or so are perhaps suggested in the comparison with Carracci's treatment of the same subject (*c.* 1585), where the monotonously expert construction of landscape in the end overwhelms the figures of saint and stag, making them look like left-over stage properties or posers in a tableau.

The decorative landscape tradition survives late into the century, dominating much of the routine work in the lesser arts, such as the *cassone* painting of Apollonio di Giovanni, as well as producing a masterpiece in the very heartland of change, *The Adoration of the Magi* of the Florentine Benozzo Gozzoli (*c.* 1460). This painting (Plate 60), which has already been mentioned for its rock formations,[128] uses winding pathways to suggest depth, as well as other refinements, but seems to regard the invention of perspective chiefly as an opportunity to cram in more and more elegant and ornamental detail. In particular areas, such as Lombardy, change was very slow to come, and elsewhere, particular subjects seem to have encouraged archaism, as in the formal and decorative love garden of April in the Salon of the Months in the Schifanoia palace, contrasted with the naturalism of other scenes in the same series.[129] One of the most extraordinary landscapes of the period is the *St John the Baptist going into the Wilderness* (Plate 58) of Giovanni di Paolo (d. 1482). Like those of Lorenzo Vecchietta's illustrations for the *Divine Comedy* (c. 1440),[130] the mountain background here seems to go back over a hundred years for its inspiration, to early Sienese versions of Byzantine landscape. Dizzy rocks curve upwards like scimitars, enclosing a foreground landscape with patchwork fields and miniature pink architecture. With no sense of space or relationship in space, figures totally out of scale with rocks, and trees painted, in the oldest tradition, as overgrown plants, it yet communicates a sense of its subject which Geertgen tot Sint Jans has quite forgotten. Furthermore, the choice is quite deliberate, as di Paolo demonstrates by painting the foreground landscape in normal convergent perspective and then allowing the saint and his attendant rocks to tower above it, quite out of proportion: it is not inverted perspective so much as paradoxical perspective, an explicit visual contradiction designed for the inward rather than the outward eye.[131]

The discovery of 'modern' perspective—that is, the concept of a painting as an imaginary window on whose surface plane are represented through linear perspective the objects that are seen outside the window—by Florentine artists, especially Masaccio (1401–29), in the early fifteenth century, and its theoretical formulation by Alberti, had at first little impact on landscape painting. Masaccio and Masolino are interested in figures and the relationship of figures in space, not in landscape, and Michelangelo was later to translate this neglect into a consistent disregard. Paolo Uccello (1397–1474), a painter much discussed in his lifetime, used certain kinds of landscape as a source of perspective trickery, such as the tessellated fields of the *Battle of San Romano* or the mechanical recession of trees and fallen logs in the Ashmolean *Hunt in the Forest* (Plate 63), but they are artificial effects; his more natural taste seems to be for the extravagant late Gothic of *St George and the Dragon*. The landscape background of Fra Angelico's *Deposition* is artificial and prim, the perspective elementary, and Botticelli's landscapes, quite late in the century, are up-dated garden paradises.

The taste for landscape, when it appears, seems to be the result of Flemish contacts. About 1450, Italian writers began to express admiration for

Flemish naturalism and 'intuitive' perspective. Cyriacus of Ancona, writing in 1449, speaks of 'blooming meadows, flowers, trees, leafy and shady hills ... [seemingly] produced not by the artifice of human hands but by all-bearing nature herself'; and Bartolommeo Fazio, in 1455–6, describes a window prospect in van Eyck, with mountains, woods and castles painted so that they appear to be fifty miles apart.[132] It was not long before this admiration was translated into painting, though it could be said, to distinguish it from Flemish naturalism, that Italian naturalism was as much the reflection of a change of taste as the operation of a new mode of vision. Domenico Veneziano (d. 1461) and Piero della Francesca (d. 1492) both had Flemish contacts, and the former exploits the new style in his *Adoration of the Magi*, with deep recession into a luminous landscape, winding pathway, and river with overlapping hill slopes, and birds against a streaked blue sky. The middle ground is still screened by the foreground figures, but this disharmony is corrected by Piero, who is the first to combine a continuous perspective with perfect control over light, whether it be sunrise, full morning or night. He also introduces into Italy, in the *Uffizi Diptych*, van Eyck's high point of view and simulated low horizons. Once established, these techniques became the common property of a host of imitators, some of them major painters in their own right, such as Pollaiuolo and Perugino, others of secondary rank, such as Ghirlandaio, Baldovinetti and Filippino Lippi. The winding river valley becomes almost a mannerism of these landscapes, sometimes in allusion to the Arno valley, but more because the converging banks, diminishing in orderly fashion, offer the nearest approach in nature to the simple conditions of one point perspective. Often a beetling crag is added in the right or left foreground to direct the eye to its distant destination. In other words, it is the mechanics of illusion that determine the choice of landscape: not landscape into art, therefore, but art into landscape. Old habits can be seen reasserting themselves too, as in Ghirlandaio's *Nativity* (Plate 65), crammed with detail of every kind, including old-fashioned simultaneous narration.

Landscape realism, it could be said, is nothing unless it is supported by a concept of reality; in the hands of these lesser painters, technical mastery degenerates into stylish exercise—landscape backgrounds were often painted in, in fact, by apprentices. The inexorable laws of supply and demand, of fashionable taste, were not likely to provide the stimulus for a more penetrating interpretation of reality, nor was a return to the classical fashion of decorating the walls of villas and palaces with illusionistic landscapes, such as those of Andrea Mantegna in the Gonzaga palace at Mantua. For Giovanni Bellini, the greatest Italian landscape painter of the later fifteenth century, the stimulus was provided by the vision of nature as an aspect of the divine. His minute attention to the detail of rock forms,[133] soil, vegetation, skies, passes beyond naturalism to a larger statement about the harmony of man and creation, a harmony which, in the *Madonna of the Meadows*, *Gethsemane* (Colour Plate VIII) and *St Francis in Ecstasy* (Plate 64), is pictorially expressed through a cool and crisp austerity of lighting. These are not, therefore, landscape backgrounds, for the landscape is part of the subject: 'A spiritual experience . . . is understood in wholly natural terms'.[134]

For Leonardo, the stimulus to a new interpretation of reality was provided by what we may loosely call 'science'; in his drawings above all, Leonardo goes in search of the causes of the forms of things, fascinated by the detailed transition of rock to soil, by leaf membranes, by the formation of storm clouds. He goes below the surface to intrinsic form, as figure painters see beyond the flesh to bone and sinew. The conclusion of the search is in pictures like those of the *Deluge*, where the composing power of the primary imagination is dissolved in the penetrating vision of the secondary.[135] The experimental nature of Leonardo's vision of landscape is well illustrated in the famous passage where he speaks of the power of arbitrary shapes, in clouds, fire and shapes on plaster, to stimulate the imagination.[136] Such optical freedom—echoed in Antony's 'Sometimes we see a cloud that's dragonish'—would have been quite intolerable to the Middle Ages.

The establishment of landscape as an independent art form had little to do with Leonardo's speculative advances. The shift of perception had been made, and the drawings of Leonardo, Dürer and Caravaggio prove it, but the rise of landscape in the early sixteenth century is more the product of a fashionable vogue than the exploration of a new mode of vision. Art theory had placed the stamp of approval on Flemish example and Italian practice—the term *paese*, 'landscape', is first being used independently to describe pictures about 1530, as by Marcantonio of Giorgione's *Tempesta*—and painters proceeded to apply themselves to the satisfaction of a new and respectable taste.[137] It is not 'the discovery of a world', for most of these painters work in readily available stereotypes of frowning rock, lush vegetation and spectacular vistas. The conceptual backing for their work is provided by no more than a revived form of pastoral, echoing Sannazzaro's *L'Arcadia* (*c.* 1500), and tricked out with classical ruins and even reminiscences of classical landscape painting. The painting of Giorgione and Titian can hardly be associated with any sort of decline, but the study of Italian landscape painting encourages the simple view that landscape is primarily a Northern possession.

There are good reasons why English art should have laid little claim to this possession in the fifteenth century. England was backward, economically and culturally, compared with Flanders and northern Italy, and contacts with the continent were not cultivated, except briefly in the 1420s, with France, and in the 1460s, with Flanders. The latter produced little—Flemish miniature art was in any case in a phase of bourgeois mass-production—but the earlier French influence comes through in some elegant miniatures in MS Harley 2278 of Lydgate's *St Edmund*, illuminated at the abbey of Bury St Edmund's, and in MS Royal 18.D.ii of Lydgate's *Troy-Book* and *Siege of Thebes*, also perhaps from Bury. Here there are blue skies and cloud effects, some competent perspective, and bluish backgrounds of hills and towered cities. Anything out of the ordinary, however, is still treated formally and decoratively: the rainbow in the Harley MS (f.72v) is arbitrarily coloured, red, blue, yellow, green, and the storm in the Royal MS (f.83v) has visible thunderbolts symmetrically displayed.

Literature shows a similar but richer mixture, as different traditions merge and overlap. Lydgate, though a patchy poet, is a good guide to early fifteenth-century taste, as in the *Complaint of the Black Knight*, where the decorative garden landscape of the *Roman de la Rose* and Chaucer's *Parlement of Foules* is still in full flourish.[138] Nature is systematically remodelled to fit concepts of human usefulness and human beauty. Its textures are those of human artefacts—jewels, carpets, velvet, even Dresden china, it seems, in the case of the wood, 'that ronge/Lyke as hyt shold shever in pesis smale'; the weather is that of long-forgotten Mediterranean lands, where flowers need protection from the heat of the sun in May and where grass needs extra moisture to thrive; the sense of enclosure is strong, and the method of assembly, as in Pisanello, is decorative, not visual. Natural reality intrudes hardly at all, though it is possible to see how it might do, for Lydgate has here largely released the garden from allegory. The setting is merely a setting, no more, without the deeper significance of the *Roman* or the *Parlement*; the well spring, as Lydgate goes on to tell us, is not the well of Narcissus or any other classical or allegorical well, but just a well. The description is not realistic, but the place, not being allegorical, can only be real, and there is thus opened up the possibility of a 'secular' landscape, as in pictures of saints in the wilderness when the painter grows more interested in the wilderness than in the saint.

Lydgate himself explores these possibilities hardly at all, though the garden of *The Churl and the Bird* has casual touches of reality which may be attributed to low-style decorum and the freedom of the poem from even residual allegorical pressures. For the most part he embroiders the traditional charms of landscape with endless topics of excellence and imagery of painting:

'With sondri floures amonge the herbes meynt,
Whiche on her stalke nature hath depeynt
With sondri hewes.'[139]

Visual detail, where it is present, seems to be drawn as much from formal styles in painting as from observation of reality:

'The nyght ypassed, at springyng of the day,
Whan that the larke with a blissed lay
Gan to salue the lusty rowes rede   rays
Of Phebus char, that so freschely sprede   chariot
Up-on the bordure of the orient . . .'[140]

The master of this painted style is Dunbar, whose bejewelled landscapes are the most extravagant literary manifestation of decorated Gothic. For Dunbar the sun is 'the goldyn candill matutyne', and the landscape that follows, in *The Goldyn Targe*, glitters with precious stones and heraldic illumination:

'The rosis yong, new spreding of thair knopis,   buds
War powderit brycht with hevinly beriall droppis;
Throu bemes rede birnyng as ruby sperkis
The skyes rang for schoutyng of the larkis;
The purpur hevyn, ourscailit in silvir sloppis,   bands
Ourgilt the treis, branchis, lef, and barkis . . .

The cristall air, the sapher firmament,
The ruby skyes of the orient,
Kest beriall bemes on emerant bewis grene;   boughs
The rosy garth depaynt and redolent   garden
With purpur, azure, gold, and goulis gent,
Arayed was by dame Flora the quene . . .'[141]

Yet there are crisp strokes of observation here, almost painted out in the rich luxuriance of colour, as a painter will subdue freshness of line to chromatic harmonies.

In other poets, perhaps less 'professional' than Dunbar, less conscious of formal tradition, the transfer of the real world of the senses can be more immediate. The poet of the *Kingis Quair*, probably James I of Scotland, is deeply indebted to Chaucer's *Parlement*, particularly in the description of the 'lusty plane' of Fortune which is the scene of the poem's central allegorical vision. But the earlier description of the garden beside the tower, where the prisoner first catches sight of his lady, has a precision of detail which Chaucer never bothers to attempt in the corresponding scene in the *Knight's Tale*:

> 'Now was there maid fast by the touris wall
> A gardyn faire and in the corneris set
> Ane herbere grene with wandis long and small
> Railit about, and so with treis set
> Was all the place and hawthorn hegis knet
> That lyf was non walking there forby   *person*
> That myght within scarse ony wight aspye.
>
> So thik the bowis and the leves grene
> Beschadit all the aleyes that there were,
> And myddis every herbere myght be sene
> The scharp grene swete jenepere
> Growing so faire with branchis here and there
> That as it semyt to a lyf without
> The bewis spred the herbere all about.'[142]

There is some attention to the observer's point of view here, though still a narrow concentration of focus. A later poem, *The Floure and the Leafe*, shifts the point of view by using the *herber* as a place to look out of, not to look at. The grove of oaks, into which the poet first passes, gives way to a little path, which leads to a 'pleasaunt herber',

> 'That benched was, and with turfes new
> Freshly turved, whereof the greene gras,
> So small, so thicke, so short, so fresh of hew,
> That most like unto green welwet it was.
> The hegge also, that yede in compas   *went around*
> And closed in all the green herbere,
> With sicamour was set and eglatere,
>
> Wrethen in fere so wel and cunningly   *twisted together*
> That every branch and leafe grew by mesure,
> Plain as a bord, of an height, by and by . . .
> And shapen was this herber, roofe and all,
> As a pretty parlour, and also
> The hegge as thicke as a castel wall . . .'[143]

The subduing of nature's forms to a cosy imitation of the civilized indoors is usual, but at this point, unexpectedly, the poem opens a vista of the surrounding fields and plains, in which the rest of the action takes place, including a curiously realistic summer hailstorm. There had been vantage points and hidden observers in allegorical love vision before, but nothing quite like this self-conscious alternation of closed and deep perspective. It might remind us of the Flemish interiors of a slightly earlier period, which suddenly open to a distant windowed prospect.

This sort of visual composition is probably more important to the growth of a sense of landscape than the casual realism which can be found almost everywhere in the fifteenth century—earlier in the same poem, for instance, where the buds of the young oak leaf are noted as 'very red', a touch of observation which drew Gilbert White's praise.[144] Even Hawes has dawn appearing

'In the depured ayre and cruddy fyrmament'[145]

where the epithet *cruddy*, if it suggests cloud effects like curdled milk, as presumably it does, is so visually apt that one suspects textual error or concealed stereotype, anything but observation on Hawes' part.[146] The importance of the *Floure and the Leafe* is that it leaps the confines of the garden fence, for the sense of landscape was even less to be nourished in late medieval gardens than in those of earlier centuries. Tastes beginning to be imported from Italy, where the design of gardens tended to lag behind the vision of painters (they were still, for instance, laid out on level ground), demanded elaborate and artificial formality, flower beds in complicated knots and parterres, fantastic topiary work, stone-built arbours, porticoes, colonnades, mazes, statues, grottoes and mechanical water devices. These tastes, represented in no doubt extreme form in the *Hypnerotomachia Poliphili* of Francesco Colonna (1467, printed 1499), a curious allegorical romance full of imaginary gardens which had a profound influence upon garden design throughout Europe,[147] are modestly reflected in a late fifteenth-century poem like the *Assembly of Ladies*, where the narrator, after wandering in a maze, finds herself in 'a streyte passage', which leads to a benched arbour enclosed by a stone wall and floored with stone tiles.[148] Here masonry and paving tiles have begun to take over the functions of hedge and greensward, which, for all man's contrivance, can still look embarrassingly natural. In Hawes, the courtyard has taken the place of the garden, and is dominated by an architecture of cheap magnificence. The Tower of Doctrine has turrets with golden images, with pipes in their mouths, which are blown by the wind so as to play the tune 'Amour de la hault pleasaunce', and in the courtyard is a fountain of fine gold and red enamel,

'And on the toppe foure dragons blewe and stoute
This doulcet water in foure partyes dyde spoute.'[149]

In the courtyard of the Tower of Chivalry there are mechanical horses which can trot and gallop like real ones by some miraculous contrivance of cogs and cords and crafty geometry.[150] Hawes's few natural landscapes conceal their echoes of Chaucer and Lydgate in a patchy tinsel of aureation:

> 'A medowe bothe gaye and gloryous
> Whiche Flora depaynted with many a colour
> Lyke a place of pleasure most solacyous
> Encensynge out the aromatyke odoure
> Of Zepherus brethe which that every floure
> Throughe his fume dothe alwaye engendre'[151]

and his one extended garden description concentrates exclusively on the artifice of flower knots, exotic topiary work and elaborately decorated fountain.[152]

A much richer seam for the development of landscape is provided by the encyclopaedic and philosophical tradition of seasons description. This tradition, with its emphasis on the ordered cycle of germination, growth and decay, the measured procession of the seasons as an aspect of universal order and as an image of human life, lies behind much medieval description of seasons and seasonal landscapes, just as it lies behind the Calendar pictures, tracing its ancestry to the philosophical vision of Virgil in the second book of *Georgics* and Boethius in the *De Consolatione Philosophiae*, and passed down to the Middle Ages in innumerable encyclopaedias and *computs*.[153] The seasons are presented in their authentic encyclopaedic setting, with appropriate moralization of man's life, in Lydgate's translation of the *Secreta Secretorum*, one of the source books for the tradition.[154] Still more explicit is Henryson's handling of the theme at the heart of the *Morall Fabillis*:

> 'All creature He maid for the behufe
> Off man and to his supportatioun
> Into this eirth, baith under and abufe,
> In number, wecht and dew proportioun;
> The difference off tyme and ilk seasoun
> Concorddand till our opurtunitie,
> As daylie be experience we may se.'[155]

Of the seasons that follow, it is winter, characteristically for a Scots poet, that is most powerfully described, though still in fairly conventional terms:

> 'Than flouris fair faidit with froist man fall,   *must*
> And birdis blyith changit thair noitis sweit
> In styll murning, neir slane with snaw and sleit.
> Thir dalis deip with dubbis drounit is,   *pools*
> Baith hill and holt heillit with frostis hair;   *covered*
> And bewis bene laifit bair off blis   *boughs*
> Be wickit windis off the winter wair;   *wild*
> All wyld beistis than from the bentis bair   *fields*
> Drawis for dreid unto thair dennis deip,
> Coucheand for cauld in coifis thame to keip.'[156]   *hollows*

The encyclopaedic tradition, along with other traditions of paradisal bounty and, more simply, of accumulation as an ornament of style, also gives stimulus to the catalogue of natural phenomena, a favourite device of medieval nature poetry. The animal catalogue of the *Kingis Quair* imitates the catalogue of trees in Chaucer's *Parlement*, attaching characterizing epithets in the same way,[157] and a poem called *How a lover praiseth his Lady* in MS Fairfax 16 presents a garden of love in lists of trees, herbs, birds and precious stones. The lists are an extraordinary medley of the homely and the exotic, and seem to operate on no principle but that of total recall:

> 'In this gardyn of al maner of kynde
> Cedres were of lyban and of Inde,
> With virres clymbyng up yn to hevene,
> Ful of shadowe, a thousand on a stevinne,   *at a time*
> Datrees, gernadez, ever blowyng orengys,
> Brasyl, almaunders, even sette yn rengys,   *in rows*
> The hard costard, the duryng wardon per,
> And damasyns yn a quarter set I-fer.'[158]

The final degeneration of this trick of style can be seen in *The Squire of Low Degree*, where lists of trees and birds are introduced, quite gratuitously, to give a tawdry glitter to the threadbare habit of romance. The original philosophical dignity of the form, however, is reasserted in *The Court of Sapience*, where the catalogues of flowers, trees, birds and animals[160] are integral to the structure of the poem, which is essentially a poetic summary of universal knowledge.

Such poems still treat Nature as a concept, and natural phenomena as a manifestation of the divine:

> 'Yit nevertheles we may haif knawlegeing
> Off God Almychtie be His creatouris
> That he is gude, fair, wyis and bening:

Exempill tak be thir jolie flouris . . .
The firmament payntit with sternis cleir,
From eist to west rolland in cirkill round,
And everilk planet in his proper spheir,
In moving makand harmonie and sound;
The fyre, the air, the watter and the ground—
Till understand it is aneuch, I wis,   *enough*
That God in all His werkis wittie is.'[161]

What is perhaps more significant, in the development of landscape, is when seasons description is detached from its philosophic setting and re-set in narrative. This is what happens in Henryson's fable of *The Preiching of the Swallow* and, on a much larger scale, in Lydgate's *Troy-Book*, where the dawn and sunset and spring transitions of classical and medieval epic are expanded into great set-pieces, counterpointing the flux of human fortune against the universal certainties. In some of these passages, such as the elaborate spring description at the end of book I,[162] Chaucer's influence is strong, but one of the paradoxes of Lydgate is that his confidence in working within a strict convention will often prompt him to experiment in a way he would not dare elsewhere, and it is out of this confidence, and out of the suggestions provided by Calendar pictures, that he extends seasons description into February and autumn landscapes for which there is little precedent in rhetorical tradition.[163]

In poetry as in painting,[164] this freedom, this extended sense of seasonal landscape, is decisively more important than any development we have seen in courtly garden description, and it is reflected in other fifteenth-century poetry, where a taste for autumn and winter openings disturbs the sway of spring,[165] hitherto so universal that even St Valentine's day poems began with spring-descriptions:

'Le doulz printemps ou tout se renouvelle
Commence anuit . . .'[166]

These are only 'preludes', of course, preludes to poems and preludes to a vision of landscape. Perhaps the nearest we come to a significant use of a seasonal motif is in Robert Henryson's *Testament of Cresseid*. Here formal Calendar associations may provide the model for a highly personal and seemingly naturalistic account of a chilly evening in early spring, when the poet turns from his window to the comfort of fireside, drink and books. The January and February activities now belong to March or April—but this is

Scotland, not France or Italy, and the adjustment is significant. The description of moonlit room and clear frosty sky is evocative in a new way:

> 'Throwout the glas hir bemis brast sa fair
> That I micht se on everie syde me by;
> The northin wind had purifyit the air,
> And sched the mistie cloudis fra the sky . . .[167]

but the image of the old man in 'doolie sessoun', bent over book and fire, is very familiar. Indeed, Henryson's explicit matching of his 'cairfull dyte' to inclement weather, followed as it is by a narrative of fearful retribution worked by a god who appears as the embodiment of the winter:

> 'His widderit weid fra him the wind out woir'
>
> (165)

shows that his attitude to the seasons and their landscape, though serious, was firmly traditional. His senses were sharp enough to register their quality: his judgment pronounced that part a limited one.

It was, however, a Scottish poet who eventually proved the strength of a treatment of the natural world both detailed and panoramic. All the traditions of late medieval poetic landscape flow together and coalesce, miraculously, in Gavin Douglas. The Prologues to certain books of his translation of the *Aeneid*[168] declare the independence of landscape description as a literary form for the first time, and manage to combine accuracy of detail and overall visual coherence in a way that makes Douglas the only poet comparable with the great Flemish landscape painters of the fifteenth and sixteenth centuries. No immediate literary precedent can be found for these descriptions of spring, summer and winter, arranged in cyclic form, and presented as extensive and self-sufficient units. Only Calendar art suggests a model. And this is borne out by the mixture of materials; seasonal labour and seasonal landscape are indivisible parts of a whole. June dawns for poet, traveller and farmer:

> 'Sone our the feildis schynys the lycht cleir,
> Welcum to pilgrym baith and lauborer.'
>
> (XIII, 169-70)

The winter day takes in man at work:

> 'Puyr lauboraris and bissy husband men
> Went wait and wery draglit in the fen'   *wet, bedraggled*
> (VII, 75-6)

as well as the raging of the storm. The references are often to Calendar motifs—the fattening of the swine, in November:

> 'fat swyne in sty,
> Sustenyt war by mannys governance
> On hervist and on symmeris purvyance;'   *summer's*
> (*ibid.* 82–4)

the retreat to food and fire in January and February:

> 'The callour ayr, penetratyve and puyr,   *fresh*
> Dasyng the blude in every creatur,
> Maid seik warm stovis and beyn fyris hoyt,   *seek, pleasant*
> In dowbill garmont cled and wily coyt,   *under-coat*
> With mychty drink and metis confortyve,
> Agane the stern wyntir forto stryve.'
> (*ibid.* 87–92)

Still acknowledging the medieval past, and in particular the medieval Calendar, in his concept of beauty as fruitfulness, Douglas is also true to older allegiances in his concept of landscape as socially significant. Although winter can rouse him, as it did the *Gawain* poet, to a kind of angry admiration for the grandeur of its wild pageants, it is still the season when 'bewte was lost, and barrand schew the landis' (*ibid.* 41), when man and beast cower from the elements. Inhabited landscape remains at the centre of his view:

> 'Baith man and beste, fyrth, flude and woddis wild
> Involvyt in tha schaddois warryn syld.'   *hidden*
> (XIII, 41–2)

But if Calendar art provided Douglas with more than a framework, it placed no greater restriction upon the range of his work than it did upon that of a painter such as Simon Benninck or, in later decades, upon that of Pieter Bruegel. Indeed, Douglas is at home in many different kinds of landscape description. The spring prologue to Book XII begins with a dazzling display of astronomical pyrotechnics, reminiscent of Statius rather than Virgil, and closer still to Dunbar's painted style:

> 'As fresch Aurora, to myghty Tytan spows,
> Ischit of hir safron bed and evir hows,   *issues, ivory*
> In crammysyn cled and granyt violat,   *dyed in grain*
> With sangwyne cape, the selvage purpurat,

Onschet the wyndois of hir large hall,
Spred all with rosys, and full of balm ryall,
And eik the hevynly portis cristallyne
Upwarpis braid, the warld till illumyn.   *flings open wide*
The twynklyng stremowris of the orient
Sched purpour sprangis with gold and asur ment, *stripes*
Persand the sabill barmkyn nocturnall,   *barbican*
Bet doun the skyis clowdy mantill wall.'

                (13–24)

The eye descends from the sky to a distant prospect of land and cityscape, suffused with light:

'For to behald, it was a glor to se
The stablit wyndis and the cawmyt see,
The soft sesson, the firmament sereyn,
The lowne illumynat ayr, and fyrth ameyn. . . . *calm, pleasant*
Towris, turettis, kyrnellis, pynnaclys hie   *battlements*
Of kyrkis, castellis and ilke fair cite,
Stude payntit, every fyall, fayn and stage,   *final, vane*
Apon the plane grund, by thar awyn umbrage.'

         (51–4, 69–72)

It rests upon the flowers underfoot:

'The dasy dyd onbreid hir crownell smaill,
And every flour onlappyt in the daill;
In battill gyrs burgionys the banwart wild, *thick grass, daisy*
The clavyr, catcluke, and the cammamyld; *clover, trefoil*
The flour delys furthspred hys hevynly hew,
Flour dammes, and columby blank and blew; *auricula*
Seir downys smaill on dent de lyon sprang *many*
The yyng greyn blomyt straberry levys amang; *young*
Gymp gerraflouris thar royn levys onschet, *graceful, 'roan'*
Fresch prymros and, the purpour violet . . . .'

           (113–22)

There are echoes of paradisal landscapes, of decorative courtly imagery,

'The lowkyt buttonys on the gemmyt treis *closed buds, budded*
Ourspredand leyvis of naturis tapestreis'

           (101–2)

of the massed effects characteristic of alliterative poetry. But all is organized
with incomparable visualizing power, and charged with a sensuous response
to detail: the range and quality of perception is newly impressive.

The description of a summer evening in the Prologue to book XIII takes
its inspiration from Virgil's nocturnes, but it has a much more expansive
and evocative sense of landscape. There is a painter's vision of fading light
and shadowy perspective:

'The lyght begouth to quynchyng owt and faill,	*began to dim*
The day to dyrkyn, declyne and devaill;	
The gummys rysis, doun fallis the donk rym,	*mist, chill damp*
Baith heir and thar scuggis and schaddois dym.	*shadows*
Upgois the bak with hir pelit ledderyn flycht,	
The lark discendis from the skyis hycht,	
Syngand hir complyng sang, efter hir gys,	
To tak hir rest, at matyn hour to rys.	
Owt our the swyre swymmys the soppis of myst,	*valley*
The nycht furthspred hir cloke with sabill lyst,	*hem*
That all the bewte of the fructuus feld	
Was with the erthis umbrage cleyn ourheld . . .'	*covered over*

(XIII, 29–40)

Little remains for the eighteenth-century landscape poets to add to this, and
perhaps nothing in the eighteenth century can compare with the sweep and
energy of Douglas's winter landscape in the Prologue to book VII:

'The soyl ysowpit into watir wak,	*soaked, running*
The firmament ourcast with rokis blak,	*clouds*
The grond fadyt, and fawch wolx all the feildis,	*yellow-brown*
Montane toppis slekit with snaw ourheildis;	*smoothed, covers*
On raggid rolkis of hard harsk quhyn stane	
With frosyn frontis cauld clynty clewis schane.	*fissures*
Bewte was lost, and barrand schew the landis,	
With frostis hair ourfret the feldis standis . . .	*patterned over*
The dolly dichis war all donk and wait,	*wretched*
The law valle flodderit all with spait,	
The plane stretis and every hie way	
Full of floschis, dubbis, myre and clay.	*bogs, puddles*
Laggerit leyis wallowit farnys schew,	*boggy fields, ferns*
Broune muris kythit thar wysnyt mossy hew,	*show, shrivelled*

Bank, bra and boddum blanchit wolx and bar.　　　*valley bottom*
For gurl weddir growit bestis hair.　　　　　　　*grim*
The wynd maid waif the red wed on the dyke,
Bedowyn in donkis deip was every sike.　　　　　*brook*
Our craggis and the front of rochis seir　　　　*many*
Hang gret ische schouchlis lang as ony speir.'

(35–42, 51–62)

Landscape is here, for the first time, the subject of poetry, and the observer's eye delights in its vision. Yet an advanced naturalism, a full awareness of landscape, are still adjusted to a strong sense of man's relation to nature and the governance of the land. In one important respect, the Prologues of Douglas and the later Flemish Calendars are the completion of a process essentially medieval as well as the inauguration of a new art form. The reconciliation of moral and aesthetic sensibilities had long been under way in the context of the labours of the months. Only here could the medieval passion for accepting responsibility be harmonized with the growing passion for observing and describing that 'mighty world of eye and ear' which earlier Christian centuries had so distrusted. To see this as the encroachment of secular upon religious interests is a half-truth; the boundaries of the old were widened to admit the new, and promises made were kept, at last, in changed conditions. The relationship of labour to landscape, and of artist to both, so differently interpreted at different times in the Middle Ages, were stabilized—not as formulas, but as declarations of creative independence.

The point is most happily made just beyond the limits of the period, not in later sixteenth-century poetry, whose Calendars were either severely practical or remodelled to classical Eclogue tradition,[169] but in five paintings of Bruegel with seasonal themes: *The Hunters in the Snow* (Plate 37), *The Gloomy Day, Hayfield, The Corn Harvest*, and *The Return of the Herd* (Plate 36).[170] Nothing medieval is denied by these studies of winter and summer months: this is the changing landscape of humanity, hunted, pruned, harvested, travelled-over, slept upon. It is the old landscape of action, filled with evidence of the needs and pleasures of ordinary mankind. There is room for the traditional labours—the singeing of the freshly killed pig in December, the pollarding of the trees in March, the hay making and fruit gathering of June, the cutting and stacking of corn in August. But in providing a deep, wide and detailed setting for such labours, Bruegel does not become over-assertive about the claims of landscape. There is none of that melodramatic exaggeration of natural features which so frequently characterizes the work of his younger contemporary, Joachim Patinir,[171] and which Bruegel himself found appropriate to certain themes.[172] In these seasonal paintings, the subject is both man and nature. Enlarging, rather than destroying medieval perspectives, Bruegel allows us the pleasure of noticing how 'the light cloud smoulders on the summer crag', high above the busy cornfields: he also makes sure that in marvelling at the dusky colours of the November woods, we do not fail to notice the weary homeward progress of man and beast.

NOTES AND BIBLIOGRAPHICAL
REFERENCES

It would be rash to attempt a bibliography for a book so diverse in its source materials as this one. However, certain secondary sources have been so important and influential that it would be ungrateful not to list them here, separately.

K. Clark, *Landscape into Art* (London, 1949)

F. Crisp, *Medieval Gardens* (2 vols, London, 1924)

E. R. Curtius, *European Literature and the Latin Middle Ages*, trans. W. R. Trask (New York, 1953; originally published in German, Berne, 1948)

J. Daniélou, *From Shadows to Reality*, trans. Dom W. Hibberd (London, 1960: originally published as *Sacramentum Futuri*, Paris, 1950)

E. H. Gombrich, *Norm and Form: Studies in the Art of the Renaissance* (London, 1966)

Marie-Luise Gothein, *A History of Garden Art*, ed. W. P. Wright (2 vols, London, 1928)

R. Hinks, *Carolingian Art* (London, 1935)

A. Katzenellenbogen, *Allegories of the Vices and Virtues in Medieval Art* (London, 1939)

M. Meiss, *French Painting in the time of Jean de Berry: the late fourteenth century and the patronage of the Duke* (2 vols, London, 1967)

—— *French Painting in the time of Jean de Berry: the Boucicaut Master* (London, 1968)

—— (ed., with J. Longnon, R. Cazelles) *Les Très Riches Heures du Duc de Berry* (London, 1969)

C. R. Morey, *Early Christian Art* (Princeton, 1953)

M. Nicolson, *Mountain Gloom and Mountain Glory* (1959; New York, 1963)

W. Oakeshott, *Classical Inspiration in Medieval Art* (London, 1959)

O. Pächt, *Early Italian Nature Studies and the Early Calendar Landscape*, *JWCI*, XIII (1950)

E. Panofsky, *Early Netherlandish Painting* (Cambridge, Mass, 1953)

—— *Renaissance and Renascences in Western Art* (Stockholm, 1960; 2nd ed., 1965)

M. Rickert, *Painting in Britain: the Middle Ages* (Harmondsworth, 1954)

J. Ruskin, *Mediaeval Landscape*, in *Modern Painters*, vol. III (*Works*, ed. Cook and Wedderburn, vol. V, pp. 248–316)

A. R. Turner, *The Vision of Landscape in Renaissance Italy* (Princeton, 1966)

R. Tuve, *Seasons and Months: Studies in a Tradition of Middle English Poetry* (Paris, 1933)

J. C. Webster, *The Labors of the Months* (Evanston and Chicago, 1938)

ABBREVIATIONS

Bibl. Nat.	Bibliothèque Nationale, Paris
B.M.	British Museum
EETS	Early English Text Society
ES	Extra Series
JWCI	Journal of the Warburg and Courtauld Institutes
MLN	Modern Language Notes

MLR   Modern Language Review
MP   Modern Philology
Pat. Lat.   Patrologia Latina, ed. J. P. Migne
PMLA   Publications of the Modern Language Association of America
SATF   Société des Anciens Textes français

CHAPTER ONE   CLASSICAL TRADITIONS

1   *Natural History*, XXXV. 71, 88, 92 (Loeb).
2   *Iliad*, trans. E. V. Rieu, Penguin Classics, 1950, p. 186.
3   *Iliad*, pp. 52, 88, 257.
4   *Iliad*, pp. 159–60. A word may be said here about the practice adopted in this study with quotations from works in foreign languages: languages with which the authors are not familiar are quoted in translation only; other languages are quoted in the original, with accompanying translation, except for medieval French, where occasional glosses are provided. This is the practice too with medieval English, where spellings are also occasionally simplified and obsolete letters systematically replaced.
5   *Iliad*, pp. 351–2.
6   *Odyssey*, trans. E. V. Rieu, Penguin Classics, 1946, pp. 204, 264, 227.
7   *Odyssey*, pp. 142, 98.
8   *Odyssey*, p. 115.
9   *Odyssey*, p. 90.
10   *Iliad*, p. 52.
11   *Aeneid*, vi. 309–10 (Loeb translation).
12   *Iliad*, p. 237.
13   *Aeneid*, xii. 688–9.
14   *Aeneid*, i. 81–123; *Odyssey*, p. 95.
15   Sir Archibald Geikie, *The Love of Nature among the Romans*, London, 1912, p. 218.
16   *Odyssey*, pp. 142, 157, 204.
17   G. Williams, *Tradition and Originality in Roman Poetry*, Oxford, 1968, p. 640.
18   *Aeneid*, i. 158–69.
19   *Aeneid*, viii. 96.
20   *Aeneid*, xi. 522, viii. 597.
21   *Aeneid*, vii. 563. See A. G. McKay, *Vergil's Italy* (Bath, 1971), p. 240.
22   See *Aeneid*, ed. J. W. Mackail, Oxford, 1930, note to i. 164, p. 14.
23   Vitruvius, *On Architecture*, VII, Preface, 11 (Loeb).
24   *Op. cit.*, V. vi. 9.
25   Mary Hamilton Swindler, *Ancient Art*, New Haven, 1929, p. 327.
26   See A. M. G. Little, 'Aeneid Landscape', a note in *American Philological Association, Proceedings for 1939*, pp. xxxviii–xxxix; A. G. McKay, *Vergil's Italy*, p. 291.
27   *Aeneid*, vii. 8.
28   *Aeneid*, viii. 22–5.
29   *Natural History*, XXXV. 138.
30   See T. B. L. Webster, *Hellenistic Poetry and Art*, London, 1964, pp. 70–1, 74–5, 160. The imagery of Medea's troubled heart, in fact (Webster, pp. 74–5), closely resembles the passage quoted from Virgil.

31 See Louisa V. Walker, 'Vergil's Descriptive Art', *Classical Journal*, XXIV, 1929, 666–78, p. 670. Even McKay, in a book dedicated to locality, admits the 'vagueness' of the locale here (*Vergil's Italy*, p. 56).

32 *Aeneid*, viii. 626–728.

33 Some illustrations in Sir Mortimer Wheeler, *Roman Art and Architecture*, London, 1964, pp. 163–7.

34 *Georgics*, ii. 150.

35 E. Fraenkel, *Horace*, Oxford, 1957, p. 110. See Horace, *Satires*, I. v. 25–6.

36 *Georgics*, ii. 156–7.

37 Fraenkel, *loc. cit.*

38 *Thebaid*, vi. 255, ii. 497, iv. 697.

39 *Thebaid*, vii. 55, x. 106. Some of these likenesses are literary in origin; others no doubt were imitated from actual painting and statuary. See T. S. Duncan, *The Influence of Art on Description in the poetry of Statius*, Baltimore, 1914, pp. 67–73.

40 *Elegies*, IV. 9. 23–36.

41 See Williams, *Tradition and Originality*, pp. 650–1.

42 *De Natura Rerum*, ii. 114–20, 317–22. See Williams, *op. cit.*, pp. 665, 667.

43 *Op. cit.*, p. 203.

44 See T. B. L. Webster, *Hellenistic Poetry and Art*, p. 165.

45 *Eclogues*, i. 51–2 (Loeb translation).

46 See *Les arts poétiques du XIIe et du XIIIe siècle*, ed. E. Faral, Paris, 1923, pp. 86–9.

47 *Georgics*, iv. 125–34.

48 *Metamorphoses*, vii. 187–8 (Loeb translation).

49 *Met.*, xi. 229.

50 *Met.*, i. 295.

51 *Tristia*, I. ii. 27.

52 *Met.*, ii. 454, iii. 407, v. 385, iii. 155, v. 587.

53 *Met.*, i. 568–9. *Tempe* is used as a catachresis for 'pleasant vale' in *Georgics*, ii. 476; Hadrian's villa at Tivoli was built in grounds that included a 'vale of Tempe'.

54 *Natural History*, IV. viii. 31 (Loeb translation).

55 L. P. Wilkinson, *Ovid Surveyed*, Cambridge, 1962, p. 82.

56 *Ars Poetica*, 17.

57 Geikie, as might be expected (*Love of Nature among the Romans*, p. 78), has some difficulty in accepting this interpretation of the poem.

58 See Gisela M. A. Richter, *Perspective in Greek and Roman Art*, London, 1970; but cf. J. White, *The Birth and Rebirth of Pictorial Space*, London, 1957; 2nd ed., 1967, p. 262: 'All the evidence points to the existence, in antiquity, of a theoretically founded system of vanishing point perspective'.

59 See C. R. Morey, *Early Christian Art*, Princeton, 1953, p. 41.

60 See A. Mau, *Pompeii: its Life and Art*, trans. F. W. Kelsey, 2nd ed., New York, 1902, pp. 280–366, 456–84.

61 See W. Oakeshott, *Classical Inspiration in Medieval Art*, London, 1959, p. 17.

62 *Natural History*, XXXV. 116.

63 *On Architecture*, VII. v. 2 (Loeb translation). He speaks also of narrative representations, as of the tale of Troy or of the wanderings of Ulysses, which we shall see evidence of in a moment.

64 Some illustrations in Wheeler, *Roman Art and Architecture*, pp. 184–7, 194–9.

65 Morey, *Early Christian Art*, p. 49.

66 Vitruvius, *On Architecture*, Introduction (Loeb), p. xxix.

67 Marie-Luise Gothein, *A History of Garden Art*, ed.. W. P. Wright, 2 vols, London, 1928, i. 101. Pliny's account is in *Letters*, V. vi.

68 Georgina Masson, *Italian Gardens*, London, 1961, p. 25.

69 *Silvae*, II. ii. 75. Cf. Vitruvius, VI. iii. 10.

70 E. Panofsky, *Renaissance and Renascences in Western Art*, Stockholm, 1960; 2nd ed., 1965, p. 121. This is not to imply that the techniques of either linear or aerial perspective are fully understood: see Richter, *op. cit.*, p. 48.

71 E. Panofsky, *Early Netherlandish Painting*, Cambridge, Mass., 1953, p. 9.

72 F. Wickhoff, *Roman Art*, trans. S. A. Strong, London, 1900, p. 178.

73 E. Auerbach, *Mimesis*, New York, 1957; first published in German, Berne, 1946, p. 50.

74 W. Dorigo, *Late Roman Painting*, London, 1971; translation of *Pittura tardoromana*, Milan, 1966, pp. 38–9 and colour plate 2.

75 Dorigo, *op. cit.*, p. 59.

76 Dorigo, *op. cit.*, chap. 6 *passim*.

77 Dorigo, *op. cit.*, pp. 274–5. See also A. Grabar, *The Beginnings of Christian Art*, London, 1967, pp. 51, 54.

78 Swindler, *Ancient Art*, p. 414.

79 Grabar, *op. cit.*, p. 233 and pl. 256.

80 Dorigo, *op. cit.*, p. 179.

81 Dorigo, *op. cit.*, p. 216.

82 Dorigo, *op. cit.*, p. 230.

83 There is a complete series of reproductions in H. Karpp, *Die Mosaiken in Santa Maria Maggiore zu Rom*, Baden-Baden, 1966; see also W. Oakeshott, *The Mosaics of Rome*, London, 1967.

84 See below, p. 64.

85 Morey, *Early Christian Art*, p. 159.

86 See Oakeshott, *Classical Inspiration*, p. 17.

87 *On Architecture*, VII. v. 4.

88 See Grabar, *The Beginnings of Christian Art*, pp. 56–7, 288–9.

89 C. Diehl, *La peinture Byzantine*, Paris, 1933, p. 8.

90 O. Demus, *Byzantine Art and the West*, London, 1970, pp. 3, 47.

91 See Morey, *Early Christian Art*, figs. 211–15.

92 Morey, *op. cit.*, p. 48.

93 Wickhoff, *Roman Art*, p. 178. These remarks are frequently echoed.

94 Morey, *op. cit.*, p. 70; see figs. 58–9.

95 E. R. Curtius, *European Literature and the Latin Middle Ages*, trans. W. R. Trask, New York, 1953; originally published in German, Berne, 1948, pp. 196–7.

96 *Shorter Poems*, v (Loeb, ii. 178: Loeb translation).

97 See Curtius, *op. cit.*, p. 195.

98 *De Raptu*, ii. 88–117.

99 *Pervigilium*, I (Loeb translation).

100 *Aeneid*, iv. 522; *Eclogues*, ii. 8.

101 Loeb translation, in the appendix to Ausonius, ii. 277.

102 *Mosella*, 63–7 (Loeb translation).

103 *Poems*, xxii, in the Loeb edition, i. 263.

104 Translation by F. J. E. Raby, *Secular Latin Poetry in the Middle Ages*, 1934, 2nd ed., 2 vols, Oxford, 1957, i. 130.

Notes and Bibliographical References
CHAPTER TWO   THE EARLY MIDDLE AGES

1 See below, pp. 62-3.

2 *Eadmeri Monachii Liber de S. Anselmi Similitudinibus*, cap. xii: 'Horum autem sensuum delectatio raro est bona, saepius vero mala' (*Pat. Lat.* 159.608).

3 *Libri Carolini*, ed. H. Bastgen, *Monumenta Germaniae Historica*, Legum sectio III, Concilia, tom. II supplementum, Hanover and Leipzig, 1924, lib. II, cap. xxiii, p. 82; also II. xxx, pp. 92-100.

4 Theophilus, *De Diversis Artibus*, trans. C. R. Dodwell, London and Edinburgh, 1961, pp. 15-16.

5 G. Duby, *L'Economie Rurale et la Vie des Campagnes dans l'Occident Médiéval*, 2 vols, Paris 1962, i. 57.

6 Duby, *op. cit.*, ii. 565-6.

7 The plan, frequently reproduced (as in Gothein, *History of Garden Art*, fig. 124), is an ideal one.

8 This is especially true of later works like the *Liber Ruralium Commodorum* (1305) of Pietro de' Crescenzi of Bologna, a treatise on agriculture and horticulture which probably draws on the author's knowledge of the royal pleasure gardens of Sicily. See Georgina Masson, *Italian Gardens*, London, 1961, pp. 52-3.

9 Gothein, *op. cit.*, i. 182.

10 See below, chaps. III and IV.

11 O. M. Dalton, *Byzantine Art and Archaeology*, Oxford, 1911, p. 244.

12 C. R. Morey, *Mediaeval Art*, New York, 1942, pp. 110-11, figs. 39-40.

13 See A. Grabar, *Byzance*, Paris, 1963, p. 23.

14 British Museum, Addit. MS 19352. See S. Der Nersessian, *L'Illustration des Psautiers grecs du Moyen Age, II: Londres, Add. 19352*, Paris, 1970.

15 See D. Talbot Rice, *The Art of Byzantium*, London, 1959, fig. 127.

16 Addit. MS 11870. For two illustrations from this MS, see G. Mathew, *Byzantine Painting*, London, 1950, pp. 13, 15.

17 See M. J. Friedländer, *On Art and Connoisseurship*, London, 1942, p. 114.

18 E.g. the Gospels of Bernward of Hildesheim, and the Lambeth Bible: see Oakeshott, *Classical Inspiration*, pl. 101.

19 See Geikie, *The Love of Nature among the Romans*, pp. 295-6; and cf. P. Birot and J. Dresch, *La Méditerranée et le Moyen-Orient*, Paris, 1953, i. 281 ff, 'L'Apennin Calcaire'. Such features are not uncommon in Mediterranean limestone areas generally.

20 F. Bologna, *Early Italian Painting*, London, 1963, p. 52 and pl. 36; O. Demus, *Romanesque Mural Painting*, London, 1970; originally published as *Romanische Wandmalerei*, Munich, 1968, p. 94 and pl. 93. See also E. W. Anthony, *Romanesque Frescoes*, Princeton, 1951, p. 113 and fig. 207.

21 See O. Demus, *Byzantine Art and the West*, pp. 230-2; and see p. 33 below.

22 See O. Demus, *The Mosaics of Norman Sicily*, London, 1949, pp. 262-4. This book contains a full programme of illustrations.

23 Demus, *Mosaics of Norman Sicily*, p. 357.

24 Both translations are from K. Jackson, *Studies in Early Celtic Nature Poetry*, Cambridge, 1935, pp. 3, 26; cf. also *Early Irish Lyrics*, ed. G. Murphy, Oxford, 1956, pp. 5, 161.

25 Jackson, *op. cit.*, p. 104. One is in the hands of the translator, of course; but comparison of Jackson's renderings with Murphy's often suggests how the former has

romanticized his original. For his 'woodland thicket', for instance, Murphy has 'a hedge of trees'.

26 This rather simplified distinction is the thesis of the paper by F. Bucher, *Medieval Landscape Painting: an Introduction*, in *Medieval and Renaissance Studies: Proceedings of the Southeastern Institute of Medieval and Renaissance Studies*, Summer 1967, ed. J. M. Headley, Chapel Hill, 1968, pp. 119–69.

27 Jackson, *op. cit.*, p. 9.

28 Murphy, *op. cit.*, pp. 7, 13.

29 See, e.g., F. J. E. Raby, *Secular Latin Poetry*, i. 205, 233, 247, 250, 302, 304. For an example of naturalistic representation in MS illustration, see the blackberry briar in the Latin *Herbal of Sextus Apuleius Barbarus*, pl. 35 in the Bodleian Picture Book of *Anglo-Saxon Illumination in Oxford Libraries*, Oxford, 1970, or f. 26 in the facsimile ed. by R. T. Gunther, Oxford, 1925; the thistle (f. 37v) is another example of drawing direct from nature—other illustrations are more derivative from classical models (see Gunther, *op. cit.*, p. xxiv).

30 Quoted by J. Carney, *Medieval Irish Lyrics*, Dublin, 1967, p. xx.

31 Murphy, *op. cit.*, pp. 224–5.

32 Oakeshott, *Classical Inspiration*, pl. 15, 69.

33 Oakeshott, *op. cit.*, pl. 71b.

34 R. Hinks, *Carolingian Art*, London, 1935, pp. 176–7.

35 Hinks, *op. cit.*, pp. 163–4.

36 F. Wormald, *The Utrecht Psalter*, Utrecht, 1953, p. 12.

37 See the facsimiles in E. T. DeWald, *The Illustrations of the Utrecht Psalter*, Princeton, 1932.

38 Panofsky, *Renaissance and Renascences in Western Art*, p. 49.

39 H. Swarzenski, *Monuments of Romanesque Art*, London, 1954, p. 25. Swarzenski reproduces the illustration to Psalm 43 from the Utrecht and all three copies in pl. 2–3; C. R. Dodwell (*The Canterbury School of Illumination 1066–1200*, Cambridge, 1954) has Psalm 30 from the three copies (pl. 1, 27, 69).

40 Compare pl. 72 and 73 in Margaret Rickert, *Painting in Britain: the Middle Ages* (Penguin, 1954), reproducing Psalms 51 and 15 from the Eadwine Psalter, and scenes of Moses and the Israelites from the Lambeth Bible.

41 Oakeshott, *Classical Inspiration*, pl. 36.

42 See Rickert, *op. cit.*, pl. 84 and 86. The influence of the mosaic style of Monreale is direct and well-attested here. See also the illustrations from some early thirteenth-century herbals in Gunther, *op. cit.*, pp. 104, 112.

43 Rickert, *op. cit.*, p. 63 and pl. 53.

44 O. Pächt, *The Rise of Pictorial Narrative in 12th-century England*, Oxford, 1962, pl.41.

45 Swarzenski, *op. cit.*, pl. 55. Such features may well be of Byzantine origin.

46 See O. Demus, *Romanesque Mural Painting*, pp. 7–8.

47 Anthony, *Romanesque Frescoes*, p. 36. Cf. Demus, *op. cit.*, p. 19.

48 *The Wanderer*, ed. R. F. Leslie, Manchester, 1966, lines 45–8. Translation from R. K. Gordon, *Anglo-Saxon Poetry*, rev. ed., London, 1954, pp. 73–4.

49 *The Seafarer*, ed. I. L. Gordon, London, 1960, lines 12–19, 31–3. Translation from R. K. Gordon, *op. cit.*, p. 76.

50 E. G. Stanley, 'Old English Poetic Diction and the Interpretation of *The Wanderer*, *The Seafarer* and *The Penitent's Prayer*', *Anglia*, LXXIII 1955, 413–66, p. 427.

51 See *The Wanderer*, ed. Leslie, pp. 31–2; and see below, pp. 59ff.

52 *Homilies of Aelfric*, ed. Thorpe, 1844, i. 162, quoted by G. V. Smithers, 'The Meaning of *The Seafarer* and *The Wanderer*', *Medium Aevum*, XXVI, 1957, 137–53, p. 145.

53 *Beowulf*, ed. F. Klaeber, New York, 1922, with revisions, lines 1357–76. Translation from R. K. Gordon, *op. cit.*, pp. 28–9.

54 As Stanley does, *op. cit.*, p. 440.

55 See Klaeber's note to line 1357 and, for a translation of the passage from the homily, S. B. Greenfield, *A Critical History of Old English Literature*, New York, 1965, p. 59. The allegorical possibilities of the mere are elaborately developed in articles by Robertson, Cabaniss and McNamee printed in *An Anthology of Beowulf Criticism*, ed. L. E. Nicholson, Notre Dame, 1963, especially pp. 184–5, 224–5, 338–46. And see below, p. 66.

56 See further the discussion of *The Phoenix*, below, pp. 65–7.

57 *Beowulf*, 222, 1132.

58 In *Egil's Saga*, trans. E. R. Eddison, Cambridge, 1930, p. 65, chap. 33.

59 *Grettis Saga*, trans. G. A. Hight, London, 1965, p. 127, chap. 48.

60 *Laxdaela Saga*, trans. T. Veblen, New York, 1925, p. 77, chap. 24.

61 *Grettis Saga*, pp. 174–5, chaps. 65–6.

62 *Egil's Saga*, p. 170, chap. 71.

63 *Njal's Saga*, trans. M. Magnusson and H. Pálsson, London, 1960, p. 166, chap. 75.

64 E.g. *Early Irish Lyrics*, ed. G. Murphy, nos. 44, 46–7, 51–2.

65 *Roland*, ed. F. Whitehead, Oxford, 1942, lines 1830–1. Translation by Dorothy Sayers, Penguin, 1957.

66 *Roland*, 1423–37: an echo of Gospel narratives of the Crucifixion.

67 As W. P. Ker does, *Epic and Romance*, London, 1896, 1908; New York, 1957, p. 56.

68 *European Literature and the Latin Middle Ages*, p. 201; and see above, p. 10.

69 Cicero, *De Inventione*, I. xxvi. 38 (Loeb translation).

70 *Ars Versificatoria*, I. 107, 111: in *Les Arts Poétiques du XIIe et du XIIIe siècle*, ed. E. Faral, Paris, 1923, pp. 146–9.

71 *Le Roman de la Rose*, ed. E. Langlois, SATF, Paris, 1920, note to line 78, vol. ii. p. 294.

72 *Op. cit.*, pp. 157–9.

73 *Ad Herennium*, IV. xxxix. 51, IV. lv. 68.

74 *Institutio Oratoria*, VIII. iii. 61.

75 *Ibid.*, IX. ii. 44.

76 See M. B. Ogle, 'Classical Literary Tradition in early German and Romance Literature', *MLN*, XXVII 1912, 233–42.

77 See above, p. 37.

78 See Curtius, *op. cit.*, p. 195: the 'mixed forest'.

79 In Helen Waddell, *Mediaeval Latin Lyrics*, 1929; Penguin, 1952, p. 154.

80 Faral, *op. cit.*, p. 149.

81 *Op. cit.*, p. 198. A kinder view might recognize certain touches of delicacy.

82 Quoted from F. J. E. Raby, *Secular Latin Poetry*, ii. 17. Nevertheless, one would agree with Peter Dronke (*Poetic Individuality in the Middle Ages*, Oxford, 1970, p. 17) that there is a good deal more in Alan than in the traditional *locus amoenus*, and also with his more general strictures on Curtius' tendency to believe that a poem can be defined in the identity of its commonplaces.

83 Waddell, *op. cit.*, p. 226.

84 William of Aquitaine, first of the *troubadours*, in *Introduction à l'Etude de l'Ancien*

Provençal, ed. F. R. Hamlin, P. T. Ricketts and J. Hathaway, Geneva, 1967, p. 56. Translation provided by Dr Ricketts.

85   See B. Q. Morgan, *Nature in Middle High German Lyrics*, Hesperia 4: Göttingen, 1912, p. 95.

86   *Poetria Nova*, 545–53: in Faral, *Les Arts Poétiques*, p. 214.

87   *Estivali sub fervore*, from the *Carmina Burana*, in E. H. Zeydel, *Vagabond Verse*, Detroit, 1966, p. 166, with translation: reprinted by permission of the Wayne State University Press.

88   In Waddell, *op. cit.*, p. 250.

89   E. Faral, *Recherches sur les Sources Latines des Contes et Romans Courtois du Moyen Age*, Paris, 1913, pp. 202, 239, 328–35, 369–72.

90   *Europäische Literatur und Lateinisches Mittelalters*, p. 200: Trask's translation, 'an elaborate vocabulary' (*op. cit.*, p. 195), is perhaps a little pallid.

91   *Yvain*, ed. W. Foerster, Halle, 1887, 760–68: translation by W. W. Comfort, *Arthurian Romances*, London, 1914, p. 190.

92   See A. C. L. Brown, *Iwain: a Study in the Origins of Arthurian Romance*, Harvard Studies, VIII, 1903; repr. New York, 1965, pp. 82–94.

93   *Erec et Enide*, ed. Foerster, Halle, 1890, 3130, 3157.

94   *Erec et Enide*, 3669–73: translation by Comfort, p. 48.

95   Ed. L. Constans, 2 vols, SATF, Paris, 1890, 2923–62.

96   W. Calin, *The Epic Quest*, Baltimore, 1966, p. 192.

97   F. Whitehead, 'Tristan and Isolt in the Forest of Morrois', in *Studies in French Language and Medieval Literature presented to Professor Mildred K. Pope*, Manchester, 1939, pp. 393–400 (p. 393).

98   *Tristan*, trans. A. T. Hatto, Penguin Classics, 1960, pp. 261–2.

99   See G. Duby, *op. cit.*, i. 244–5.

100   'Tho was yonge Gamelyn glad and blithe y-nough / Whan he fond his merry men under woode-bough' (773–4): in *Middle English Verse Romances*, ed. D. B. Sands, New York, 1966, p. 177.

101   *Tristan*, trans. Hatto, p. 49.

102   *Thebaid*, iv. 797.

103   Ed. cit., lines 2141–8, quoted also in Curtius, *European Literature*, p. 201: the translation is by the present author.

CHAPTER THREE   THE LANDSCAPE OF PARADISE

1   Honorius of Autun, *Elucidarium*, Pat. Lat. 172, col. 1117.

2   *Religious Lyrics of the Fifteenth Century*, ed. C. Brown, Oxford, 1939, p. 115 (spelling normalized).

3   *The Travels of Sir John Mandeville*, ed. A. W. Pollard, Dover Publications, New York, 1964, p. 201.

4   *Alexandri Iter ad Paradisum*, a twelfth-century Latin prose work, translated and quoted by M. Lascelles, in 'Alexander and the Earthly Paradise in Medieval English writings', *Medium Aevum*, V, 1936, 36–7.

5   *Sybilline Oracles*, Proem, 84, quoted by Zofda Ameisenowa, 'The Tree of Life in Jewish Iconography', *JWCI*, II, 1938–9, 331.

6   *Mandeville's Travels*,   p. 202.

7   See above, pp. 48–52.

8   *Mandeville's Travels*, p. 201.

9   *Floire et Blanceflor*, ed. E. du Méril, Paris, 1856, 1747–9, 1753–8.

10 *Le Roman de la Rose*, ed. E. Langlois, 5 vols, SATF, Paris, 1914–24, 1567, 1569–70 translated as *The Romaunt of the Rose* (lines 1597, 1599–1600), in *The Poetical Works of Chaucer*, ed. F. N. Robinson, 2nd ed., Cambridge, Mass., 1957. All reference to Chaucer is from this edition.

11 *Pearl*, ed. E. V. Gordon, Oxford, 1953, 113–14, 117–19.

12 *Pearl*, 83–4, 137–44.

13 J. Chydenius, *The Typological Problem in Dante: a Study in the History of Medieval Ideas*, Helsingfors, 1958, p. 24.

14 *Luke*, 23 : 43.

15 *On the Allegories of the Sacred Laws*, in *Works of Philo Judaeus*, trans. C. D. Yonge, London, 1854, i. 63.

16 *Questions and Solutions to those Questions which arise in Genesis*, in *Works*, iv. 286, 289.

17 *De Paradiso*, in *Pat. Lat.* 14, cols. 279 ff.

18 *The Book of Vices and Virtues*, ed. W. N. Francis, EETS, 217, 1942, p. 93.

19 Quoted in J. Daniélou, *From Shadows to Reality*, trans. Dom W. Hibberd, London, 1960, p. 25. The work was originally published as *Sacramentum Futuri*, Paris, 1950.

20 *Ibid.*, p. 27.

21 *Ibid.*, p. 27.

22 *Commentary on the Canticles*, Sermon 8, quoted in *From Glory to Glory: Texts from Gregory of Nyssa's Mystical Writings*, sel. J. Daniélou, trans. H. Musurillo, London, 1962, pp. 227–8.

23 *Ibid.*, p. 156.

24 See J. J. Rorimer, *The Unicorn Tapestries at the Cloisters*, New York, 1962, plate 33.

25 *From Glory to Glory*, p. 232.

26 *Ibid.*, p. 228.

27 *Ibid.*, p. 231.

28 See above, p. 27, and below, p. 77.

29 *Pat. Lat.* 3, cols. 27–8, translated in *From Shadows to Reality*, p. 28.

30 See above, p. 18.

31 Bede, *Hexameron, Pat. Lat.* 91, col. 44. See also Avitus, *De Mosaicae Historiae Gestis*, Bk. 1, ll. 211–14, *Pat. Lat.* 59 : 328.

32 See Curtius, *op. cit.*, p. 186; H. R. Patch, *The Other World*, Cambridge, Mass., 1950, pp. 25–6, 135 ff.

33 *Purgatorio*, xxviii. 139–43, ed. Rizzoli, 1949: translation by Dorothy Sayers, Penguin, 1955. All quotation and translation from Dante is from these editions.

34 *Carmen de Ave Phoenice*, lines 1, 9–10, 25: text from *The Phoenix*, ed. N. F. Blake, Manchester, 1964. Authors' translation.

35 Hildegard of Bingen, *Liber Divinorum Operum Simplicis Hominis*, in *Pat. Lat.*, 197, col. 749.

36 *Phoenix*, ed. Blake, pp. 30–31.

37 See also below, p. 113.

38 See also above, p. 42.

39 See the facsimile of *The Cædmon Manuscript*, ed. I. Gollancz, Oxford, 1927.

40 *Genesis*, 215–17, 221–6, in *The Junius Manuscript*, ed. G. P. Krapp, New York, 1931. Authors' translation.

41 Compare the account of the Utrecht Psalter and its copies, above, p. 39.

42 See A. Katzenellenbogen, *Allegories of the Virtues and Vices in Medieval Art*, London, 1939, pls. 38–41.

43 St Jerome, *Epistola IX, De Assumptione Beatae Mariae Virginis*, in *Pat. Lat.* 30, col. 132. See also *Epistola X*, which pictures the Virgin 'inter paradisi amoenitates', *loc. cit.*, col. 144.

44 Honorius of Autun, *Speculum Ecclesiae*, in *Pat. Lat.* 172, col. 833.

45 Honorius of Autun, *Expositio in Psalmis*, Psalm 1:3, in *Pat. Lat.* 172, cols. 277.

46 Ed. J. Walter, Strasbourg and Paris, 1952.

47 *Ed. cit.*, plate 38.

48 Cf. plate 43 in Katzenellenbogen, *op. cit.*, which reproduces an even more austere version of this illustration.

49 See B.M. MS Arundel 44, f. 13r.

50 *De Conversione ad Clericos*, in *Pat. Lat.*, 182, col. 847.

51 See above, p. 61.

52 *Book of Vices and Virtues*, ed. Francis, p. 93.

53 *Paradiso*, xxiii. 71, xxxi. 97, xxx. 124.

CHAPTER FOUR   THE ENCLOSED GARDEN

1 *Paradiso*, xxvi. 64–6. See above, p. 74.

2 See P. Dronke, *Medieval Latin and the Rise of the European Love-Lyric*, vol. I, Oxford, 1965, chap. v.

3 See, e.g., no. 26 in *Introduction à l'Etude de l'Ancien Provençal*, ed. F. R. Hamlin, P. T. Ricketts and J. Hathaway, Geneva, 1967.

4 *Cligès*, ed. W. Foerster, Halle, 1884, 6400–24; translation by W. W. Comfort, *Arthurian Romances*, London, 1914, p. 174.

5 See above, p. 27.

6 *Liberate Roll*, 34 Henry III, memb. 6, 20 June.

7 H. N. Wethered, *A Short History of Gardens*, London, 1933, pp. 122–3.

8 Quotation in Marie-Luise Gothein, *A History of Garden-Art*, ed. W. P. Wright, 2 vols, London, 1928, i. 40.

9 Gothein, *A History of Garden-Art*, i. 143.

10 See B.M. Addit. MS 18113, f. 40v (1396) and B.M. Addit. MS 25900 (1490), plate 15 in B. Robinson, *Persian Miniature Painting*, London, 1967.

11 E.g. *Romaunt of the Rose* 54–70, *Pearl* 71–2, Lydgate's *Complaint of the Black Knight* 51–2 (see Appendix).

12 *Romaunt* 602–4.

13 See E. Cerulli, *Il Libro della Scala*, Vatican, 1949, and M. Manzaloui, 'English Analogues of the *Liber Scalae*', *Medium Aevum*, XXXIV, 1965, 21–35.

14 B.M. Addit. MSS 27695, 28841 and Egerton 3127. The Latin texts in this collection draw some of their material, significantly, from the history of Cyprus and Sicily.

15 M. Meiss, *Painting in Florence and Siena after the Black Death*, Princeton, 1951, pp. 140–1.

16 I am indebted for this plate-reference to Lord Clark. And see also B. Gray, *Persian Painting*, London, 1947, p. 10, plates 5 and 6.

17 *The Haft Paikar, or The Seven Beauties*, trans. C. E. Wilson, London, 1924, i. 235–6.

18 *Ibid.*, i. 114.

19 *Lailī and Majnūn*, trans. from the Persian of Nizāmī by J. Atkinson, rev. L. Cranmer Byng, London, 1905, pp. 160–1.

20 Prose parable by the twelfth-century Sūfī writer Shibāb al-Dīn Suhravardī Maqtūl: translated and quoted by A. J. Arberry, *Classical Persian Literature* London, 1958,, pp. 107–8.

21 Gothein, *op. cit.*, i. 150.

22 *Makhzanol Asrār*, *The Treasury of Mysteries*, trans. Gholām Hosein Dārāb, London 1945, pp. 101, 104, 112.

23 *Ibid.*, p. 105.

24 Lorenzo de' Medici Il Magnifico, *Opere*, ed. A. Simioni, Bari, 1913, i. 42: translation in A. R. Turner, *The Vision of Landscape in Renaissance Italy*, Princeton, 1966, p. 39.

25 'She said it was more a case of "père-Robert" than of "Jennet-pear" ' (a kind of pear ripening early on St John's day). From *Secular Lyrics of the XIVth and XVth centuries*, ed. R. H. Robbins, Oxford, 1952, p. 15.

26 *The Decameron*, trans. R. A. Aldington, London, 1957, p. 284.

27 *Ibid.*, p. 10.

28 *Ibid.*, p. 159.

29 *Ibid.*, p. 158.

30 *Ibid.*, p. 544.

31 See above, p. 58.

32 See M. Meiss, *Painting in Florence and Siena after the Black Death*, pp. 74ff.

33 See M. Meiss, *French Painting in the time of Jean de Berry: the Late Fourteenth Century and the Patronage of the Duke*, 2 vols, London, 1967, pl. 319, 320.

34 *Ed. cit.*, lines 48–9; Chaucerian translation, *ed. cit.*, lines 52–3.

35 Cf. p. 49 above.

36 *Decameron*, p. 544.

37 Authors' translation.

38 *Roman*, 19938.

39 Chaucer, *Knight's Tale*, 3007–3010, based on Boethius, *De Consolatione Philosophiae*, book IV, prose 6.

40 See E. S. Greenhill, 'The Child in the Tree', *Traditio*, X, 1954, 323–71.

41 In Alan of Lille, *De Planctu Naturae*, pr. T. Wright, *Anglo-Latin Satirical Poets of the 12th Century*, (Rolls Series, no. 59, 1872), ii. 429–522.

42 See Rosemond Tuve, *Allegorical Imagery: some Medieval Books and their Posterity*, Princeton, 1966, pp. 276 ff; J. V. Fleming, *The Roman de la Rose: a Study in Allegory and Iconography*, Princeton, 1969, chap. I.

43 Laurent de Premierfait, quoted in Fleming, *op. cit.*, p. 62.

44 H. Martin, *Le Boccace de Jean sans Peur*, Brussels, 1911, p. 11.

45 Sir Gilbert Haye's *Buik of King Alexander*: quoted from B.M. Addit. MS 40732 by M. Lascelles, 'Alexander and the Earthly Paradise', *Medium Aevum*, V, 1936, p. 90.

46 The visual expression of such an acceptance can be found in fourteenth-century wall paintings from Italy—courtly figures, male and female, transfixed by arrows of love, but willingly enduring their state. See A. Morassi, 'Una Camera d'Amore nel Castello di Avio', *Festschrift für Julius Schlosser*, Zurich, etc., 1927, pp. 99 ff.

47 Wallace Stevens, *Sunday Morning*.

48 See below, p. 193.

49 See above, p. 58.

50 From Sir Gilbert Haye's *Buik of King Alexander*, quoted in Lascelles, *op. cit.*, p. 89.

51 See above, p. 72.

52 See above, p. 59.

53 Charles d'Orléans, *Rondeau: Le Temps a laissé*, trans. P. T. Lesley, quoted in Panofsky, *Early Netherlandish Painting*, i. 69.

54 Gregory of Nyssa: see above, p. 63.

55 See J. Chydenius, *The Typological Problem in Dante*, p. 107.

56 *Paradiso*, xxxiii. 144–5.

57 See chapter 5, below.

58 *English Lyrics of the XIIIth century*, ed. C. Brown, Oxford, 1932, p. 1.

59 The 'Goldenes Rössel', Altötting, Pilgrimage Church, Upper Bavaria. See plate 85 in G. Henderson, *Gothic*, Penguin, 1967.

60 In the church of St Martin, Colmar (*c.* 1473): fig. 7 in F. Crisp, *Medieval Gardens*, 2 vols, London, 1924.

61 See Crisp, fig. 78: the illustration was used in the Italian version of *P. Crescentiüs de Agriculture Vulgarüs*, Venice, 1511.

62 See C. A. Luttrell, '*Pearl*: Symbolism in a Garden Setting', *Neophilologus*, XLIX, 1965, 160–76, and Pan of sky, *op. cit.*, pls. 198, 226.

63 See below, p. 186.

64 B.M. Addit. MS 18850, ff. 9v, 192ʳ.

65 Paris, Bibl. Nat. MS fr. 616: see *Livre de la Chasse: Réproduction réduite des 87 miniatures du ms. français 616*, Paris, 1910.

66 *Ibid.*, pl. 68, 72.

67 *Ibid.*, pl. 87; and see *La Chasse de Gaston Phebus*, ed. J. Lavallée, Paris, 1854, p. 274.

68 See also fig. 98 in Crisp, *Medieval Gardens*: 'Parc au Cerfs', from a later fifteenth-century tapestry.

69 Butler's *Lives of the Saints*, ed. H. Thurston and D. Attwater, London, 1956, iv. 247–8.

70 See Crisp, *Medieval Gardens*, figs. 44, 45.

71 For the 'Boucicaut workshop', see M. Meiss, *French Painting in the time of Jean de Berry: the Boucicaut Master*, London, 1968.

72 See Meiss, *op. cit.*, pl. 381, 448.

73 *Ibid.*, pl. 379.

74 Boccaccio, *Teseida*, vii. st. 52; Chaucer, *Parlement of Foules*, 196.

75 *Ayala Hours*, Lisbon, f. 63a.

76 See Crisp, *Medieval Gardens*, fig. 69.

77 For this MS in general, see *Les Très Riches Heures du Duc de Berry*, ed. J. Longnon, R. Cazelles and M. Meiss, London, 1969.

78 *Ibid.*, pl. 20 and commentary.

79 Now in the Musee D'Unterlinden, Colmar.

80 Henry Hawkins, *Partheneia Sacra*: see below, note 89.

81 Rorimer, *The Unicorn Tapestries*, pl. 33, 34.

82 Ed. M. R. James, Oxford, 1926.

83 *Poems*, ed. J. Norton-Smith, Oxford, 1966, p. 26.

84 Henry Hawkins, *op. cit.*

85 For this MS see the facsimile edition, *Das Breviarum Grimani*, ed. S. de Vries and S. Morpurgo, 14 vols, Leiden, 1903–8 and M. Salni, *The Grimani Breviary*, London, 1972.

86 *Cant.* 4:4, 4:15; *Ecclus.* 24:17–19.

87 See Rosemary Freeman, *English Emblem Books*, London, 1948.
88 *Religious Lyrics of the XVth century*, ed. C. Brown, p. 67.
89 *Partheneia Sacra*, facsimile ed., with introduction by I. Fletcher, Hand and Flower Press, Aldington, 1950, p. 2.
90 *Ibid.*, pp. 31–2.
91 *Ibid.*, p. 12.
92 *Ibid.*, p. 11.
93 Andrew Marvell, *The Garden*. For Marvell's poem, seen in a traditional garden context, see S. Stewart, *The Enclosed Garden: The Tradition and the Image in Seventeenth-century Poetry*, Wisconsin U.P., 1966.
94 Anthony Stafford, *The Female Glory*, 1635, prefatory poem, quoted in Freeman, *op. cit.*, p. 182.
95 Bartholomew Griffin's *Fidessa*, 1596.

CHAPTER FIVE THE LANDSCAPE OF THE SEASONS

1 Hart Crane, *Voyages* (11).
2 Virgil, *Georgics*, i. 424–6 (Loeb translation).
3 Lucretius, *De Rerum Natura*, v. 747: 'crepitans hanc dentibus Algor'.
4 Ovid, *Metamorphoses*, ii. 27–30 (Loeb translation).
5 *Georgics*, ii. 401–2.
6 *Georgics*, i. 302: 'invitat genialis hiems curasque resolvit'. See also ii. 259, 406, 520.
7 See J. C. Webster, *The Labors of the Months*, Evanston and Chicago, 1938, pp. 9 ff.
8 *De Rosis Nascentibus*, attrib. Ausonius (Loeb ed., author's trans.).
9 Propertius, *Elegies*, IV. v. 61–2. Author's translation.
10 *De Rerum Natura*, v. 199, 220–1: translation by R. E. Latham, Penguin, 1951, p. 177.
11 *Ibid.*, v. 620.
12 *Ibid.*, v. 1203: translation, p. 208.
13 *Georgics*, i. 121–3, 145–6.
14 See above, ch. 3.
15 *Genesis* 3:17. For fuller discussion of this verse, and its complicated history, see Marjorie Nicolson, *Mountain Gloom and Mountain Glory*, 1959; New York, 1963, pp. 84 ff.
16 *Tristia*, III. iv. 48.
17 *The Wanderer*, 101–7: author's translation. See above, p. 41.
18 *The Seafarer*, 14–15: see above, p. 41.
19 *Ibid.*, 53–5.
20 Helen Waddell, *Medieval Latin Lyrics*, Oxford, 1929, pp. 272–3.
21 *Genesis*, 805–8, 810–11, in *The Junius Manuscript*, ed. G. P. Krapp, London and New York, 1931. Author's translation.
22 *Ibid.*, 952 ff.
23 Lucretius, *De Rerum Natura*, v. 1203.
24 *De Cons. Phil.*, IV, pr. 6, 45 ff. Chaucer's translation, *ed. cit.*
25 *Ibid.*, IV, m. 6, 25–33.
26 *Ibid.*, II, m. 3, 5–8.
27 *Ibid.*, II, pr. 5, 32–4.
28 *Ibid.*, 36–43.
29 *Ibid.*, I, pr. 5, 6–7.

30 Ambrose, *De Paradiso*, in *Pat. Lat.*, 14, col. 314.

31 *Liber Divinorum Operum Simplicis Hominis*, in *Pat. Lat.* 197, col. 857.

32 *Ibid.*, col. 886.

33 *Genesis*, 3:17–18.

34 *Secular Lyrics of the XIVth and XVth centuries*, ed. R. H. Robbins, Oxford, 1955, p. 62. Each line refers to a month of the year.

35 See Webster, *op. cit.*, chap. iii, and E. Mâle, *L'Art Religieux du XIIIe siècle en France*, Paris, 1925, pp. 65 ff.

36 Rosemond Tuve, *Seasons and Months*, Paris, 1933, p. 45.

37 *Cleanness*, ed. I. Gollancz, Oxford, 1921, 523–7.

38 *Troilus and Criseyde*, ii. 50–54.

39 For these Torre dell' Aquila frescoes, see O. Paecht, 'Early Italian Nature Studies and the Early Calendar Landscape', *JWCI*, XIII, 1950, 38 ff.

40 See P. D'Ancona, *The Schifanoia Months at Ferrara*, trans. L. Krasnik, Milan, 1955.

41 B.M. MS Cotton Tiberius B. v, part 1, ff. 3–8v.

42 See also below, p. 144.

43 MS Montecassino 132, facsimile edition of the illustrations by A. M. Amelli, *Miniature illustranti L'Enciclopedia Medioevale di Rabano Mauro*, Montecassino, 1896, LIII, LV.

44 *Parlement of Foules*, 130.

45 See Tuve, *Seasons and Months*, pp. 128–9.

46 *Piers Plowman*, ed. W. W. Skeat, Oxford, 1886, B. xiv. 164–5.

47 *Ibid.*, C. xiii. 192, xvi. 292, B. xiv. 112.

48 *Ibid.*, C. x. 78, B. xiv. 161–2.

49 *Ibid.*, B. xvii. 226–8.

50 *Ibid.*, C. xiii. 219–23.

51 See E. Mâle, *op. cit.*, figs. 33, 34, 37, 39.

52 B.M. Addit. MS 27944, f. 124v.

53 *Early Medieval French Lyrics*, ed. C. C. S. Abbott, London, 1932, no. 73.

54 *Ibid.*, no. 86.

55 Roy Campbell, *Autumn*.

56 See Tuve, *Seasons and Months*, pp. 159–60.

57 *Kyng Alisaunder*, ed. G. V. Smithers, EETS 227, 237, 1952–7, 457–62.

58 Corpus Christi College, Cambridge, MS 53.

59 As in the so-called Paduan Psalter, Fitzwilliam Museum, Cambridge, MS 36–1950, f. 12v. Webster (*Labors of the Months*, p. 78) cites one example of baking for the December 'labour', from the twelfth-century cathedral of Senlis.

60 *Ed. cit.*, p. 139-42.

61 *Ibid.*, 5745–50.

62 B.M. MS Cotton Tib. B. v., part I, ff. 5v, 7,

63 See below, p. 168.

64 B.M. MS Royal 2.B. vii, ff. 72r–83r.

65 B.M. Addit. MS 42130, ff. 170r–173v.

66 *Piers Plowman*, C. ix. 310–15.

67 See Paecht, 'Early Italian Nature Studies', pp. 46–7.

68 Folgore da San Gemignano, *Rime*, ed. G. Navone, 1881, no. 9, p. 20: trans. R. Aldington, *A Wreath for San Gemignano*, London, 1946, p. 25.

69 Browning, *De Gustibus*.

70 *Rime*, no. 7, p. 51: translation, p. 23.

71 *Rime*, no. 5, p. 11.

72 *Rime*, no. 4, p. 9: translation, p. 20.

73 *Rime*, no. 2, p. 5: translation, p. 18.

74 *Rime*, no. 13, p. 29.

75 Paecht, *op. cit.*, p. 47.

76 *Rime*, no. 7, p. 15: translation, p. 23.

77 *Rime*, no. 5, p. 11: translation, p. 21. And cf. the discussion of Petrarch below, p. 182.

78 See *Les Très Riches Heures de Duc de Berry*, ed. cit., pl. 5, 6, 7.

79 Deschamps, *Lay de Franchise*, in *Oeuvres*, ed. de Queux de Saint-Hilaire and G. Raynaud, SATF, 1878–1903, vol. II, p. 204.

80 See above, p. 138.

81 See Panofsky, *Early Netherlandish Painting*, pp. 33–4, and p. 373, n.2.

82 The Calendar of the first volume of the *Belleville Breviary* (Paris, Bibl. Nat. MS lat. 10483/4) was used as the model for seven other manuscripts, which are fully listed in K. Morand, *Jean Pucelle*, Oxford, 1962, p. 44. Plates for the purposes of the present volume have been taken from the *Petites Heures* of Jean de Berri (Bibl. Nat. MS lat. 18014) and the *Grandes Heures* of Jean de Berri (Bibl. Nat. MS lat. 919).

83 All of the Calendar illustrations from the Prayer Book of Bonne of Luxembourg, (New York, Cloisters Collection, MS 69.86) are reproduced in the *Bulletin* of the Metropolitan Museum of Art, New York, for February 1971.

84 Paecht, *op. cit.*, p. 46.

85 Paecht, *op. cit.*, pp. 31–7, and pl. 10a, b.

86 *Ibid.*, pl. 11d, 12c.

87 See Sir M. Conway, 'Giovannino de' Grassi and the Brothers van Limbourg', *Burlington Magazine*, XVIII, 1910, 144 ff.

88 Paecht, *op. cit.*, pl. 12c.

89 *Meditationes Vitae Christi*, trans Nicholas Love, 1410, ed. L. F. Powell, Oxford, 1908, pp. 48–9.

90 See M. Meiss, *French Painting in the time of Jean de Berry: the late Fourteenth Century*, p. 171.

91 Brussels, Bibl. Royale MS 11060/1, presented by Jean de Berri to the duke of Burgundy in 1403/4.

92 See M. Meiss, *French Painting in the time of Jean de Berry: the Boucicaut Master*, London, 1968.

93 See Meiss, *The Boucicaut Master*, figs. 30–32, 35.

94 *Ibid.*, fig. 54.

95 See above, p 112, and p. 134. The French translation is by Jean Corbechon, *Le Livre de la Propriété des choses*: Fitzwilliam Museum MS 251.

96 See above, p. 107.

97 Musée Jacquemart-André MS 2: see Meiss, *The Boucicaut Master*, pp. 7–22, pl. 1–44, and pls. 48a, b above.

98 See above, pp. 102–8.

99 See *Les Très Riches Heures*, ed cit., pl. 2.

100 *Sir Gawain and the Green Knight*, ed. R. A. Waldron, London, 1970, 44–7, 55.

101 See below, p. 180.

102 *Piers Plowman*, C. xvi. 293–4.

103 *The Adoration of the Kings, in Snow*: Winterthur, collection Oskar Reinhart.

104 See Tuve, *Seasons and Months*, pp. 123–4.

105 *Franklin's Tale,* 1243–7, 1250–54.

106 *Ibid.,* 1513; and see p. 99 above.

107 See, for instance, the July miniature, *Les Très Riches Heures, ed. cit.,* pl. 8.

108 *Ibid.,* Preface by M. Meiss, p. 11.

109 Wood chopping is known for February in a few thirteenth- and fourteenth-century MSS: cf. Bibl. Nat. MS lat. 1077. See Tuve, *Seasons and Months,* p. 161.

110 *Rime, ed. cit.,* no. 2, p. 5.

111 Those of the *Petites Heures* and the Brussels Hours, for instance: see above, p. 145.

112 For the frescoes of the Torre dell'Aquila, see Paecht, 'Early Italian Nature Studies', pp. 38 ff, and above, p. 131.

113 *Rime, loc. cit.*

114 See above, p. 145.

115 See Sir M. Conway, 'Giovannino de' Grassi and the brothers Van Limbourg', and Paecht, 'Early Italian Nature Studies', pp. 40–1.

116 In the *Watch over the Tomb* miniature, for instance, from their *Belles Heures* (c. 1410: New York, Cloisters), f. 152v: in the edition of J. Porcher, Paris, 1953, pl. 81.

117 B.M. MS Yates Thompson 37, f. 118v: reproduced in M. Meiss, *French Painting in the time of Jean de Berri: the Late XIVth century,* fig. 264.

118 *Ibid.,* text vol., pp. 220–1.

119 See, for instance, L. M. C. Randall, *Images in the Margins of Gothic Manuscripts,* California U.P., 1966, figs. 83, 641,701, etc.

120 Dylan Thomas, *A Winter's Tale.*

121 See Sir M. Conway, *op. cit.,* p. 149, pl. 2.

122 B.M. MS Add. 18850, ff. 1r et seq.

123 Bibl. Nat. MS lat. 9471: see J. Porcher, 'Two Models for the "Heures de Rohan"', *JWCI,* VIII, 1945, 1–6.

124 See especially pp. 197–205.

125 See above, p. 110.

126 Stefano di Giovanni, called Sassetta, 1392–1450: Metropolitan Museum of Art, New York; for the Dijon *Nativity* (Musée de la Ville), see Panofsky, *Early Neth. Painting,* pl. 88, figs. 201–2; the Bellini *Madonna* is in the National Gallery, London.

127 As, for instance, in the background of Joachim Patinir's *Flight into Egypt,* Korinklijk Museum voor Schone Konsten, Antwerp.

128 See the sequence in B.M. Addit. MS 38126, an early sixteenth-century Flemish Book of Hours (reproduced in B.M. postcard series): Visitation, f. 66v, Annunciation to Shepherds, f. 79v, and Crucifixion, f. 39v. It is interesting that the Calendar miniatures show more seasonal variation—f. 2r has a robust winter vignette for January.

129 See the Calendar miniatures in B.M. Addit. MS 24098, an early sixteenth-century Book of Hours (reproduced in B.M. postcard series), ff. 18v–29v.

130 *Ibid.,* ff. 29v, 18v.

131 See note 85 to chapter 4, above; and see also P. Durrieu, 'Les Très Riches Heures et le Bréviaire Grimani', *Bibliothèque de l'Ecole de Chartres,* LXIV, 1903, 321–8.

132 Part of the series is contained in B.M. Addit. MS 18855, and part in the Salting Bequest, Victoria and Albert Museum, London, E4575–1910 verso.

133 See C. de Tolnay, *Pierre Bruegel l'Ancien,* Brussels, 1935, pp. 38 ff, and F. Grossman, *The Paintings of Peter Bruegel,* London, 1955, pl. 79–109 and accompanying notes.

CHAPTER SIX   LATE MEDIEVAL

1   C. R. Leslie, *Memoirs of the Life of John Constable*, ed. J. Mayne, London, 1951, p. 327. The classic study of the history of representation in art and its relationship with the psychology of perception is E. H. Gombrich, *Art and Illusion* (London, 1960).

2   Kenneth Clark, *Landscape into Art*, London, 1949, chap. II.

3   See above, p. 158.

4   See S. Gardner, *English Gothic Foliage Sculpture*, Cambridge, 1927, esp. p. 35.

5   N. Pevsner, *The Leaves of Southwell*, Penguin Books, 1945, pp. 53–65.

6   Quoted in Pevsner, *op. cit.*, p. 53.

7   See the facsimile of Bodley 130, ed. R. T. Gunther, Oxford, 1925, and see above, p. 35. For the *De arte venandi*, see C. H. Haskins, *Studies in the History of Medieval Science*, 1924, pp. 299–326.

8   *Op. cit.*, p. 23. See also above, pp. 19, 35.

9   C. E. Raven, *English Naturalists from Neckam to Ray*, Cambridge, 1947, p. 26.

10   *Ibid.*, p. 3.

11   See above, pp. 131–4.

12   Colour reproduction in the Skira *Gothic Painting*, 1954, p. 34.

13   *Gothic Painting*, p. 24.

14   Illustrations in Margaret Rickert, *Painting in Britain: the Middle Ages*, pl. 123–4. And see above, p. 138.

15   *Gothic Painting*, p. 25. And see above, p. 139.

16   *Gothic Painting*, p. 38.

17   See above, p. 143.

18   See M. Aubert, *High Gothic Art*, London, 1964, title page.

19   For a full discussion of the symbolic and spiritual implications of this picture and the following one, see above, pp. 108–11.

20   Rickert, *Painting in Britain*, pl. 161.

21   In *English Lyrics of the XIIIth Century*, ed. C. Brown, Oxford, 1932, p. 154. Similarly *Alysoun* ('Bytuene mersh and averil'), p. 138,

22   *Ibid.*, p. 119.

23   *Ibid.*, pp. 145–6, with emendation of MS *wynter wele* to *wynne wele* ('wealth of joys'), line 11, from *The Harley Lyrics*, ed. G. L. Brook, Manchester, 1948, p. 43.

24   See above, p. 50.

25   *English Lyrics of the XIIIth century*, p. 55.

26   *Ibid.*, p. 108.

27   *Harley Lyrics*, ed. Brook. p. 54: a variant version appears in Brown, *op. cit.*, p. 120.

28   *The English Religious Lyric in the Middle Ages*, Oxford, 1968, p. 64.

29   'An Autumn Song', in *Harley Lyrics*, ed. Brook, p. 60.

30   A typical example in *Amis and Amiloun*, 529–40.

31   *Ywain and Gawain*, ed. A. B. Friedman and N. T. Harrington, EETS, 254, 1964, 238–42. Cf. *Yvain*, 280.

32   *Sir Gawain and the Green Knight*, ed. R. A. Waldron, York Medieval Texts, London, 1970, 720–3.

33   See J. Finlayson, 'Rhetorical "Descriptio" of Place in the Alliterative *Morte Arthure*', *MP*, LXI, 1963, 1–11, pp. 7–11.

34   Chapter 5 above, pp. 136–8, deals in detail with these associations; the emphasis here is on the literary and rhetorical associations of such passages.

35 *Kyng Alisaunder*, ed. G. V. Smithers, EETS, 227, 237, 1952–7, 2543–7.
36 *Kyng Alisaunder*, 5745–7, and see above, p. 138.
37 Viz.41–8 (there is evidence of Chaucer's influence here), 963–78.
38 *Arthour and Merlin*, ed. E. Kölbing, Leipzig, 1890, 3059–64.
39 *Kyng Alisaunder*, Introduction, pp. 37–9.
40 T. B. L. Webster, *Hellenistic Poetry* and *Art*, 1964, gives examples from Homer and cites others from Callimachus and Apollonius of Rhodes (p. 70).
41 *Aeneid*, vii. 25.
42 *Aeneid*, xii. 113–15 (Loeb translation).
43 *Aeneid*, iv. 584–5. Cf. *Aeneid*, ix. 459; *Georgics*, i. 447.
44 *Aeneid*, iv. 522. Cf. viii. 26, x. 216.
45 *Thebaid*, iii. 407–14 (Loeb translation).
46 *Kyng Alisaunder*, Introduction, p. 39. There are also echoes, as in all seasons description in narrative, of larger themes of mutability: see D. Mehl, *The Middle English Romances of the 13th and 14th centuries*, London, 1968, p. 238.
47 See also above, p. 139.
48 See above, chapter 4.
49 See Rosemond Tuve, 'Spring in Chaucer and before him', *MLN*, LII, 1937, 9–16; also *Seasons and Months: Studies in a Tradition of Middle English Poetry*, Paris, 1933.
50 *Troilus and Criseyde*, ii. 50–6.
51 *Troilus*, v. 8, 274, 1016, 1107.
52 *Troilus*, ii. 820–2.
53 *Canterbury Tales*, I. 1491–6.
54 See *Book of the Duchess*, 162; *Knight's Tale*, I. 1977, 1979, 1991.
55 As Claes Schaar shows clearly, *The Golden Mirror: Studies in Chaucer's Descriptive Technique and its Literary Background*, Lund, 1955, pp. 372–7 385–7.
56 Ed. W. W. Skeat, in *Chaucerian and Other Pieces*, Oxford, 1897, lines 59–65.
57 *Le Dit dou Vergier*, 42–5: in *Oeuvres*, ed. E. Hoepffner, 3 vols, SATF, 1908–21, vol. I, p. 14.
58 In his essay on 'Medieval Landscape' in *Modern Painters*, vol. III (*Works*, ed. Cook and Wedderburn, V. 248–316), p. 257.
59 *La Fonteinne Amoureuse*, 1354 (*Oeuvres*, vol. III, p. 191).
60 Lines 81–106, *Oeuvres*, II. 162.
61 Lines 1393–1422, *Oeuvres*, I. 110.
62 Line 829, *Oeuvres*, II.30. The garden at Hesdin had been created by Robert of Artois on his return from the crusades in 1270; it was modelled on the gardens he had seen in Sicily, the only place where the realities of the oriental pleasure garden could be found in medieval Europe. See Georgina Masson, *Italian Gardens*, London, 1961, p. 51, and for arbours, see also chapter 4 above.
63 E.g. *La Fonteinne Amoureuse*, 1345; *Remede de Fortune*, 814.
64 Lines 25–33: in *Oeuvres*, ed. A. Scheler, 3 vols, Brussels, 1870–2, vol. II, p. 195. Author's translation.
65 *La Cour de May*, 160 (*Oeuvres*, III. 6).
66 *La Cour de May*, 361–4.
67 *Lay du Desert d'Amours* in *Oeuvres Complètes*, ed. de Queux de Saint-Hilaire and G. Raynaud, 11 vols., SATF, 1878–1903, vol. II, p. 182.
68 *Balades* 764–7.
69 *Balade* 419.

70 *Balade* 316.

71 *Balade* 315.

72 *Balades* 1143, 1161.

73 *Balade* 483 ('Sur le château de Cachan'). Cf. *Balades* 61, 144, 454, 483.

74 *Balade* 897. Cf. *Balades* 781–2, 790, 801, 812, 827, *Rondel* 637.

75 *Tristia*, III. iv. 52 (Loeb translation).

76 *Georgics*, iii. 354–5.

77 E.g. *Autres Balades*, IX, X, XXV, XXVIII, LII: in *Oeuvres poétiques*, ed. M. Roy, 3 vols, SATF, 1886–96, vol. I.

78 Lines 81–211 (*Oeuvres poétiques*, II. 161–5).

79 L. LeFrançois-Pillion, *L'Art du XIVe siècle*, Paris, 1954, p. 145.

80 *Ballades*, LXIII, XLIII, CV: in *Poésies*, ed. P. Champion, 2 vols, Classiques français du Moyen Âge, 1923–7, vol. I, pp. 88, 64, 165.

81 See Italo Siciliano, *François Villon et les thèmes poétiques du Moyen Âge*, Paris, 1934, p. 35: also Chapter VI, 'Pastoureaux'.

82 *Morte Arthure*, ed. E. Brock, EETS, 8, 1871, 3038–42.

83 *Wars of Alexander*, ed. W. W. Skeat, EETS, ES 47, 1886, 503–6.

84 *Parlement*, ed. M. Y. Offord, EETS, 246, 1959, 40–2.

85 See above, p. 166.

86 *Winner and Waster*, ed. I. Gollancz, Select Early English Poems III, Oxford, 1930, 35–43.

87 Lines 920–32.

88 Lines 2501–8. Björkman's edition, Heidelberg, 1915, has 'mornynge myste' in line 2506, but the MS reading seems in every way preferable.

89 *Historia Destructionis Troiae*, ed. N. E. Griffin, Cambridge, Mass., 1936, p. 6; *Destruction of Troy*, ed. G. Panton and D. Donaldson, EETS, 39, 56, 1869–74, 326–48; Lydgate, *Troy-Book*, ed. H. Bergen, EETS, ES 97, 103, 106, 126, 1906–20, i. 1265–1309; *Laud Troy Book*, ed. J. E. Wülfing, EETS, 121–2, 1902–3, 539–52.

90 *Destruction of Troy*, 4625–33. Cf. 1983, 3686, 12487, and imitation in *Siege of Jerusalem*, 53–72.

91 *Destruction of Troy*, 9636–9. Cf. 7618.

92 See above, pp. 147–52.

93 Lines 504–35, 713–32. See D. A. Pearsall, 'Rhetorical *Descriptio* in *Sir Gawain*', *MLR* L, 1955, 129–34.

94 See above, p. 31.

95 See A. R. Turner, *The Vision of Landscape in Renaissance Italy*, Princeton, 1966, p. 9, and pl. 9–10. Cf. an analogous effect (mentioned to me by Mrs Hazel Jones-Lee) in the alliterative *Wars of Alexander* 1527–8, in the description of Jerusalem arrayed to greet Alexander: 'And qua so lukis fra with-out, and with-in haldis, / It semyd as the cite to se ane of the sevyn hevyns'.

96 *Purgatorio*, xi. 94–6.

97 *Decameron*, vi. 5 (*Everyman* translation, 2 vols, 1930, ii. 73). See E. Panofsky, *Renaissance and Renascences*, pp. 11–15.

98 M. Meiss, *Painting in Florence and Siena after the Black Death*, Princeton, 1951.

99 See above, p. 175.

100 *Renaissance and Renascences*, p. 142.

101 Book vii, stanzas 51–60.

102 See above, p. 82. *Decameron*, iii (translation, i. 153–4).

103   *Decameron*, vi. 10 (translation, ii. 92).

104   See Edith G. Kern, 'The Gardens in the *Decameron* Cornice', *PMLA*, LXVI, 1951, 505–23, p. 514.

105   See *Letters from Petrarch*, selected and translated by M. Bishop, Bloomington, Indiana: London, 1966, pp. 23, 70, 87–9.

106   *Letters*, p. 49. See Clark, *Landscape into Art*, p. 7.

107   *Piers Plowman*, ed. W. W. Skeat, Oxford, 1886, C. XIV. 135–8, 174–7.

108   *Piers Plowman*, C. XV. 169–99.

109   *Li Contes dou Pellicam*, 103–9: in *Dits*, ed. A Scheler, 3 vols., Brussels, 1866–7, vol. I, p. 35.

110   Lynn Thorndike's salty comment, 'All Petrarch's account proves is his capacity for story-telling and sentimental ability to make a mountain out of a molehill' ('Renaissance or Prenaissance?' *Journal of the History of Ideas*, IV, 1943, 65–74, p. 72), misses this point.

111   See Marjorie Nicolson, *Mountain Gloom and Mountain Glory*, 1959; New York, 1963, pp. 39–40, 81–92.

112   *Ibid.*, p. 49.

113   Margaret Aston, *The Fifteenth century: the prospect of Europe*, London, 1968, p. 54.

114   See above, pp. 30–32.

115   *Letters*, p. 35.

116   *Letters*, p. 152.

117   *Paradiso*, xxii. 135; *Teseida*, xi. 1–3; *Troilus and Criseyde*, v. 1807–27.

118   As in Langland, or in the later alliterative *Death and Liffe*, ed. I. Gollancz, Select Early English Poems, Oxford, 1930, lines 39ff.

119   J. H. Whitfield, *Petrarch and the Renascence*, Oxford, 1943, p. 90.

120   See above, chapter 5.

121   *Early Netherlandish Painting*, Cambridge, Mass., 1953, p. 49.

122   See above, p. 32.

123   Panofsky, *op. cit.*, p. 180.

124   M. J. Friedländer, *Landscape, Portrait, Still-Life: their Origin and Development*, trans. R.F.C. Hull, Oxford, 1949, p. 55.

125   *Ibid.*, p. 20.

126   *Op. cit.*, p. 319.

127   *European Painting in the 15th century*, Studio Books, London 1961, p. 232.

128   See above, p. 31.

129   See above, p. 131.

130   *A Sienese Codex of the Divine Comedy*, ed. J. Pope-Hennessy, London, 1947.

131   See J. White, *The Birth and Rebirth of Pictorial Space*, London, 1957; 2nd ed., 1967, p. 111.

132   See Panofsky, *Early Netherlandish Painting*, pp. 2–3.

133   See above, p. 32.

134   A. R. Turner, *The Vision of Landscape in Renaissance Italy*, p. 65.

135   Coleridge's terms: and see E. H. Gombrich, 'Leonardo's method for working out compositions', in *Norm and Form: Studies in the Art of the Renaissance*, London, 1966, p. 62.

136   See Clark, *Landscape into Art*, pp. 45–6; E. H. Gombrich, *Art and Illusion*, pp. 154–61.

137   See E. H. Gombrich, 'The Renaissance Theory of Art and the Rise of Landscape', in *Norm and Form*, pp. 107–21.

138 See Appendix.

139 *Troy-Book*, ed. H. Bergen, EETS, ES 97, 103, 106, 126, 1906–20, i. 1275–7.

140 *Troy-Book*, i. 1197–1201.

141 *The Goldyn Targe*, 22–7, 37–42: in *Poems*, ed. J. Kinsley, Oxford, 1958. For extended quotation see Appendix.

142 *Kingis Quair*, ed. A. Lawson, London, 1910, stanzas 31–2.

143 Lines 50–9, 64–6, in *The Floure and the Leafe and the Assembly of Ladies*, ed. D. A. Pearsall, London, 1962.

144 See *The Floure and the Leafe*, ed. cit., note to line 35.

145 *The Passetyme of Pleasure*, ed. W. E. Mead, EETS, 173, 1927, line 62.

146 See Eleanor P. Hammond's note to the line in *English Verse between Chaucer and Surrey*, Durham, North Carolina, 1927, p. 488.

147 Georgina Masson, *Italian Gardens*, London, 1961, pp. 60–3. In the facsimile of the 1499 print, published by Gregg, 1969, see especially the description of the 'delitiosa & amoenissima insula', beginning sig. t iiii.

148 See Appendix.

149 *Passetyme of Pleasure*, 391–2.

150 *Passetyme*, 3010.

151 *Passetyme*, 64–9.

152 See Appendix.

153 *Georgics*, ii. 323–35; Boethius, book II, metre 8. See Tuve, *Seasons and Months*, and see above, chapter 5.

154 Lydgate and Burgh's *Secrees of the old Philisoffres*, ed. R. Steele, EETS, ES 66, 1894, 1296–1491.

155 Lines 1671–8, in *Robert Henryson: Poems*, ed. C. Elliott, Oxford, 1963, p. 51.

156 *Morall Fabillis*, 1696–1705. For fuller quotation, see Appendix.

157 *Kingis Quair*, stanzas 155–7.

158 'How a Lover praiseth his Lady', 25–32: ed. Eleanor P. Hammond, *MP*, XXI, 1924, 379–95. In line 4, *stevinne* ('time') is a conjecture for MS *stepinne* (*p* being a mistake for *ph = f = v*).

159 Lines 27–62, in *Middle English Verse Romances*, ed. D. B. Sands, New York, 1966, p. 252.

160 *The Court of Sapience*, ed. R. Spindler, Leipzig, 1927, 1212–1463; extracts in Hammond, *English Verse between Chaucer and Surrey*, pp. 263–4.

161 Henryson, *Morall Fabillis*, 1650–3, 1657–63. For fuller quotation, see Appendix.

162 See Appendix.

163 See Appendix.

164 See above, chapter 5, *passim*.

165 E.g. Lydgate's *Temple of Glas*, Henryson's *Testament of Cresseid*, George Ashby's *A Prisoner's Reflections*, *The Assembly of Ladies*, Hawes' *Example of Virtue*.

166 Christine de Pisan, *Cent Balades d'Amant et de Dame*, LXXII (*ed. cit.*, iii. 281).

167 *Testament*, 15–18, in *Poems*, ed. Elliott, p. 90.

168 *Virgil's Aeneid, translated into Scottish verse by Gavin Douglas*, ed. D. F. C. Coldwell, 4 vols, Scottish Text Society, Third series, 25, 27–8, 30, 1957–64. See especially Prologues VII (winter), XII (spring) and XIII (summer evening), all quoted in the Appendix.

169 Thomas Tusser's *Five Hundred Points of Good Husbandry*, for instance, or Spenser's *Shepheardes Calender*.

170 See *The Paintings of Pieter Bruegel*, ed. F. Grossman, London, 1955, pl. 79–109. The paintings are recorded in 1566 as belonging to Niclaes Jonghelinck, of Antwerp, who probably commissioned them.

171 See, for instance, his *Flight into Egypt*, in the Koninklijk Museum, Antwerp.

172 *The Landscape with the Martyrdom of St Catherine*, for example, or *The Conversion of St Paul*.

APPENDIX

I *Lydgate: Complaint of the Black Knight, 36–84*

> And by a ryver forth I gan costey
> Of water clere as berel or cristal
> Til at the last I founde a lytil wey
> Towarde a parke enclosed with a wal
> In compas round; and by a gate smal
> Whoso that wolde frely myghte goon
> Into this parke walled with grene stoon.
>
> And in I went to her the briddes songe
> Which on the braunches bothe in pleyn and vale
> So loude song that al the wode ronge
> Lyke as hyt shold shever in pesis smale.
> And, as me thoghte, that the nyghtyngale
> With so grete myght her voys gan out wrest
> Ryght as her hert for love wolde brest.
>
> The soyle was pleyn, smothe and wonder softe,
> Al oversprad wyth tapites that Nature
> Had made herselfe, celured eke alofte
> With bowys grene the floures for to cure
> That in her beaute they may long endure
> Fro al assaute of Phebus fervent fere
> Which in his spere so hote shone and clere.
>
> The eyre atempre and the smothe wynde
> Of Zepherus among the blosmes whyte
> So holsom was and norysshing be kynde
> That smale buddes and round blomes lyte
> In maner gan of her brethe delyte
> To yif us hope that their frute shal take
> Ayens autumpne redy for to shake.

I saw ther Daphene closed under rynde,
Grene laurer and the holsom pyne,
The myrre also that wepeth ever of kynde,
The cedre high, upryght as a lyne,
The philbert eke that lowe doth enclyne
Her bowes grene to the erthe doune
Unto her knyght icalled Demophoune.

Ther saw I eke the fresshe hawethorne
In white motele that so soote doth smelle,
Asshe, firre and oke with mony a yonge acorne,
And mony a tre mo than I can telle.
And me beforne I saw a litel welle
That had his course (as I gan beholde)
Under an hille with quyke stremes colde.

The gravel gold, the water pure as glas,
The bankys round, the welle environyng,
And softe as veluet the yonge gras
That therupon lustely cam spryngyng.
The sute of trees aboute compassyng
Her shadow cast, closyng the welle rounde
And al the erbes growyng on the grounde.

(*John Lydgate: Poems*, ed. J. Norton-Smith,
Oxford, 1966, pp. 48–9)

2 *Dunbar: The Goldyn Targe, 10–45*

Full angellike thir birdis sang thair houris
Within thair courtyns grene, in to thair bouris
   Apparalit quhite and rede wyth blomes suete;
Anamalit was the felde wyth all colouris,
The perly droppis schake in silvir schouris
   Quhill all in balme did branch and levis flete;
   To part fra Phebus did Aurora grete,
Hir cristall teris I saw hyng on the flouris,
   Quhilk he for lufe all drank up wyth his hete.

For mirth of May, wyth skippis and wyth hoppis
The birdis sang upon the tender croppis,
   With curiouse note, as Venus chapell clerkis;
The rosis yong, new spreding of thair knopis,
War powderit brycht with hevinly beriall droppis;
   Throu bemes rede birnyng as ruby sperkis
   The skyes rang for schoutyng of the larkis;
The purpur hevyn, ourscailit in silvir sloppis,
   Ourgilt the treis, branchis, lef, and barkis.

Doune through the ryce a ryvir ran wyth stremys
So lustily agayn thai lykand lemys
   That all the lake as lamp did leme of licht,
Quhilk schadowit all about wyth twynkling glemis,
That bewis bathit war in secund bemys
   Throu the reflex of Phebus visage brycht:
   On every syde the hegies raise on hicht,
The bank was grene, the bruke was full of bremys,
   The stanneris clere as stern in frosty nycht.

The cristall air, the sapher firmament,
The ruby skyes of the orient,
   Kest beriall bemes on emerant bewis grene;
The rosy garth depaynt and redolent
With purpur, azure, gold, and goulis gent,
   Arayed was by dame Flora the quene
   So nobily that joy was for to sene;
The roch agayn the rivir resplendent
   As low enlumynit all the leves schene.

              (*William Dunbar: Poems*, ed. J. Kinsley,
              Oxford, 1958)

3 *The Assembly of Ladies*, 47–70

   So com I forth in to a streyte passage,
   Whiche brought me to an herber feyre and grene
   Made with benchis ful craftily and clene;

That, as me thought, myght no creature
Devise a bettir by proporcioun.
Save it was closed wele, I yow ensure,
With masonry of compas environ
Ful secretly, with steyres goyng down
In myddes the place, a tornyng whele, sertayne,
And upon that a pot of margoleyne;

With margarites growyng in ordynaunce
To shewe hem self as folk went to and fro,
That to behold it was a grete plesaunce;
And how they were accompanyed with mo,
Ne m'oublie-mies and sovenez also;
The poore penses ne were nat disloged there—
No, no, God wote, theyr place was every where.

The floore beneth was paved faire and smoth
With stones square of many dyvers hewe
So wele joyned that, for to sey the soth,
Al semed on, who that non other knewe.
And underneth the streames, newe and newe,
As silver newe bright spryngyng in such wise
That whens it com ye cowde it nat devise.

(*The Floure and the Leafe and The Assembly of Ladies*,
ed. D. A. Pearsall, London, 1962)

4 *Hawes: The Pastime of Pleasure, 2008–30*

Than in we went to the gardyn gloryous,
Lyke to a place of pleasure moost solacyous,

With Flora paynted, and wrought curyously
In dyvers knottes of mervaylous gretenes.
Rampande Lyons stode up wondersly
Made all of herbes with dulcet swetenes,
With many dragons of mervaylous lykenes
Of dyvers floures made full craftely
By Flora couloured with colours sundry.

Amyddes the garden so moche delectable
There was an herber fayre and quadrante
To paradyse ryght well comparable,
Sette all aboute with floures fragraunt,
And in the myddle there was resplendysshaunt
A dulcet sprynge and mervaylous fountayne
Of golde and asure made all certayne.

In wonderfull and curyous symylytude
There stode a dragon of fyne golde so pure
Upon his tayle of myghty fortytude
Wrethed and skaled all with asure,
Havynge thre hedes dyvers in fygure
Whiche in a bath of the sylver grette
Spouted the water that was so dulcette.

> (*The Passetyme of Pleasure*, ed. W. E. Mead,
> EETS, 173, 1927)

5 Henryson: Morall Fabillis, 1650–1712

Yit nevertheles we may haif knawlegeing
Off God Almychtie be His creatouris
That he is gude, fair, wyis and bening:
Exempill tak be thir jolie flouris
Rycht sweit off smell and plesant off colouris,
Sum grene, sum blew, sum purpour, quhyte and reid,
Thus distribute be gift off His Godheid.

The firmament payntit with sternis cleir,
From eist to west rolland in cirkill round,
And everilk planet in his proper spheir,
In moving makand harmonie and sound;
The fyre, the air, the watter and the ground—
Till understand it is aneuch, I wis,
That God in all His werkis wittie is.

Luke weill the fische that swimmis in the se;
Luke weill in eirth al kynd off bestiall;
The foulis fair sa forcelie thay fle,

Scheddand the air with pennis grit and small;
Syne luke to man, that He maid last off all,
Lyke to His image and His similitude:
Be thir we knaw that God is fair and gude.

All creature He maid for the behufe
Off man and to his supportatioun
Into this eirth, baith under and abufe,
In number, wecht and dew proportioun;
The difference off tyme and ilk seasoun
Concorddand till our opurtunitie,
As daylie be experience we may se.

The somer with his jolie mantill off grene,
With flouris fair furrit on everilk fent,
Quhilk Flora Goddes, off the flouris quene,
Hes to that lord as for his seasoun lent,
And Phebus with his goldin bemis gent
Hes purfellit and payntit plesandly
With heit and moysture stilland from the sky

Syne harvest hait, quhen Ceres that goddes
Hir barnis benit hes with abundance;
And Bachus, god off wyne, renewit hes
The tume pyipis in Italie and France
With wynis wicht and liquour off plesance;
And Copia Temporis to fill hir horne,
That never wes full off quheit nor uther corne.

Syne wynter wan, quhen austerne Eolus,
God off the wynd, with blastis boreall
The grene garment off somer glorious
Hes all to-rent and revin in pecis small;
Than flouris fair faidit with froist man fall,
And birdis blyith changit thair noitis sweit
In styll murning, neir slane with snaw and sleit.

Thir dalis deip with dubbis drounit is,
Baith hill and holt heillit with frostis hair;
And bewis bene laifit bair off blis

Be wickit windis off the winter wair;
All wyld beistis than from the bentis bair
Drawis for dreid unto thair dennis deip,
Coucheand for cauld in coifis thame to keip.

Syne cummis ver, quhen winter is away,
The secretar off somer with his sell,
Quhen columbie up-keikis throw the clay,
Quhilk fleit wes befoir with froistes fell;
The mavis and the merle beginnis to mell;
The lark onloft with uther birdis haill
Than drawis furth fra derne over doun and daill.

(*Robert Henryson: Poems*, ed. C. Elliott,
Oxford, 1963, pp. 50–2)

6 Lydgate: Troy-Book, i. 3907–41

Whan that the soote stormis of Aprille,
Un-to the rote ful lawe gan distille
His lusty licour, with many holsom schour,
To reise the vertu up in-to the flour;
And Phebus was ascendyng in his spere,
And on the brest smote his bemys clere
Of the Ram, ful colerik at al,
Halvynge in ver the equinnoccial;
Whan May kalendis entre in for-sothe,
And Zephirus, ful agreable and smothe,
The tendre braunchis enspireth and dothe springe,
And every busche is lusty blossumynge,
And from the hil the water is revolvid
Of snowys white, that Phebus hath dissolvyd,
And the bawme vapoureth up a-lofte
In-to the eyre of the erbes softe,
The Rotis vertu, with colde of wynter hid,
Hath hool his myght and his force kyd,
Oute of the erthe in erbe and every tree
Schad in the braunchis his humydite,
Areised only with the sonnys hete,

And with the moysture of the reynes swete;
Whan silver welles scheden oute her stremys
In the ryvers, gilt with the sonne bemys,
And Flora had with newe grene ageyne
Hir lyvere schad up-on every playn,
And nyghtyngales, that al the wode rong,
Ful amorously welcomed in hir song
The lusty sesoun, fresche and desyrous,
Namly to hertis that ben amerous,
And the see is calme and blaundisching
From trouble of wynde or wawy boilyng,
And from tempest is smothe to eskape—
The same sesoun Grekys furth hem schape
Towardis Troye.

(*Troy-Book*, ed. H. Bergen, EETS, ES 97,
103, 106, 126, 1906–20)

7 *Lydgate: Troy-Book, ii. 5067–91*

The tyme neigheth after this nat yore,
That breme wynter with his frostis hore
Gan t'aswagen of his bitter colde;
Whan Appollo passid was the holde
Of the signe that we calle Aquarie,
And in the Fissche, fer in Februarie
I-ronne was to-ward the Ariete;
And that sesoun, with his feynte hete,
On hillis highe gan his bemys smyte,
Makyng the snow with faire flakis whyte
In-to water kyndely relente,
Whiche from above to the valey went,
That newe flodis of the sodeyn thowe
The grene mede gan to overflowe,
And the yis gan stoundemele distille
Doun fro the hil the brokis for to fille
With fomy stremys of the wawes smale,
By broke bankis as thei dide avale;
Whan lusty ver, with his yonge grene,

Is recounforted by the sonne schene,
Whiche lite and lite his hewes ay amendeth,
Up in his spere as Titan up ascendeth;
Whan Marche aprocheth, and branchis overal
Gynne buddyn out, and the equinoccial
Of ver is halved, the sesoun amerous . . .

8 *Gavin Douglas, translation of the Aeneid.*
Prologue to book VII, 12–84

The frosty regioun ryngis of the yer,
The tyme and sesson bittir, cald and paill,
Tha schort days that clerkis clepe brumaill,
Quhen brym blastis of the northyn art
Ourquhelmyt had Neptunus in his cart,
And all to schaik the levis of the treis,
The rageand storm ourweltrand wally seys.
Ryveris ran reid on spait with watir broune,
And burnys hurlys all thar bankis doune,
And landbrist rumland rudely with sik beir,
So lowd ne rumyst wild lyoun or ber;
Fludis monstreis, sik as meirswyne or quhalis,
Fro the tempest law in the deip devalis.
Mars occident, retrograde in his speir,
Provocand stryfe, regnyt as lord that yer;
Rany Oryon with his stormy face
Bewavit oft the schipman by hys race;
Frawart Saturn, chill of complexioun,
Throu quhais aspect darth and infectioun
Beyn causyt oft, and mortal pestilens,
Went progressyve the greis of his ascens;
And lusty Hebe, Junoys douchtir gay,
Stude spulyeit of hir office and array.
The soyl ysowpit into watir wak,
The firmament ourcast with rokis blak,
The grond fadyt, and fawch wolx all the feildis,
Montane toppis slekit with snaw ourheildis;
On raggit rolkis of hard harsk quhyn stane
With frosyn frontis cauld clynty clewis schane.

Bewte was lost, and barrand schew the landis,
With frostis hair ourfret the feldis standis.
Seir bittir bubbis and the schowris snell
Semyt on the sward a symylitude of hell,
Reducyng to our mynd, in every sted,
Gousty schaddois of eild and grisly ded.
Thik drumly skuggis dyrknyt so the hevyn,
Dym skyis oft furth warpit feirfull levyn,
Flaggis of fire, and mony felloun flaw,
Scharpe soppys of sleit and of the snypand snaw.
The dolly dichis war all donk and wait,
The law valle flodderit all with spait,
The plane stretis and every hie way
Full of floschis, dubbis, myre and clay.
Laggerit leyis wallowit farnys schew,
Broune muris kythit thar wysnyt mossy hew,
Bank, bra and boddum blanchit wolx and bar.
For gurl weddir growit bestis hair.
The wynd maid waif the red wed on the dyke,
Bedowyn in donkis deip was every sike.
Our craggis and the front of rochis seir
Hang gret ische schouchlis lang as ony speir.
The grond stud barrant, widderit, dosk or gray,
Herbis, flowris and gersis wallowyt away.
Woddis, forestis, with nakyt bewis blowt,
Stude stripyt of thar weid in every howt.
So bustuusly Boreas his bugill blew,
The deyr full dern doun in the dalis drew;
Smale byrdis, flokkand throu thik ronys thrang,
In chyrmyng and with cheping changit thar sang,
Sekand hidlis and hyrnys thame to hyde
Fra feirfull thuddis of the tempestuus tyde;
The watir lynnys rowtis, and every lynd
Quhislit and brayt of the swouchand wynd.
Puyr lauboraris and bissy husband men
Went wait and wery draglit in the fen.
The silly scheip and thar litil hyrd gromys
Lurkis undre le of bankis, woddis and bromys;
And other dantit grettar bestiall,
Within thar stabillis sesyt into stall,
Sik as mulis, horssis, oxin and ky,

Fed tuskyt barys and fat swyne in sty,
Sustenyt war by mannys governance
On hervist and on symmeris purvyance.

> (*Virgil's Aeneid, translated into Scottish verse
> by Gavin Douglas*, ed. D. F. C. Coldwell,
> 4 vols, Scottish Text Society, Third series,
> 25, 27–8, 30, 1957–64)

9 *Gavin Douglas, translation of the Aeneid:*
Prologue to book XII, 25–140

Eous the steid, with ruby hamys red,
Abuf the sey lyftis furth hys hed,
Of cullour soyr, and sumdeill broun as berry,
Forto alichtyn and glaid our emyspery,
The flambe owtbrastyng at his noys thyrlys;
Sa fast Pheton with the quhyp hym quhyrlys,
To roll Apollo hys faderis goldyn char,
That schrowdith all the hevynnys and the ayr;
Quhill schortly, with the blesand torch of day,
Abilyeit in hys lemand fresch array,
Furth of hys palyce ryall ischit Phebus,
With goldyn croun and vissage gloryus,
Crysp haris, brycht as chrisolyte or topace,
For quhais hew mycht nane behald hys face,
The fyry sparkis brastyng from hys eyn,
To purge the ayr, and gylt the tendyr greyn,
Defundand from hys sege etheryall
Glaid influent aspectis celicall;
Befor hys regale hie magnificens
Mysty vapour upspryngand, sweit as sens,
In smoky soppys of donk dewis wak,
Moich hailsum stovys ourheldand the slak;
The aureat fanys of hys trone soverane
With glytrand glans ourspred the occiane,
The large fludis lemand all of lycht
Bot with a blenk of hys supernale sycht.
Fortobehald, it was a glor to se
The stablit wyndis and the cawmyt see,

The soft sesson, the firmament sereyn,
The lowne illumynat ayr, and fyrth ameyn;
The sylver scalyt fyschis on the greit
Ourthwort cleir stremys sprynkland for the heyt,
With fynnys schynand broun as synopar,
And chyssell talys, stowrand heir and thar;
The new cullour alychtnyng all the landis,
Forgane thir stannyris schame the beriall strandis,
Quhil the reflex of the diurnall bemys
The beyn bonkis kest ful of variant glemys;
And lusty Flora dyd hyr blomys spreid
Under the feit of Phebus sulyart steid;
The swardit soyll enbroud with selcouth hewys,
Wod and forest obumbrat with thar bewys,
Quhois blisfull branschis, porturat on the grund,
With schaddoys schene schewe rochis rubicund;
Towris, turettis, kyrnellis, pynnaclys hie
Of kyrkis, castellis and ilke fair cite,
Stude payntit, every fyall, fayn and stage,
Apon the plane grund, by thar awyn umbrage.
Of Eolus north blastis havand no dreid,
The sulye spred hir braid bosum on breid,
Zephirus confortabill inspiratioun
Fortill ressave law in hyr barm adoun;
The cornys croppis and the beris new brerd
With glaidsum garmont revestyng the erd;
So thik the plantis sprang in every peyce,
The feildis ferleis of thar fructuus fleyce;
Byssy Dame Ceres and proud Pryapus,
Rejosyng of the planys plentuus,
Plenyst sa plesand and mast propyrly,
By natur nurysyt wondir nobilly,
On the fertill skyrt lappys of the grund
Strekyng on breid ondyr the cyrkyll round;
The variand vestur of the venust vaill
Schrowdis the scherald fur, and every faill
Ourfret with fulyeis of figuris full divers,
The spray bysprent with spryngand sprowtis dispers,
For callour humour on the dewy nyght,
Rendryng sum place the gers pilis thar hycht,
Als far as catal, the lang symmyris day,

Had in thar pastur eyt and knyp away;
And blisfull blossummys in the blomyt yard
Submittis thar hedis in the yong sonnys salfgard;
Ive levys rank ourspred the barmkyn wall,
The blomyt hawthorn cled hys pykis all;
Furth of fresch burgionys the wyne grapis yyng
Endlang the treilyeis dyd on twystis hyng;
The lowkyt buttonys on the gemmyt treis
Ourspredand leyvis of naturis tapestreis,
Soft gresy verdour eftir balmy schowris
On curland stalkis smylyng to thar flowris;
Behaldand thame sa mony divers hew,
Sum pers, sum paill, sum burnet, and sum blew,
Sum greyce, sum gowlys, sum purpour, sum sangwane,
Blanchit or broune, fawch yallow mony ane,
Sum hevynly culloryt in celestiall gre,
Sum watry hewit as the haw wally see,
And sum depart in freklys red and quhite,
Sum brycht as gold with aureat levys lyte.
The dasy dyd onbreid hir crownell smaill,
And every flour onlappyt in the daill;
In battill gyrs burgionys the banwart wild,
The clavyr, catcluke, and the cammamyld;
The flour delys furthspred hys hevynly hew,
Flour dammes, and columby blank and blew;
Seir downys smaill on dent de lyon sprang
The yyng greyn blomyt straberry levys amang;
Gymp gerraflouris thar royn levys onschet,
Fresch prymros, and the purpour violet;
The roys knoppys, tutand furth thar hed,
Gan chyp, and kyth thar vermel lippys red,
Crysp scarlet levis sum scheddand, baith atanys
Kest fragrant smell amyd from goldyn granys;
Hevynly lylleis, with lokrand toppys quhyte,
Oppynnyt and schew thar creistis redymyte,
The balmy vapour from thar silkyn croppys
Distilland hailsum sugurat hunny droppys,
And sylver schakaris gan fra levys hyng,
With crystal sprayngis on the verdour yyng;
The plane pulderit with semly settis sound,
Bedyit full of dewy peirlys round,

So that ilk burgioun, syon, herb and flour
Wolx all enbalmyt of the fresch liquour,
And bathit hait dyd in dulce humouris fleyt,
Quharof the beys wrocht thar hunny sweit,
By myghty Phebus operations,
In sappy subtell exalations.

10 *Gavin Douglas, translation of the Aeneid:*
Prologue to book XIII, 1–66

Towart the evyn, amyd the symmyris heit,
Quhen in the Crab Appollo held hys sete,
Duryng the joyus moneth tyme of June,
As gone neir was the day and supper doyn,
I walkyt furth abowt the feildis tyte,
Quhilkis tho replenyst stud full of delyte,
With herbys, cornys, catal, and frute treis,
Plente of stoir, byrdis and byssy beys,
In amerant medis fleand est and west,
Eftir laubour to tak the nychtis rest.
And as I lukit on the lift me by,
All byrnand red gan walxin the evyn sky:
The son enfyrit haill, as to my sight,
Quhirlit about hys ball with bemys brycht,
Declynand fast towart the north in deid,
And fyry Phegon, his dun nychtis steid,
Dowkit hys hed sa deip in fludis gray
That Phebus rollis doun undir hell away;
And Esperus in the west with bemys brycht
Upspryngis, as forrydar of the nycht.
Amyd the hawchis, and every lusty vaill,
The recent dew begynnys doun to scaill,
To meys the byrnyng quhar the son had schyne,
Quhilk tho was to the neddir warld declyne:
At every pilis poynt and cornys croppis
The techrys stude, as lemand beryall droppis,
And on the hailsum herbis, cleyn but wedis,
Lyke cristal knoppis or smal silver bedis.
The lyght begouth to quynchyng owt and faill,
The day to dyrkyn, declyne and devaill;
The gummys rysis, doun fallis the donk rym,

Baith heir and thar scuggis and schaddois dym.
Upgois the bak with hir pelit ledderyn flycht,
The lark discendis from the skyis hycht,
Syngand hir complyng sang, efter hir gys,
To tak hir rest, at matyn hour to rys.
Owt our the swyre swymmys the soppis of myst,
The nycht furthspred hir cloke with sabill lyst,
That all the bewte of the fructuus feld
Was with the erthis umbrage cleyn ourheld;
Baith man and beste, fyrth, flude and woddis wild
Involvyt in tha schaddois warryn syld.
Still war the fowlis fleis in the air,
All stoir and catall seysit in thar lair,
And every thing, quharso thame lykis best,
Bownys to tak the hailsum nychtis rest
Eftir the days laubour and the heyt.
Clos warryn all and at thar soft quyet,
But sterage or removing, he or sche,
Owder best, byrd, fysch, fowle, by land or sey.
And schortlie, every thing that doith repar
In firth or feild, flude, forest, erth or ayr,
Or in the scroggis, or the buskis ronk,
Lakis, marrasis, or thir pulys donk,
Astabillit lyggis still to slepe, and restis;
Be the smaill byrdis syttand on thar nestis,
The litill mygeis, and the urusum fleys,
Laboryus emmotis, and the bissy beys;
Als weill the wild as the taym bestiall,
And every othir thingis gret and small,
Owtak the mery nychtgaill, Philomeyn,
That on the thorn sat syngand fra the spleyn;
Quhais myrthfull notis langyng fortil heir,
Ontill a garth undir a greyn lawrer
I walk onon, and in a sege down sat,
Now musyng apon this and now on that.

INDEX

1

1 *Pastoral Scene* (*the Ram at the Temple*), from
Pompeii. Museo Nazionale, Naples. Wall
painting, before AD 79.

2 *Pastoral Scene* (*a Sacred Grove*), from the
villa of Agrippa Postumus near Pompeii.
Museo Nazionale, Naples. Wall painting,
before AD 79.

3

3 *Harbour*, from Stabiae. Museo Nazionale, Naples. Wall painting, before AD 79.

4a, b *Two Scenes of Odysseus in the Land of the Laestrygonians*, from the Odyssey Landscapes. Biblioteca Apostolica Vaticana. Wall paintings, first century AD.

5 *Battle of the Centaurs and Leopards*, from Hadrian's villa at Tivoli. Staatliche Museen, Berlin. Mosaic, *c.* AD 130.

6 *The Corridor of the Great Hunt* (detail), at Piazza Armerina, Sicily. Mosaic, fourth century.

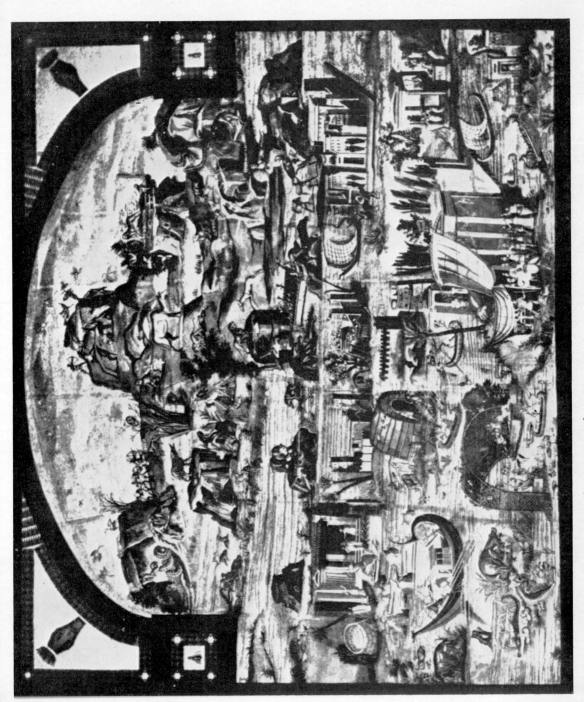

7 *Barberini Mosaic. Museo Nazionale, Palestrina. Second century.*

8 *The Good Shepherd*. Mausoleum of Galla Placidia, Ravenna. Mosaic, c. 450.

9 *Abraham and the Three Angels*, and *The Sacrifice of Isaac*. S. Vitale, Ravenna.
Mosaic, sixth century.

11 *David the Harper*, from the Paris Psalter. Bibliothèque Nationale, Paris, MS grec 139, f. 1v. Ninth century?

10 *Shepherds Tending their Flocks*, from the *Vergilius Romanus: Georgics III*. Biblioteca Apostolica Vaticana, MS Vat. lat. 3867, f. 44v. Early fifth century.

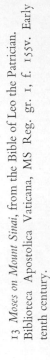

13 *Moses on Mount Sinai*, from the Bible of Leo the Patrician. Biblioteca Apostolica Vaticana, MS Reg. gr. 1, f. 155v. Early tenth century.

12 *Moses on Mount Sinai*, from the Paris Psalter. Bibliothèque Nationale, Paris, MS grec 139, f. 422v. Ninth century?

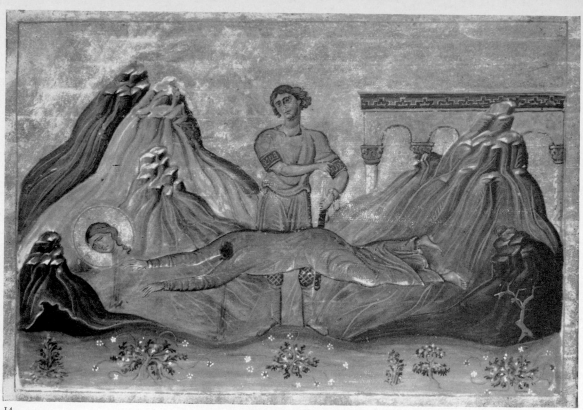

14

15a

15b

16

14 *The Martyrdom of St Hermione*, from the Menologion of Basil II. Biblioteca Apostolica Vaticana, MS Vat. gr. 1613, pag. 12. 979–84.

15a, b *Moses on Mount Sinai*, and *The Death of Moses*, from an Octateuch. Topkapu Saray Library, Istanbul, cod. 8, ff. 257v, 471v. Twelfth century.

16 *St Matthew*, from the Ebbo Gospels. Bibliothèque Municipale, Epernay, MS 1, f. 18v. Ninth century. Photo: Bibliothèque Nationale, Paris.

17

Deduc me dñe inuia iusticia   suis. secundum multitudi   tj tuae coronasti nos
ppt . inimicos meos   nem impietatum eorum

INCIPIT INCARMINIBᵁ   PRO OCTAVA   PSALMVS   DAVID . VI .   18

19

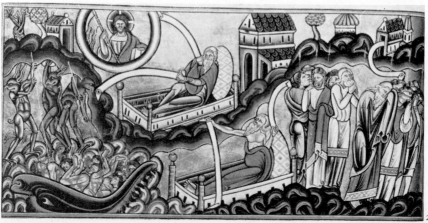

20

17 *Illustration for Psalm 6*, from the Utrecht Psalter. Bibliotheek der Rijksuniversiteit, Utrecht, MS 32. *c.* 830.

18 *Illustration for Psalm 6*, from British Museum, London, MS Harley 603, f. 3v. Early eleventh century.

19 *Illustration for Psalm 6*, from the Eadwine Psalter. Trinity College, Cambridge, MS R.17.1, f. 11v. *c.* 1146.

20 *Illustration for Psalm 6*, from Bibliothèque Nationale, Paris, MS lat. 8846, f. 11v. *c.* 1200.

21 *Garden of Paradise*. Städelsches Kunstinstitut, Frankfurt. *c.* 1410.

22

23a

Côuir nir sêug ava adam et poita eu puadis ciuslbe et fait eue re son aulie erleur detseur le fmi

23b

22 *Paradise*, by Herri met de Bles (*c.* 1480–1550). Rijksmuseum, Amsterdam.

23a, b *The Fall and Expulsion from Eden*, from
(a) *Les Très Riches Heures de Jean de Berri*. Musée Condé, Chantilly, MS 65,
f. 25v. Before 1416. Photo: Bibliothèque Nationale, Paris.
(b) The Bedford Hours. British Museum, London, Addit. MS 18850, f. 14.
c. 1423.

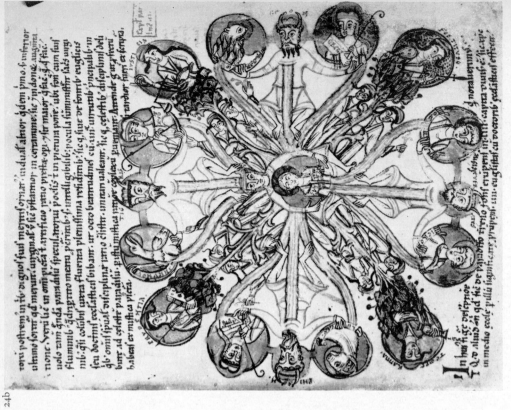

24b

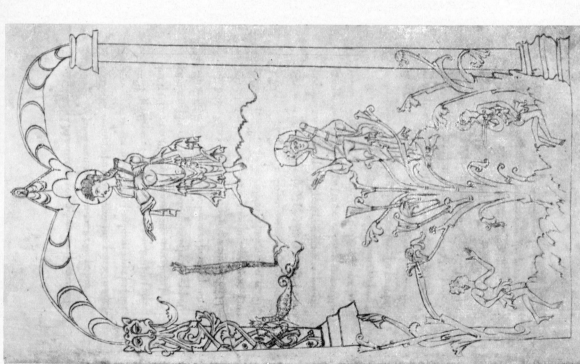

24a

24a, b (a) *Adam and Eve in Eden, accused by God*, from Bodleian Library, Oxford, MS Junius XI, p. 41. Tenth to eleventh century.
(b) *Paradise*, from the *Speculum Virginum*. British Museum, London, MS Arundel 44, f. 13. Mid-twelfth century.

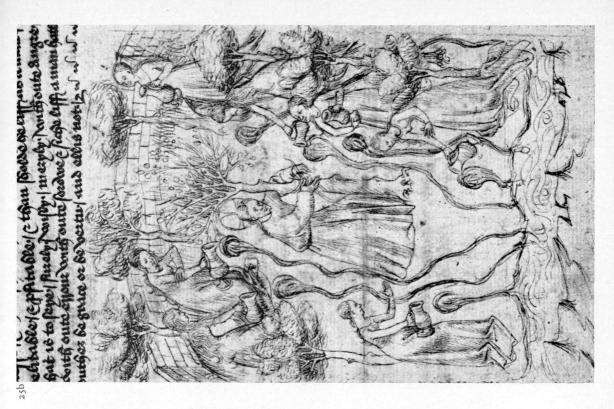

25a, b *The Paradise of Virtues*, from
(a) *Somme le Roi*. British Museum, London MS Addit. 54180, f. 130. Thirteenth century.
(b) *Somme le Roi*, Bodleian Library, Oxford, MS 283, f. 99v. Fifteenth century.

26 *Paradise*, by Giovanni di Paolo (1402–82) (detail). Metropolitan Museum of
Art, New York, Rogers Fund 1906.

27

27 *Garden of Eden*, and *Ascent to the Empyrean*, by Hieronymus Bosch (d. 1516).
Palazzo Ducale, Venice.

28 *The Triumph of Death,* by Francesco Traini (?). Camposanto, Pisa. Fourteenth century.

29

30a

31

b30

29 *Bihzad in the Garden*, from British Museum, London, Addit. MS 18113, f. 11v. *c.* 1396.

30a, b *Bel Acueil leads the Lover to the Rose*, and *The Lover attains the Rose*, from *Le Roman de la Rose*. British Museum, London, MS Harley 4425, ff. 36, 184v (details). Fifteenth century.

31 *Lovers in a Garden*, from British Museum, London, MS Harley 4431, f. 376 (detail). Fifteenth century.

32b

32a

32a, b (a) *Madonna in the Rose Garden*, by Stefano da Zevio (Stefano da Verona).
Museo di Castelvecchio, Verona. Early fifteenth century.
(b) *Madonna in the Rose Arbour*, by Stefan Lochner (d. 1451). Wallraf-Richartz-
Museum, Cologne. Photo: Rheinisches Bildarchiv, Kölnisches Stadtmuseum.

33

33 *Deer Enclosure*. The King's Manor, University of York, on loan from
P. F. Craggs, Esq. Tapestry, Tournai, 1525. Photo: David Whiteley.

34a

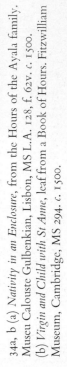

34b

34a, b (a) *Nativity in an Enclosure*, from the Hours of the Ayala family. Museu Calouste Gulbenkian, Lisbon, MS L.A. 128, f. 62v. *c.* 1500.
(b) *Virgin and Child with St Anne*, leaf from a Book of Hours. Fitzwilliam Museum, Cambridge, MS 294. *c.* 1500.

35a, b *The Enclosed Garden*, from
(a) *Speculum Humanae Salvationis*. Bibliothèque Nationale, Paris, MS 9584.
(Ed. M. R. James, Oxford, 1926, chap. III, pl. 3).
(b) The Grimani Breviary. Biblioteca Nazionale Marciana, Venice, f. 831.
(Ed. S. de Vries and S. Morpurgo, *Das Breviarum Grimani*, Leiden, 1903–8,
pl. 1581). c. 1500.

35a

35b

36 *The Return of the Herd*, by Pieter Bruegel (d. 1569). Kunsthistorisches Museum, Vienna.

37 *The Hunters in the Snow*, by Pieter Bruegel (d. 1569). Kunsthistorisches Museum, Vienna.

38a, b *April: the Triumph of Venus*, and *March: Vine-pruning* (details), from the Salone dei Mesi, Palazzo Schifanoia, Ferrara. 1470.

39

40a

40b

39 *April*. Torre dell' Aquila, Trento. *c.* 1410.

40a, b *May*, and *October*, from British Museum, London, MS Cotton Tiberius
B.v. (part i), ff. 5, 7v (details). Eleventh century.

41a

41b

41c

41a–e *January, February, May, July,* and *October,* from the Peterborough Psalter. Corpus Christi College, Cambridge, MS 53, ff. 1, 1v, 3, 4, 5v (details). *c.* 1320.

41d

41e

42a

42b

42a–f *December Pig Killing with Capricorn, February Warming with Pisces, April Flower Picking with Taurus*, from Queen Mary's Psalter. British Museum, London, MS Royal 2.B.VII, ff. 82v–83, 72v–73, 74v–75 (details). Early fourteenth century.

42c

42d

42e

42f

43a

**Quoniam tu dominus altiſſi
ſuper omnem terram: nimis er
tus es ſuper omnes deos**

43a, b (a) *Harvest Waggon*, from the Luttrell
Psalter. British Museum, London, Addit. MS
42130, f. 175v (detail). *c.* 1340.
(b) *Threshing*, from Queen Mary's Psalter.
British Museum, London, MS Royal 2.B.VII,
f. 165v (detail). Early fourteenth century.

43b

44a, b, c (a) *December*, from the Belleville Breviary. Bibliothèque Nationale, Paris, MS lat. 10483, f. 6v (detail). *c.* 1325.
(b) *February*, from the *Petites Heures de Jean de Berri*, Bibliothèque Nationale, Paris, MS lat. 18014, f. 1v (detail). *c.* 1388.
(c) *February*, from the Prayer Book of Bonne de Luxembourg (detail). Metropolitan Museum of Art, New York, Cloisters Collection, 1969. *c.* 1345.

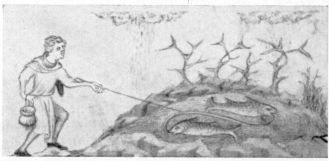

44c

45a

45b

45c

45d

46a

46b

45a–d (a, c) *March*, and *September*, from the *Grandes Heures de Jean de Berri*.
Bibliothèque Nationale, Paris, MS lat. 919, ff. 2, 5 (details). *c.* 1409.
(b, d) *August*, and *November*, from the *Petites Heures de Jean de Berri*. Bibliothèque Nationale, Paris, MS lat. 18014, ff. 4v, 6 (details). *c.* 1388.

46a, b (a) *Nativity*, from the *Petites Heures de Jean Berri*. Bibliothèque Nationale,
Paris, MS lat. 18014, f. 38 (detail). *c.* 1388.
(b) *February*, from the *Petites Heures de Jeanne d'Evreux* (detail). Metropolitan
Museum of Art, New York, Cloisters Collection, Purchase 1954. *c.* 1325–8.

47a

47b

48a

48b

49

47a, b *Visitation*, and *Flight into Egypt*, from the Brussels Hours. Bibliothèque Royale Albert Ier, Brussels, MS 11060/61, ff. 54, 106. *c.* 1390.

48a, b *Visitation*, and *Flight into Egypt*, from the Boucicaut Hours. Musée Jacquemart-André, Paris, MS 2, ff. 57, 90. *c.* 1405–8. Photo: Bulloz.

49 *Martyrdom of St Denis and companions at Montmartre, with Paris in the background*, from the Châteauroux Breviary. Bibliothèque Municipale, Châteauroux, MS 2, f. 364. Before 1415.

50a, b (a) *February*, from the *Très Riches Heures de Jean de Berri.* Musée Condé, Chantilly, MS 65, f. 2v. Before 1416. Photo: Bibliothèque Nationale, Paris. (b) *January.* Torre dell' Aquila, Trento. *c.* 1410.

51b

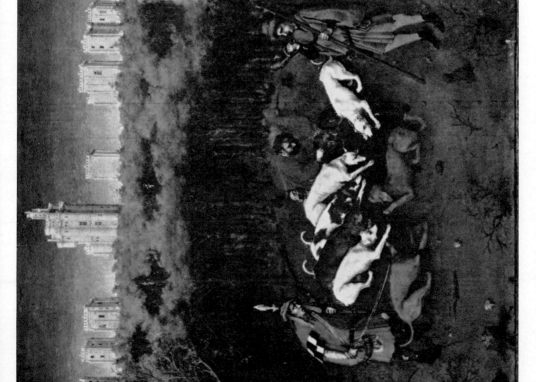

51a

51a, b (a) *December*, from the *Très Riches Heures de Jean de Berri*. Musée Condé, Chantilly, MS 65, f. 12v. Before 1416. Photo: Bibliothèque Nationale, Paris. (b) *December*, from the Grimani Breviary. Biblioteca Nazionale Marciana, Venice, f. 12v. (Ed. S. de Vries and S. Morpurgo, *Das Breviarum Grimani*, Leiden, 1903–8, pl. 23.) *c.* 1500.

52a

52a, b, c (a) *December*, from the *Belles Heures de Jean de Berri*. Metropolitan Museum of Art, New York, Cloisters Collection, Purchase 1954, f. 13 (detail). *c.* 1410–13.
(b) *December*, from the *Grandes Heures de Rohan*. Bibliothèque Nationale, Paris, MS lat. 9471, f. 17v (detail). *c.* 1418.
(c) *December*, from the Grimani Breviary. Biblioteca Nazionale Marciana, Venice, f. 13. (Ed. S. de Vries and S. Morpurgo, *Das Breviarium Grimani*, Leiden, 1903–8, pl. 24.) *c.* 1500.

52b

52c

54 *St Francis and the Poor Man*, by Giotto (?). Upper Church of S. Francesco at Assisi. Fresco, *c.* 1300.

53 *The Flight into Egypt*, by Giotto. Cappella dell' Arena, Padua. Fresco, 1305.

57

56

55 *The Effects of Good Government, in the Country* (detail), by Ambrogio Lorenzetti. Palazzo Pubblico, Siena. Fresco, 1337–40.

56 *The Madonna and Chancellor Rollin*, by Jan van Eyck. Musée du Louvre, Paris. Cliché des Musées Nationaux. *c.* 1425.

57 *The Visitation*, from the Infancy Altarpiece, by Dirc Bouts. Museo del Prado, Madrid. *c.* 1445.

58

58 *St John the Baptist going into the Wilderness*, by Giovanni di Paolo (1402–82). National Gallery, London.

59 *The Flight into Egypt*, predella from the panel of the Adoration, by Gentile da Fabriano. Galleria degli Uffizi, Florence. 1423.

60 *The Adoration of the Magi* (detail), by Benozzo Gozzoli. Palazzo Medici-Riccardi, Florence. 1459.

61 *The Annunciation to the Shepherds*, from the *Grandes Heures de Rohan*. Bibliothèque Nationale, Paris, MS lat. 9471. c. 1418.

59

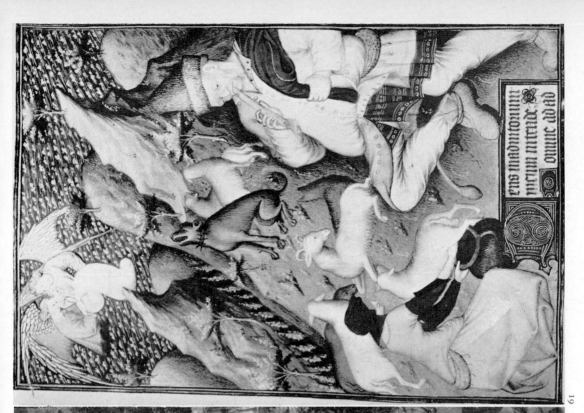

62

63

64

62 *St Eustace*, by Pisanello. National Gallery, London. Early fifteenth century.

63 *The Hunt in the Forest*, by Paolo Uccello (1397–1475). Ashmolean Museum, Oxford.

64 *St Francis in Ecstasy*, by Giovanni Bellini (d. 1516). Copyright: the Frick Collection, New York.

65 *The Nativity*, by Domenico Ghirlandaio. S. Trinità, Florence. 1485.

66 *The Transfiguration*, by Giovanni Bellini (d. 1516). Museo Civico Correr, Venice.